Paraguay under Stroessner

PARAGUAY UNDER STROESSNER

PAUL H. LEWIS

The University of North Carolina Press *Chapel Hill*

© 1980 The University of North Carolina Press
All rights reserved
Manufactured in the United States of America
ISBN 0-8078-1437-7
Library of Congress Catalog Card Number 79-28554

Library of Congress Cataloging in Publication Data

Lewis, Paul H
  Paraguay under Stroessner.

  Bibliography: p.
  Includes index.
  1. Paraguay—Politics and government—1938–
2. Stroessner, Alfredo, Pres. Paraguay, 1912–
3. Totalitarianism. I. Title.
F2689.L48   989.2'072   79-28554
ISBN 0-8078-1437-7

FOR ANNE

Contents

Preface

By any measure General Alfredo Stroessner is a successful dictator. He has governed his country for more than a quarter of a century, an unusually long time for any politician to remain in office. With the passing in recent years of Francisco Franco in Spain, Antonio de Salazar in Portugal, Mao Tse-tung in China, and Josip Broz Tito in Yugoslavia, only Enver Hoxha of Albania, and Kim Il Sung of North Korea outrank Stroessner in tenure. Moreover, he has been in power longer than any current Latin American ruler, including Fidel Castro, and has governed longer than any Paraguayan head of state. That record is all the more astonishing when one considers that in the past one hundred years the average term in office for Paraguayan presidents (excluding Stroessner) is less than two years.

This accomplishment cannot be dismissed simply as the result of dictatorial repression. Brute force as a means of attaining and holding power is easily resorted to in an authoritarian regime, but it is never enough in the long run. A successful dictator, like every other politician, needs brains and a manipulative instinct. Especially in the present era, when pressures for modernization tend to make all political systems more unstable, a dictator must either have organizational and managerial talent or know how to co-opt it.

Therefore, the study of Stroessner and his regime is also a study in politics. At bottom, politics is concerned with power, and if this book is about anything, it is about power—how it is won, wielded, and defended. To understand Stroessner is to understand something basic to all governments.

Researching a closed political system such as Stroessner's presents several difficulties. Information is kept secret by official sources, accusations by opponents are often difficult to substantiate, and the American investigator is held in suspicion by people on both sides. It is hard for Paraguayans to believe that anyone except a CIA man could possibly be interested in them. As a result, the picture presented in the following pages will have gaps that might have been filled in easily if the government had been a democratic one. Nevertheless, enough information exists to make a study of Stroessner and his regime possible—although it requires piecing together scattered bits of data.

The study is divided into four parts. Part 1 deals with the background to Stroessner's dictatorship and attempts to explain how it was made possible by Paraguay's history and culture, giving special emphasis to the period just before Stroessner's takeover—an era characterized by a failed attempt to bring about democracy, a civil war, and a chain of violent and unstable dictatorships.

Part 2 describes Stroessner as a political leader. Stroessner is essentially the sort of political buccaneer that Latin Americans call a *caudillo*. Given the personalistic nature of *caudillo* rule, the task of stabilizing a regime falls squarely on the top man himself. Therefore, it is important to know how Stroessner handles himself in political situations, how he made his way to power, and how he deals with threats to his authority. To show these some of the confrontations he has faced are described in detail.

Part 3 deals with the dictatorial machine, describing its fundamental parts and operating principles, how its key personnel are recruited and kept loyal, and what groups constitute the pivotal parts of the machinery. In addition this section shows how Stroessner balances those parts and how he uses patronage, corruption, and economic development policy to keep the machine well greased.

Part 4 looks at the political opposition. It begins by describing its treatment under Stroessner and in this context discusses the subjects of police brutality and torture. Each opposition group is described with respect to its program and internal cohesion, but special attention is given to the Liberal party and the Roman Catholic church, potentially the two most dangerous opponents of the regime. Finally, the study ends with a conclusion summarizing the data, presenting Stroessner as a figure in the unfolding of Paraguay's evolution, and venturing some guesses as to the country's future course.

During the four years that I was working on this project, I received help from a number of sources. I am indebted to the National Endowment for the Humanities for a summer grant to Argentina in 1973 to interview Paraguayan exiles, to the Tulane University Graduate School for a summer grant to Paraguay in 1974, and to the American Philosophical Society for a summer grant in 1977 to do further research for a final draft. I also owe a great deal to my wife, Anne, who read and criticized the manuscript and encouraged me all along the way. I hope that the result is worthy of them and of the reader's attention.

PART 1. THE BACKGROUND

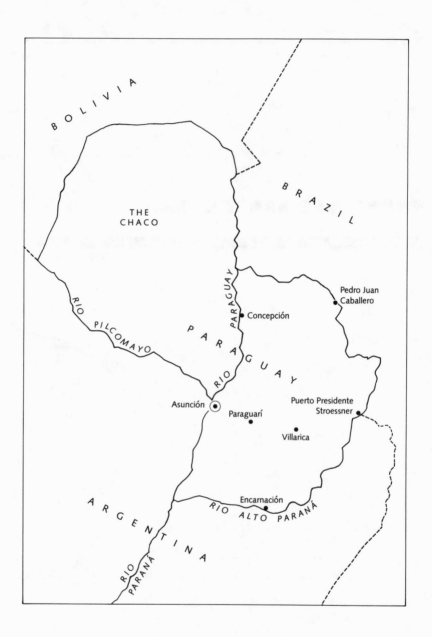

Chapter 1. An Authoritarian Political Culture

The Tradition of Dictatorship

General Alfredo Stroessner's dictatorship follows a long tradition of authoritarian rule in Paraguay. From its founding as a Spanish colony in the early sixteenth century through more than 160 years as an independent republic, Paraguay has never known democratic government. Free elections, fair party competition, and representative institutions are not part of the country's experience. Instead, Paraguayan history is an unbroken sequence of dictatorships. Some of those were paternalistic tyrannies—popular dictatorships like those of ancient Greece—whose policies could claim the support of the poor. Others were oligarchies that served only the interests of the rich few. In either case, the overwhelming majority of Paraguayan governments came to power illegally, maintained themselves through fraud and coercion, and ended violently. And most of them were short-lived. Stroessner has been in power more than twenty years, making his the second longest regime in the country's history; if he survives until 1980, it will be the longest. Thus, his dictatorship is exceptional only in its relative durability.

The earliest dictatorships, those before 1870, were stable. Doctor José Gaspar Rodríguez de Francia, who guided Paraguay to independence from Spain in 1811, ruled peacefully for some twenty-five years as the country's first dictator. A handpicked congress granted him absolute powers for life and accorded him the official title of "El Supremo." Similarly, Francia's successor, Carlos Antonio López, was also made dictator for life by a popular assembly. His title was "El Excelentisimo," and he died in office after eighteen years of unchal-

lenged rule. This period of stability finally came to an end with Carlos
Antonio's son, Francisco Solano López, who involved Paraguay in a
disastrous war with Argentina and Brazil and died in battle in 1870.
All three of these early presidents were absolute tyrants. Any opposition to them resulted in jail, exile, confiscation of property, or death.
Although their governments brought internal peace at a time when
the rest of Spanish America was going through anarchy and many of
their social policies were popular with the masses, these gains cost
the people even their most basic liberties.

Paraguayan governments after 1870 brought neither internal peace
nor liberty, although they were still dictatorships. Managed elections
or the direct seizure of power was the means by which every succeeding president achieved office. Forty-four men occupied the presidency
in the eighty-five years between the death of Solano López and Alfredo Stroessner's coup in 1954—one president every twenty-three
months. Moreover, of those forty-four, more than half (twenty-four)
were forced from office by violence or the threat of violence. Many of
the remainder were simply provisional presidents who headed care-
taker governments while the real contestants for power fought it out.
Sixteen of the twenty-four presidents who were overthrown served for
less than a year, and five of them were in office for less than a month.

The period of greatest instability was from 1910 to 1912. Those
two years saw seven different presidents and nine different administrations, two of the presidents returning to office a second time. Extreme instability was typical also of the more recent dictatorships.
Eleven different presidents served in the nineteen years between the
end of the Chaco War with Bolivia in 1935 and General Stroessner's
takeover in 1954. Furthermore, since the beginning of this century
Paraguay has experienced two revolutions of such scale and intensity
as to justify calling them civil wars.

Such chronic political instability cannot be blamed solely on the
scheming of generals. As a military dictator, General Stroessner is not
so much in the mainstream of Paraguay's political tradition as one
might suppose. Direct military rule was not all that common in the
past. Only nine of the forty-four presidents since 1870 were army
men. Moreover, the officers' average tenure in power—about two
and a half years—was only slightly longer than that of the civilians.
Nevertheless, military support has always been crucial to achieving
power. Although military men seldom occupied the presidency, their
influence on politics was important, if not preponderant. Both of
Paraguay's traditional political parties, the National Republican Association (the Colorado party) and the Liberal party, included mili-

tary chiefs in their directorates. No civilian could come to power without army support, and he could maintain himself in office only so long as that support lasted. Politics inside the barracks had much to do with the dizzying rise and fall of administrations.

Neither the periods of Colorado dominance nor the periods of Liberal dominance were characterized by political stability. The Colorados were in power for a total of thirty-three years between 1870 and 1954. During that time seven of their seventeen presidents were overthrown. The Liberal party and its forerunners, the "Legionnaires," held office for some forty-two years. Of their twenty-four presidents, fourteen were forcibly deposed. Three presidents during that period were nonpartisan military *caudillos*; two of them headed short-lived regimes, and the third managed to hold on for eight years before being bumped out of office. The Liberals have been accused most often of bringing weak, unstable government to Paraguay. The charge is accurate. From the time they ousted the Colorados in 1904 until their feuding factions plunged the country into civil war in 1922, the Liberals were responsible for some fifteen different administrations. It was a time of near anarchy. Nonetheless, the Colorados' recent record is hardly better. Coming to power in 1948 following the country's second civil war in this century, the Colorados put six presidents into office in six years—seven presidents including General Stroessner, who finally imposed order on the situation.

All of this demonstrates that Paraguay has no tradition of constitutional government or liberal democratic procedures to draw upon. On the contrary, the fundamental political norms of the culture are authoritarian, and they are universally shared. Groups out of power may proclaim their democratic ideals and condemn the government as a dictatorship, but the historical record shows that all of the major parties, when in power, have tried to silence their opponents. And when out of power not one has hesitated to knock at the barracks door.

The reason why dictatorship is as normal to Paraguay as representative government is to Britain, Canada, or the United States lies in the social setting within which politics take place. Therefore, to understand Stroessner's dictatorship it is necessary to look at the society that produced his brand of leadership. That is the task of this chapter. However, since every society is the result of a certain process of evolution, chapter 2 will recount Paraguay's historical development, and chapter 3 will round out this review of the political background to Stroessner's rise by describing the crisis conditions that existed in Paraguay immediately prior to his takeover.

Paraguayan Society at Midcentury

An overview of Paraguayan society before Stroessner should begin by introducing a few facts about the country's geography—facts which are crucial for setting the political stage. First, Paraguay is a landlocked country in the heart of the South American continent. Its total area of 157,047 square miles makes it about the size of California. The Paraguay River, which begins in Brazil's Mato Grosso and flows southward to join the Paraná River, divides the country into two very distinct regions. Some two-thirds of the land lies to the west of the river in a scrubby, desolate region known as the Chaco. Beginning in steamy floodplains along the riverbanks, the Chaco gets progressively drier as it stretches westward, ending in a hot, arid wasteland on the Bolivian border. Besides some Mennonite colonies, whose assiduously worked truck farms occupy the transition zone, the only other inhabitants of this region in the 1950s were soldiers scattered among frontier forts, a few cowboys on the large cattle ranches, and some nomadic Indians.

The land to the east of the Paraguay River is, by contrast, rolling, red-clay country, with some low mountains of not more than two thousand feet in elevation, thick forests, and open, undulating fields, which are well watered by many streams. The climate is tropical, and the soil is very fertile. So beautiful is the countryside that more than one traveler has described Paraguay as a tropical paradise. Despite its apparent natural advantages, however, Paraguay has had a tragic history of poverty, strife, and oppression—for geography has been unkind in other ways. For example, Paraguay's territory is defended by no important natural barriers, yet it is surrounded by powerful neighbors, all of whom are larger in both area and population. Brazil lies to the north and east, Argentina to the south and west, and Bolivia to the northwest. All of these countries have gone to war with Paraguay in the past. Argentine troops marched into Paraguay in 1810, ostensibly to liberate the country from Spanish rule, but in reality to incorporate it into the new Argentine Republic. In 1865 Argentina joined with Brazil in the War of the Triple Alliance against Solano López, which nearly finished Paraguay as an independent state. Thousands of Paraguayans, including civilians, died, much territory was lost, and Brazilian troops occupied the country for the next six years. Then, just as Paraguay was recovering from that disaster, Bolivia put forward its claims to the Chaco and began to erect forts in that region. Another bloody war eventually resulted, which lasted from 1932 to 1935. Although Paraguay won this time, it was exhausted by the struggle.

In addition to wars, Paraguay has been subject to constant diplomatic and economic pressure. For most of its history, the only feasible access to the outside world was down the Paraná River, which flows south to the Atlantic through Argentine territory. Thus, commerce could be shut off at any time by a hostile government in Buenos Aires. The alternative route overland through Brazil was seldom taken because of bad roads. Subject as they were to economic blockades, Paraguayan governments were usually quick to placate their powerful neighbor to the south. Much of Paraguay's trade was with Argentina, and a large portion of its farm and ranchland was in Argentine hands. Poorly marked boundaries also led to frequent border clashes with Argentine and Brazilian troops.[1]

The constant need to defend Paraguay's borders from threatening neighbors has tended to enhance the position of the army, perhaps to an exaggerated degree. From the earliest years following independence, a tradition of viewing the nation's military forces as the backbone of the society and an emphasis on keeping them strong at any cost have developed. Doctor Francia created a garrison state, and his government placed all the country's economic and social resources at the disposal of his army. His successors, the two Lopezes, strengthened the army even more and perfected the system of state economic regulation to supply it. Although the War of the Triple Alliance ended Paraguay's pretensions to military power, once the occupation forces were withdrawn the army assumed the role of maker of governments. Under its commander, General Bernardino Caballero, who also founded the Colorado party, Paraguay followed the old formula of strongman rule to the end of the nineteenth century.

When the Liberals came to power in 1904, however, they propounded a new doctrine of limited government, constitutional freedoms, and civilian rule. Therefore, the army's role in politics was to have been reduced. But despite the Liberals' democratic principles the party quickly degenerated into a group of squabbling factions, each claiming power for itself and seeking support for those claims in the military. Coups were frequent. Continual plotting and strife brought a succession of weak presidents to office, while sapping the army's discipline. Worse still, the Bolivians were taking advantage of this chaos to occupy larger and larger areas of the Chaco. While their army was preparing for war by hiring German advisers and buying new equipment, the Paraguayan Liberals, afraid of making their generals too powerful, preferred to keep the military budget low and to depend on peace negotiations. When war finally came, Paraguay was woefully unprepared. Luckily, disease, supply problems, and lack of morale among the Indian peasants who served as common soldiers undermined the Bolivian invasion. Fighting from interior lines, the Paraguayan army pushed the enemy back; but even so the soldiers often had to equip themselves with arms left behind by the retreating Bolivians. After the war a bitter and rebellious faction of the army overthrew the Liberal government, proclaiming it a traitor to the country's sovereignty.

The 1936 revolution split the armed forces between those who favored change and those whose fortunes were tied to the Liberal party. One army officer after another came to power, until finally the country exploded again in a civil war. After the bloodletting came another period of civilian rule, this time with the Colorado party taking over in 1948. But, as with the Liberals, factionalism split the Colorado politicians so badly that another series of unstable governments resulted—with the army playing a major role in each turnover. At last, with Stroessner's seizure of power in 1954, the military assumed direct control once more.

Geography, therefore, has helped to fashion a praetorian tradition in Paraguay. But it has also helped to keep the country poor. Although Paraguay possesses a favorable climate, good soil, and mineral deposits, its situation as a landlocked nation distant from world markets has made those advantages difficult to exploit profitably. Also, the distribution of the land has been extremely lopsided, resulting in a vast number of poor subsistence farmers and a tiny elite of great estate owners. Table 1 gives the distribution of farmland at the time of Paraguay's last agricultural census, in 1956, shortly after Stroessner came to power.

Thus, the Paraguayan rural sector, which comprises most of the country's economic life, was (and still is) dominated by large farmers and ranchers who produced the main commercial products consumed at home or shipped abroad: beef, cotton, timber, tobacco, yerba mate (a bitter green tea greatly prized in southern South America), quebracho extract (obtained from the quebracho, or "axebreaker," tree and used in tanning), and leather. Their output accounted for the modest $30.7 million worth of exports registered in 1953. At the other extreme was the large mass of *minifundistas* living, for the most part, outside the market economy. Many of them did not even own the land they worked. Commonly they were squatters who practiced a shifting type of farming in the remote backlands. They would move on to a corner of some large estate, erect a simple hut, clear a patch of land, and live there until the soil gave out. They were seldom expelled because the big *latifundios* were so vast and, as a rule, so inefficiently run that their owners had little idea of what was going on in the distant outreaches of their property. Already living the life of

TABLE I. *Land Distribution in Paraguay*

Category	Number of Farms	Percentage of All Farms	Percentage of All Land
Minifundio (0–10 hectares)	103,666	69.2	2.3
Small farms (10–99 hectares)	41,011	27.4	5.0
Medium farms (100–999 hectares)	3,391	2.3	6.0
Large farms (1,000–4,999 hectares)	1,015	0.7	13.2
Latifundios (over 5,000 hectares)	534	0.4	73.5

Source: República del Paraguay, Ministerio de Agricultura y Ganadería, *Censo Agropecuario, 1956*, p. 14. The categories of farms are the author's, and the table has been collapsed for brevity. One hectare equals about 2.5 acres.

aristocrats, the *latifundistas* had little incentive to maximize their profits or to put more than a small fraction of their land into cultivation. Therefore, it was used by the squatters, whose lives were spent moving from place to place throughout the interior. Buying little and selling little, they used the same primitive farming methods as had earlier generations. The results of this backward rural economy were, according to a contemporary observer, that "less than one percent of the land in Paraguay is sown to the most important field crops in the country. What land is used is by no means cultivated as intensively as it might be. The average farmer's equipment is an axe, a hoe, and a machete. Despite the efforts of the government to sell plows at cost, only two or three percent of all farmers have breaking plows. The ox is the only source of power other than human."[2] The predominance of subsistence agriculture meant that the average per capita income in 1953 was only $200.

In the mid-1950s most of Paraguay's 1.3 million people lived on farms or in villages; only 20 percent were classified as urban—that is, living in towns of twenty thousand inhabitants or more. Asunción, the capital, with a population of over two hundred thousand, was the largest city by far. Even so, the pace of life there was that of a sleepy tropical outpost. Spread over seven hills and overlooking a harbor on the eastern shore, it was laced by shady streets lined with orange trees. Its colonial-style stuccoed buildings were low and brightly colored, with quiet interior gardens. In the period discussed here the horse cart and the ox cart were far more common than the automobile. Indeed, there were fewer than five thousand vehicles of all types in the country, of which about half were private cars. The telephone was an even rarer luxury. Fewer than half the homes in Asunción had electricity, and almost none had running water. The populace— rich and poor alike—obtained drinking water from peddlers, who brought it into the city on muleback. The few homes that had inside toilets or showers operated them from a cistern atop the roof; most homes depended on outhouses and wells.[3]

Like most people in the tropics, *asunceños* rose early to work, for in the middle of the day the heavy, humid heat was so pulverizing that everything closed down for a siesta, which lasted until evening. In the early 1950s, before the automobile and motorcycle invaded the downtown streets, many people went downtown and back in ancient trolley cars that clanged and rattled loudly or in even more decrepit wooden-sided buses. Quite a few people went barefoot: the shoeshine boys, the cigar-smoking peasant women who sold little *chipá* cakes of cornmeal and cheese on the street corners, the old men who lounged on the benches in the park. Occasionally an extra dash of color was added when Indians came into town from the Chaco, complete with native dress, to trade their handicrafts for supplies.

Yet however backward and countrified Asunción might have seemed to an outsider in 1954, it was the center of government, trade, industry, and culture for the people of Paraguay. Most of the goods entering or leaving the country passed through its harbor. What little manufacturing Paraguay had took place there—mainly small establishments engaged in food processing, simple textiles, pharmaceuticals, and furniture making. The average factory employed only about twelve workers and often had to shut down for part of the day because of shortages of electric power.[4] The commercial quarter ran from the harbor up a hill and thence along the Calle Palma to the heart of town. It consisted chiefly of seed stores, dry goods stores, hardware stores, and tourist shops. Interspersed with these were the larger baroque-style buildings that housed the government ministries and banks. Overlooking the harbor, above the docks, was the Presidential Palace, with its two wings flanking a spacious courtyard in front of which was chained a Bolivian tank captured in the Chaco War. Across the street were the police headquarters and barracks. To one side of the palace was the Military College, where cadets were trained; to the other side was a pretty park, at the opposite end of which was the Congress building, considerably smaller and less imposing than the Presidential Palace. Diagonally across the park from the Congress stood the National Cathedral.

This was the public aspect of the capital at the time Stroessner was rising to power. Private life, on the other hand, revolved around the family, and among the educated classes, who alone counted politically, it took place behind the blank stuccoed walls that shut off the home from the outside. The concept of family extended beyond the parents and children to include distant relations, and even godparents and godchildren. These ties were close and powerful. To the average Paraguayan anyone not connected with his family—save perhaps for a few very close friends—was viewed with a certain reserve, if not suspicion. The family, not the general community, was his haven, his support, and the object of his loyalty.

This pride in family had many virtues, but it also stunted the growth of civic spirit. Even public associations such as political parties tended to be based on clusters of families. That might explain why Paraguayan politics were so bitter and vicious, for they involved not only—nor even chiefly—clashes of principle. Rather, they involved blood relationships, which tinged the political struggle with deep personal emotions. Once a party took power, such relationships made nepotism, favoritism, and corruption inevitable. After all, from the Paraguayan's point of view it was only natural that for those in office the claims of family or friends should take precedence over those of strangers. To apply impersonal criteria to such things as hiring for a job, granting a loan, awarding a contract, or deciding a lawsuit would be not only alien but also disloyal and therefore reprehensible.

It should be remembered, too, that in a country where economic opportunities were so limited a job in the government was a much desired source of income. Politics was largely a struggle to control scarce resources so as to allocate them to one's family and friends. Getting power required the construction of an intricate web of personal connections. Family relationships might branch out to include rich landowners, merchants, army officers, or intellectuals, all of whose talents could be marshaled in a political contest. The head of such a family would loom large in party affairs. But seldom could any individual dominate the political scene by himself. It was necessary to ally with other influential men. Over generations these alliances had become more or less traditional, forming the basis for the two main parties, the Colorados and the Liberals. Nevertheless, given the construction of such parties, they were bound to be divided into various personal factions. Once a party got into power the *caudillos*, or factional bosses, often quarreled over the division of the spoils. That was a frequent cause of instability in government. Meanwhile, those in the opposing party fared even worse. Disconnected from those in power, they had no political leverage. In fact, their freedom and property were in danger. It was common practice to jail or exile opponents and to expropriate their property. If a party's triumph came after a particularly violent struggle, the defeated leaders might even be killed. In brief, the opposition was protected by no objective rule of law. Plundered and persecuted, it could only wait for the day when political fortunes changed—and work for that day by conspiring against the regime. When the turnover finally came, the incumbents could expect little mercy from their enemies.

For the most part, politics concerned only the educated classes in the capital. Outside of Asunción the vast majority of Paraguayans lived isolated from and indifferent to modern life. They had no radios, no telephones, and received no newspapers—nor could they have read them if any had been available. Communications with the city were difficult: in 1953 the country had fewer than one hundred miles of paved road. Most roads in the interior were mere dirt tracks, impassable in the rainy season. Thus, rural Paraguayans had almost no impact on their country's political life. Exceptions to this arose when, on occasion, the peasants were mobilized by party leaders. Clientalistic traditions many generations old may have made a peasant family identify itself with one of the great landowning families. Thus the individual peasant might have called himself a Liberal or Colorado. He might have worn a blue or a red poncho and been ready to sacrifice himself as cannon fodder in the country's partisan struggles whenever his *patrón* told him to do so. But unless stirred by his "betters," he had few ties to national politics and little sustained interest in it.

The small provincial towns also had little political influence. According to the 1950 census, only three of them had more than ten thousand inhabitants: Concepción, in the north, on the Paraguay River; Encarnación, in the south, on the Paraná River; and Villarica, in the mountains of central Paraguay.[5] None of them had more than twenty thousand people. The typical provincial capital was little more than a sleepy village with cows grazing on the grassy central square, chickens pecking around the steps of rude, unpainted houses, and dogs sleeping in the dirt streets. It was easy for the police to control such villages. They had no trouble spotting outsiders or learning of suspicious goings-on.

By contrast, it was easy to be involved in politics in Asunción, even if one was in the opposition. The city was more heterogeneous, each individual in it was less conspicuous, and the possibilities for political contacts were more numerous. The heads of the political parties, labor unions, businessmen's groups, and farmers' and ranchers' associations, the archbishop of the Catholic church, and the National University, with its traditionally volatile students, were all located there, as well as the local and foreign newspapers, radio, magazines, movies, lectures, and occasional public rallies. Despite censorship, there was an opposition press—although it often had to go underground.

In the capital, too, were the key foreign embassies: the Argentine, Brazilian, and American embassies especially. Also, the largest cavalry and infantry garrisons were nearby, as were navy and air force bases, the heavily armed police, the Military College, and the General Staff headquarters. Personal contacts inside these could be used by disgruntled politicians to instigate a revolt against the incumbents. Since the 1870s the quick, sudden coup had been a frequent route to power. The large number of turnovers in the Presidential Palace testified to the efficacy of this tactic. To guard against this those in power tried to put trusted friends in sensitive military commands, and they formed personal networks of friends and clients who worked as spies (*pyragüés*, or "hairy soles," in the local Indian language) to supplement the efforts of the police in discovering plots.

This was the paradox of Paraguayan life in the mid-1950s. The casual visitor to Asunción could envy the apparent calm of its shaded streets and secluded courtyards. He could admire its handsome *mestizo* people—a mixture of Spaniard and Guaraní Indian—and note with surprise that the population retained its aboriginal heritage so much that the Guaraní language was spoken as often as Spanish in the capital, while in the countryside Guaraní predominated. He could take pleasure too in the distinctive music inspired by that heritage: the languid *polcas* and *guaranías* played on the Indian harp. Finally he might leave with souvenirs of the native lace and pottery, thinking to himself that here was a simple, tropical Arcadia. What the casual visitor could not see (unless he was unlucky) was the dark side of Paraguayan society—the political hatreds, the incessant conspiring, the persecutions, and the sordid double-dealings that constituted everyday political life. Behind the peaceful facade was a violent tradition, all the more vicious at times because it involved emotional ties and personal rivalries. That was the political school in which Stroessner trained and became an expert.

Stroessner did not, of course, invent the rules of that political game. He played them as he found them. But in mastering them so well he may have succeeded in changing the nature of the game. In any case, his long rule, spanning more than two decades, has inevitably witnessed changes in Paraguay. Some of the features described here are still present today; others have disappeared or been greatly modified. Such changes, and their ramifications for politics, will be discussed in the later chapters. For the present, let us keep in mind this picture of Paraguayan society on the eve of Stroessner's takeover, and then proceed in the next chapter to trace the historical events which helped to fashion it.

Chapter 2. The Making of a Political Tradition

The Early Tyrants

When Paraguay gained independence from Spain in 1811, few of its inhabitants had any experience in government. Spain's imperial administration had been highly centralized and suspicious of any initiative on the part of the colonists. *Criollos*—Spaniards born in America—were usually excluded from positions in the colonial governments. Instead, trusted officials were sent out from the mother country to be viceroys, governors, judges, and tax collectors, and they were frequently transferred to prevent their acquiring local attachments. Until 1776 Paraguay was administered by a crown-appointed governor, who was immediately responsible to the viceroy in Peru. After that, the colony became part of the new Viceroyalty of La Plata, whose capital was Buenos Aires. The *criollos'* only opportunity for representation was the town council, or *cabildo*. The *cabildo*, however, seldom met and had no real power.

The colony was poor and isolated. It contributed no gold, other precious metals, or lucrative crop to the crown's treasury, so therefore it was neglected. Even among the relatively well-to-do *criollos* few were educated or even literate. Most were ignorant about the world outside their remote tropical province. The native Guaraní Indians worked the plantations as slaves or lived under paternalistic tutelage in the Jesuit missions. At best they were treated like helpless children; at worst they were mercilessly exploited. Consequently, when independence came, the Paraguayan population was hardly fit for self-government.

What is more, neighboring countries posed serious threats to the young nation's independence. In Buenos Aires the *criollo* patriots had thrown off Spanish rule, but were now claiming the old authority of the viceroyalty to govern Paraguay as a province of the new Argentine Republic. One attempt had already been made to incorporate the country when, in 1810, General Manuel Belgrano invaded Paraguayan territory to "liberate" it from Spanish rule. That had failed, thanks to the Paraguayan militia, but the *porteños* (as the people of Buenos Aires are called) were still determined to bring all of the old viceregal territories under their control. Brazil threatened as well. For two hundred years the Brazilians had been expanding westward, and a weak and disorganized Paraguay could do little to hinder that movement. Finally, added to these external threats, some groups inside Paraguay had loyalties elsewhere: old Spanish families who refused to accept the new republic and merchants whose commercial relations with Buenos Aires made them favor incorporation into Argentina.

At first Paraguay was governed by a junta composed mainly of militia officers, but those uneducated and unsophisticated men soon showed themselves incapable of running a government. They knew nothing of finances, administration, or diplomacy. They were even unable to maintain internal order. At last, in desperation, they turned to one of the few *criollos* who had a university education and experience in government—Doctor José Gaspar Rodríguez de Francia. Francia accepted the responsibility, however, only on the assurance that he would have a completely free hand. Then, having been granted temporary dictatorial powers, he proceeded to confound the Argentine diplomats, build up the country's defenses, put an end to the internal disorders, and arrange the finances on a sound basis. In 1814 a grateful congress met and made him dictator for life, with the official title of "El Supremo." That was the beginning of a long, harsh tyranny. And it was also a fateful beginning for Paraguay's political development.[1]

A solitary, ascetic bachelor, Francia devoted himself singlemindedly to governing Paraguay. The backbone of his policy, one which he pursued at all costs, was to keep the country independent. To do that he turned the society into a barracks state in which everything was channeled toward maintaining a strong army. Every male *criollo* and Indian between seventeen and sixty was required to serve; out of a population of around 375,000 Francia was able to field a force of some 5,500 regular troops and 25,000 reservists.[2] To insure that the army was fed and supplied he had the state take over most of the farmland by confiscating the property of the upper classes. Then he leased it to peasants under terms that gave the government the right to say what would be planted and how much it could sell for. Some farms and ranches were worked directly by the army. He pursued a similar policy with industry. Having sealed off the country's borders to prevent an invasion, Francia was forced to pursue a policy of economic autarky. That meant setting up state factories to supply the army's—and, incidentally, the civilians'—needs. The prices of all goods were fixed by the government, and no foreign trade was permitted except by Francia's rarely granted leave. In fact, no one was allowed to leave or enter Paraguay. Even going from one village to the next required a passport from the police.[3]

Such an unnatural regime required a vast network of repression to make it work. All mail was censored, public meetings were banned, and the publication of books or newspapers was forbidden. Spies were everywhere. The chief targets of Francia's hatred were the rich Spaniards and *criollos*. Their political leaders were arrested, and wholesale confiscations soon reduced these families to poverty. When "El Supremo" caught them plotting against him, he ordered a general roundup of suspects. Dozens of executions followed. Many others were sent to concentration camps deep in the jungle or else to the city's dungeons, where they languished and died. Those who were able to evade the police escaped into exile. With the ruination of the upper class went Paraguay's modest school system. Within a short time the nation sunk to the level of a brute, benighted society.

According to his own views, however, Francia was successful. When he finally died in 1840, after a quarter century in power, Paraguay was still an independent republic whose existence was secured by a strong army. Moreover, the nation's finances were sound, for he had been both honest and parsimonious. His own life had been ascetic, and he had imposed the same discipline on his people. Francia could boast, too, that Paraguay had escaped the debilitating anarchy that had plagued its neighbors. The elimination of the old elites, together with Francia's system of state socialism, kept the country politically and culturally more homogeneous and egalitarian. Moreover, having a stake in the system of public leaseholds, the proud, simple peasantry were fanatically patriotic.

Francia's successor, Carlos Antonio López, continued the same autocratic policies. Although there was a congress, it was hand-picked by López, who ruled as an absolute dictator. The system of state socialism was kept too. The government's landholdings were extended, accounting for almost 98 percent of the entire territory. The army was increased to between seven thousand and eight thousand men, not counting reserves. But while Francia's rule had seen some economic contraction, a change of administrations in Argentina after 1852 resulted in lessened tensions, which allowed Paraguay to break out of its diplomatic and commercial isolation. Trade increased revenues, which were plowed into internal improvements: dockyards, a river fleet, a telegraph system, a railroad, several new industries, and many grand public buildings. When he died in 1862, Carlos Antonio López left Paraguay a more prosperous and militarily stronger nation.

The dead president was succeeded by his younger son, Francisco Solano López, who was also head of the army and claimed the title of "Marshal." Posterity is sharply divided over Solano López's character and intentions. The unfavorable view, shared by most foreign historians and liberal-minded Paraguayans of the last century, holds that he was a bloodthirsty despot who sacrificed his countrymen to his grandiose but futile dreams of empire. The favorable interpretation, created by modern nationalistic Paraguayan historians, argues that López was a patriot who died fighting to defend the nation from foreign imperialism. This latter view prevails among Paraguayans today. For them, "El Mariscal" is their greatest national hero.[4]

The truth probably lies somewhere in between. Argentina and Brazil did have expansionist designs on Paraguay, but it is also true that Solano López's character was impetuous and barbarous. Unlike his predecessors, he entangled Paraguay in dubious foreign alliances. When Brazil attacked Uruguay in December 1865, López felt compelled to go to the latter's defense and declare war. To invade Brazil, however, he had to cross a corridor of Argentine territory. When the Argentines refused him permission, he sent his army across anyway, and then found himself fighting two formidable powers.

The War of the Triple Alliance (Argentina, Brazil, and the Uruguayan puppet regime) lasted until 1870. Long years of military preparedness allowed Paraguay to hold out valiantly against great odds, but ultimately the war began to go against López. As it did, his megalomania swelled. He committed frightful cruelties to spur his people to greater sacrifices. Yet in the end it was hopeless. Paraguay was invaded, Asunción was burned, and López was forced to flee into the jungle. Even though all was lost, he continued to fight on, until on 1 March 1870 he was killed at Cerro Corá, near the Brazilian border. He fell shouting, "I die with my country!" But it would have been more accurate to say that his country had died with him. Out of a population of around 550,000 at the beginning of the war more than half were dead, and of those left only 14,000 were males.[5] The numb, devastated survivors could hardly have cared when the victorious Argentines and Brazilians proceeded to plunder what was left, lopping off nearly 160,000 square kilometers of territory and saddling the empty treasury with a staggering war debt of 19 million gold pesos.

Dictatorship and Chaos

In fact, Paraguay might have ceased to exist altogether, except that Argentina and Brazil soon renewed their old rivalry for regional supremacy. Brazil's army, which occupied the country for the next six years, assumed the role of political arbiter by selecting puppet presidents. But Argentina also had influence, for most of the Paraguayan politicians scrambling for office had once been exiles in Buenos Aires. They had come back to their homeland as members of the Paraguayan Legion, a military detachment that had formed in exile during the war and had fought alongside the Argentine army.

The Legionnaires were descendants of the old Paraguayan upper class, which had fled the country during the rule of Francia and the Lopezes. They were determined to do away with every vestige of the old despotic socialist state. One of their first acts in 1870 was to draw up a democratic constitution, after which they began selling off the state's lands and businesses. Most of the buyers were foreigners. Such generosity earned the Legionnaire governments good credit abroad, and the British banking firm of Baring Brothers was willing to extend two very large loans. Unfortunately for Paraguay, the Legionnaires seized most of this money as their personal spoils; little of it ever reached the treasury or went to any good use. The country was simply left with another enormous debt.[6]

Meanwhile, Legionnaire *políticos* began to quarrel among themselves over the presidency. Only the Brazilian army could settle such disputes and provide for an orderly transfer of power. But by 1876 the cost of maintaining the army of occupation was becoming a burden to Brazil, and the troops were removed. Less than a year later the incumbent president, Juan Bautista Gill, was overthrown and killed in a Paraguayan army revolt led by General Bernardino Caballero.

This time, however, the triumphant faction was led by a nationalist, not a Legionnaire. Caballero had fought by Solano López to the last, and he was a hero to all those who still waved the bloody shirt and called all Legionnaires traitors. For the next twenty-seven years he imposed a semblance of order on Paraguay, first as president of the republic (1880–86), and then as head of the armed forces. Unfortunately for his nationalist policy, however, Caballero inherited a bankrupt treasury whose only immediate source of revenue was the continued sale of public properties. Consequently, the extensive state landholdings, the railroad, the factories, and the mines were sold off—often at bargain prices. Most of the beneficiaries of these sales were foreign speculators, for the vast bulk of the Paraguayan people were still impoverished by the war. In this way huge tracts of land passed into the hands of foreign absentee landlords. The helpless peasants now lost the protection of the old paternalistic state; they were thrown onto the mercy of the great *latifundistas*, who ran their estates like feudal fiefdoms.[7]

The Legionnaires were not content to remain out of power for long, however, and in Captain Benigno Ferreira they had a military leader every bit as resourceful as Caballero. Ferreira had been an exile under Solano López and had helped to found the Paraguayan Legion in Buenos Aires at the beginning of the war. He was so pro-Argentine that the Brazilian occupation army had deported him in 1874. Wisely, he remained across the border after Caballero came to power, but spent his time lobbying the government in Buenos Aires to help him equip another army to invade Paraguay. Meanwhile, in 1887 a group of anti-Caballero politicians formed a club called the Centro Democrático, which claimed to oppose the dictatorship on liberal principles. A few years later, as if to emphasize its liberalism, the Centro changed its name to the Liberal party. Rejecting the authoritarian socialist tradition that Caballero represented, the Liberals claimed a commitment to parliamentary democracy and free enterprise.

Quick to recognize the advantages of a formal organization, Caballero responded a few months later by establishing the National Republican Association. Because it adopted red as its symbolic color, in contrast to the blue banner of the Liberals, the association became known more popularly as the Colorado party. The Colorados were not united, however. As time went on Caballero began to lose his grip and factions began to appear. Some Colorados had gotten rich through land speculation and had grown conservative. Others were disgruntled because they had not profited enough. Still others were tired of Caballero's long domination of the political scene and wanted to get him out of the way. Also, years in power made the Colorados careless. They became lax about admitting questionable elements into their party. Some of those who entered their ranks were former Legionnaires who now claimed to have changed. However, some of those who slipped into positions of power continued to seek out their old friends in the Liberal Party.

Caballero purged the government in 1902, but it was already too late to restore discipline. Two years later, with backing from the Argentines, Ferreira launched an armed invasion which met only minimal resistance. At last the Liberals were in power.[8]

Instead of installing a democracy, however, the Liberals merely replaced the strong rule of army men with the weak rule of civilians.[9] No one, not Ferreira nor even the party's great writer and propagandist, Cecilio Báez, was able to keep Liberalism from splintering into petty factions. All conspired against the rest, and some even sought the support of the ousted Colorados. The army was also a presence, of course, since every ambitious *caudillo* had to have his contacts inside the garrisons for the purpose of staging a coup. Some military men took advantage of this to seize power for themselves. Colonel Albino Jara, who tried to impose his own personalist rule in 1911, is one example. In all, fifteen different men occupied the presidency in the eighteen years from 1904 to 1922. Then order broke down completely, and a civil war erupted between the two main Liberal factions which was to ravage the country for fourteen months.

The period from 1924 to 1936 saw a gradual return to orderly government. Backed by the military, the next three Liberal administrations followed with relatively little disturbance. But the country was bankrupt, for each revolt had destroyed more property and had left the state more deeply in debt. Moreover, the political calm was deceptive. The Colorados refused to participate in elections, and a growing number of Liberal dissidents also withheld their allegiance from the system. Many of the latter were on the left, politically. They had grown increasingly critical of a society in which so much property was in foreign hands while the peasantry was held in bondage through debt servitude.

The most serious threat to the government, however, was the steady encroachment of Bolivian soldiers in the disputed Chaco territory. That immense wasteland lying between the Andes and the Paraguay River was claimed by both countries, but years of weak, unstable government in Paraguay had given the Bolivians their opportunity to advance a chain of forts all the way to the headwaters of the river. The German-trained and equipped Bolivian armies were also better prepared for war. When the Paraguayans finally awoke to this invasion, they unleashed their indignation on the Liberals for their flaccid diplomacy. The country's plight was suddenly dramatized in December 1928 when a frustrated major named Rafael Franco led his little garrison of Chaco troops to attack and destroy the Bolivians' Fort Vanguardia. At that, the Bolivians seized two Paraguayan forts, and the two sides were on the verge of war. But when it realized that Paraguay had no plans for mobilization and was lacking in arms, munitions, foods, and medical supplies, the government could do nothing but sign a humiliating treaty that promised, among other things, the rebuilding of Fort Vanguardia for the Bolivians. Though a popular hero by this time, Major Franco was dropped from the army.[10]

Nationalist agitation against the Liberal government of President José P. Guggiari was fanned by a new political organization, the Liga Nacional Independiente (Independent National League), which demanded stepped-up preparations for war. The worst antigovernment riots broke out on 23 October 1931, when a mob of students tried to storm Guggiari's home. The demonstrators were fired on by soldiers, and ten were killed. That event was to have long-lasting ramifications, for the students composed the army's reserve officer corps. When the Chaco War finally came, in July 1932, this resentful youth joined with the long-suffering regular officers to plot a postwar Paraguay much different from that under the Liberal rule of the previous quarter-century. The pivotal figure in their plans was none other than Rafael Franco, who had been recalled to the army at the outbreak of the war, promoted to colonel, and given command of the Second Army Corps.

The Nationalist Revolution

To the outside world the overthrow of President Eusebio Ayala's Liberal government on 17 February 1936, just after it had guided the country to a glorious military victory, was a startling surprise. In less than four years the ill-prepared Paraguayan forces, taking advantage of superior esprit de corps and familiarity with the terrain, had swept the Bolivians out of the Chaco. But few foreigners realized that, in the army's view, the victory had been won in spite of—not because of— the Liberals. The government's popularity plummeted even further when it voted down pensions for disabled war veterans while rewarding Marshal José Felix Estigarribia, the commander in chief, with a handsome bonus. Also, the fighting spirit of the Paraguayan peasant soldiers stirred all nationalists to demand social reforms. The Liberals, however, were opposed to such legislation, which they claimed went against their laissez-faire principles.

Colonel Franco was still at the center of most anti-Liberal plots. His bold tactics and his humane treatment of the soldiers under his command made him a greater hero than ever. Now, as head of the Military College, he continued to criticize the government for not taking a tougher stand at the Chaco peace talks. At first, President Ayala ignored him, but when it became clear in early February 1936 that

Franco really was involved in a conspiracy, he was put on an airplane and sent to Argentina. However, that only spurred on the other plotters, who now feared discovery. Having secured the support of the big Campo Grande cavalry base outside the capital, they launched their coup before dawn on 17 February. By the end of the day, President Ayala had surrendered, bringing to an end thirty-two years of Liberal rule. On the following day, Franco was called back from exile to head the government.

A true military *caudillo* with great popular appeal, Franco loved to enthuse the crowds with his balcony oratory. But his government was doomed from the beginning, composed as it was of holders of every shade of dissident opinion who shared nothing but a hatred of the Liberals. Anselmo Jover Peralta, the minister of justice and education, was a socialist. Juan Stefanich, the foreign affairs minister, headed the Liga Nacional Independiente. Hence, he was a nationalist, but lukewarm about social reform. Gómez Freire Esteves and his brother Luís—the interior and treasury ministers—were leaders of an old Liberal faction called the *cívicos.* They wanted a corporate state along the lines of Mussolini's Italy. Finally, the Colorados were represented by Bernardino Caballero, a grandson of the great general, who was minister of agriculture.

Though divided internally, the revolutionary government nevertheless accomplished three important things. First, it made a real start toward agrarian reform with the law of May 1936, which provided for the expropriation of *latifundios* and the resale of land on easy terms to the peasantry. Over the next few months some two hundred thousand hectares (about half a million acres) were distributed to about ten thousand families. Second, it promulgated a labor code that gave the workers the right to unionize and strike and guaranteed them a wide range of social insurance benefits. Encouraged by the newly created Labor Department, some seventy-three unions formed and combined into a great national association, the Paraguayan Workers' Confederation (CPT). Third, to restore the nation's pride even more, the Franco government recovered the body of Francisco Solano López from its unmarked grave at Cerro Corá and reburied it with high honors in a small baroque chapel, now designated the Pantheon of Heroes, in downtown Asunción.[11]

Despite these accomplishments, though, the revolutionary government gradually lost popularity. It wasted much time and disillusioned many of its original supporters with bitter intrigues among its cabinet ministers. Jover Peralta was the first to be ousted—largely at the army's insistence, for he had been a pacifist during the war. Then the Freire Esteves brothers tried to steer the government toward fascism.

On 10 March 1936, the interior minister published the infamous Decree Law Number 152, which declared the Paraguayan revolution to be "the same type as the totalitarian social transformations of contemporary Europe." That touched off a storm of protest from the public—and from other cabinet ministers—which soon drove its authors out of the government. Finally, when Stefanich convinced Franco to set up an entirely new political party to embody the principles of the revolution, Caballero and the Colorados withdrew their support from the regime. In the end, Franco's government rested on the all too narrow base of the Liga Nacional Independiente, and that was not enough. Another military revolt took place on 13 August 1937, led by Colonel Ramón Paredes, who had been in touch with the exiled Liberal leaders. The coup was justified on the grounds that Franco needed to be liberated from his "bad advisers." However, when he refused to cooperate with Paredes, the plotters had no choice but to remove him from office and send him out of the country.

Although the revolutionary government had fallen, the expectation of reforms was still strong, possessing a momentum that would be hard to stop. Yet the Liberals returned to power convinced that they could turn back the clock, and they sought to cloak their intentions by replacing Franco with another war hero, Marshal Estigarribia. But Estigarribia soon became aware that counterrevolutionary policies would never work. Determined to place the Liberal party in the mainstream of popular opinion rather than in opposition to it, he gathered about him a group of brilliant young men—the so-called New Liberals—who were committed to social reform. That brought him into a head-on collision with the traditional Liberals who controlled Congress. A stalemate resulted. To break it, Estigarribia finally dissolved Congress and declared himself absolute dictator. Moreover, to advertise his government's desire for change he scrapped the Constitution of 1870, with its liberal democratic and laissez-faire principles, and replaced it with the Constitution of 1940.[12]

The new constitution provided for an all-powerful state, with authority concentrated in the executive. The government had broad powers to intervene in the economy, which it justified by such high-sounding phrases as "the exploitation of man by man is forbidden," "in no case will the private interests prevail over the general interests of the nation," and "all citizens are obliged to collaborate for the good of the state and the nation." The constitution also provided for a unicameral congress, but it possessed few powers. Far more important was the new Council of State, a kind of corporative chamber modeled after Mussolini's Corporate State to represent group interests, such as farmers, businessmen, bankers, the military, and the Catholic church. Like its Italian model, Estigarribia's corporate state was to have sweeping powers to suppress any private association, to suspend individual liberties, or to take any exceptional action considered to be in the state's interest.[13]

Unfortunately for the New Liberals, Estigarribia died in an airplane accident less than a month after the new constitution was promulgated. Back came Colonel Paredes and the old Liberals, who put up the defense minister, General Higinio Morínigo, as their temporary presidential straw man. That was a mistake, for although Morínigo had seemed a genial type with no great ambition, he soon showed himself to be a masterful politician. First he outmaneuvered Paredes and his military clique by shuffling commands. Once he was independent of them, he turned on the old Liberals, calling them traitorous "Legionnaires," and declared their party to be outlawed.

Morínigo set himself up as a nonpartisan dictator whose only real base of support was the armed forces. His chief collaborators were three pro-Fascist officers who called themselves the Frente de Guerra: Colonel Victoriano Benítez Vera, the head of Campo Grande; Colonel Bernardo Aranda, the chief of the army's general staff; and Colonel Pablo Stagni, the air force commander. But Morínigo also enjoyed some popular support, for he was a country boy who knew the peasants well and spoke fluent Guaraní. He delighted his audiences by pointing to Paraguay's tricolor flag and exclaiming, "I am neither red [Colorado] nor blue [Liberal], but white—here, just in the middle." His popularity was heightened, too, by the prosperity that accompanied World War II, when the Allies were buying Paraguay's farm exports in unprecedented quantities. For those who refused to go along with his rule, there were only two choices: exile or one of the many concentration camps that were built out in the Chaco. To make sure that such dissidents were few, the press was tightly censored and *pyragüés* were everywhere.[14]

The Coalition Government

The political atmosphere suddenly changed with the defeat of the Axis in World War II. It was no longer easy for pro-Fascist regimes like Morínigo's to ignore pressures for democratic reforms. In neighboring Bolivia the right-wing government of Colonel Gualberto Villaroel fell in July 1946 after a bloody revolt that ended with the president hanging from a lamp post. Morínigo took the cue and began to loosen up. To accomplish this, however, he had to ditch the Frente de Guerra and seek support from the more moderate elements in the military.

His first step was to get control of the Campo Grande. He sent Colonel Benítez Vera out of the country as Paraguay's representative to Juan Perón's presidential inauguration. While the unsuspecting colonel was in Buenos Aires, Morínigo took control of the cavalry base. The inauguration ceremonies had already begun when Benítez Vera was informed of what had happened. To the surprise of his Argentine hosts he hurriedly excused himself and took a speedboat back to Paraguay. Disembarking outside of Asunción, he made his way to the Campo Grande, where he rallied the troops and deposed Morínigo's new commander. Caught off guard in his turn, Morínigo called on General Juan Rovira, the head of the Military College, to assume the defense of the capital. Rovira was a liberal officer who, as it turned out, had the firm support of the majority of the armed forces. Not only was he able to call on the infantry regiment in Asunción and the artillery regiment in nearby Paraguarí, but he even caused two of the three cavalry regiments at the Campo Grande to defect. Benítez Vera's invasion of the capital was stalled, but he was hoping for air force support to tip the advantage in his favor once more. It never came, for Colonel Stagni was already under arrest. Upon learning this, Benítez Vera surrendered, and the revolt was over. The clash of troops had resulted in only five men killed: two officers and three enlisted men.[15]

Paraguay now entered a period of liberalization. Having eliminated the right-wing colonels, the moderate military officers put pressure on Morínigo to prepare the country for a return to constitutional government. Chief among these reformers were General Rovira, General Amancio Pampliega, the defense minister, and General Vicente Machuca, the army's popular commander. Press censorship was ended officially on 13 June, and on 20 July, Morínigo revoked his decree banning all political party activities. Then, a few days later, an even more startling announcement was made. The government had reached an agreement with the Colorado party and Colonel Franco's followers—now known as the Febreristas, after the February Revolution—to form a coalition cabinet. That was to be the first step toward holding elections for a constitutional convention that would liberalize the state. There would be a general amnesty for all parties, even the Liberals and Communists. After the convention general elections would be held, and Morínigo would hand over his powers to the new democratic government. As for Morínigo himself, he said that he was ready to resume his duties as an army officer, or if that were unacceptable he would gladly retire to his farm. Maybe he would even go abroad for awhile, just to remove any doubts about his sincere intentions. In any case, Paraguay was going to experiment with democracy.

The coalition government began its work in an atmosphere of public optimism. The press was free, exiles were returning, political prisoners were freed, and labor unions were enjoying a new era of autonomy. Morínigo fixed 25 December 1946 as the date for the constitutional convention. Each party prepared for the coming elections amid a fever of political activity—with rallies, marches, speeches, and posters.

Beneath this atmosphere of excitement, however, was a note of suspicion. Morínigo was a wily manipulator who had double-crossed his rivals many times before. Was this just another one of his maneuvers to lure people into a false sense of security, so that he could strike when their guard was down? And even if he was sincere, how about the different parties competing for power? Would they really forget the hatreds of the past and submit their political fortunes to the test of the ballot box? And would they respect the results if they lost?

The Febrerista movement, organized since October 1945 as the Concentración Revolucionaria Febrerista, reflected all these suspicions. It was deeply divided from the outset over the propriety of taking part in the coalition government. Many of those who had suffered under Morínigo felt betrayed by their leaders. The leaders themselves had argued bitterly inside the executive committee over the proposal—which had passed by only a single vote. The main proponents of the coalition were Arnaldo Valdovinos, who became the minister of agriculture, as well as minister of industry and commerce, and José Soljancic, who took over the public health ministry. Valdovinos, a hotheaded leftist, had long been a thorn in the side of the party's copresidents, Colonel Franco and Juan Stefanich. He had been exiled during the February Revolution because of his newspaper articles scourging the Franco government for its slow pace on reform. Soljancic, a more diplomatic sort, headed the Febrerista Committee of Revolutionary Organization, whose job in recent years had been to keep the Febrerista exiles in touch with underground student and worker organizations inside Paraguay. Between them, these two men were finally able to convince the reluctant party chiefs that a coalition government was a wedge for getting back into power.

Even so, the Febrerista leaders were not willing to pin all their hopes on working inside the legal system, especially as there was a quicker route to power. Many of them were former military officers who still had personal contacts inside the armed forces. A coup was not out of the question. But whether they were working toward elections or planning to overthrow the government, the Febreristas' principal asset was Colonel Franco. Not only was he a hero and a model to many of the officers but he still had an enormous personal following among the people. On 4 August, the day of his return from exile, more than twenty thousand persons—an enormous crowd for Asunción—stood at the harbor, waiting to greet him. Significantly, they also lined the streets leading to the Presidential Palace. The atmosphere was tense. Morínigo had left town to take a "holiday" at his private residence in the country and had sent an aide to greet Franco. Only a small guard patrolled the palace.

For a brief hour Paraguay's political fate rested in Franco's hands as he stepped off the river steamer, amid clamorous applause, and went to the balcony of the customshouse to speak to the crowd. He could have shouted, "To the Palace! Down with Morínigo!" and the expectant mob probably would have obeyed him. There was little to stop them, and as later events were to show, the military probably would have supported such a coup. But instead, Franco was restrained. He said simply, "I call for everyone to collaborate in establishing tranquility in Paraguay." On that note of moderation he entered a waiting car and drove to his home. It was an unusual gesture of statesmanship for Paraguay, but it also may have been an egregious blunder.[16]

The other coalition partner, the Colorado party, was also divided between moderates and radicals. Its leader at this time was the aged and respected Doctor Juan Mallorquín. So long as this patriarch was alive, unity prevailed, but just below the surface lay a deep and widening gulf between two very different wings of the party. One of these was led by Mallorquín's apparent successor, Federico Cháves, the party's vice-president. The son of a Portuguese immigrant, Cháves was a tall, aristocratic man of sixty-five who had distinguished himself as a lawyer and judge. He was known as a political moderate who spoke for the "democratic" wing of the party. Although a strong party man, he nonetheless felt that the Colorados would have to learn how to compromise if democracy were going to take root. He believed in the coalition government. Accordingly, in the negotiations with Morínigo to parcel out cabinet seats he agreed to a parity with the Febreristas in order to get their participation—even though he was certain that the Colorados' following was more numerous. As a result, the cabinet consisted of three Colorados, three Febreristas, and two military men without partisan affiliations.[17] Cháves himself got the public works portfolio.

The other wing of the party was headed by a tough militant named Juan Natalicio González. Short, dark, Indian featured, and self-educated, González was the exact opposite of the courtly Cháves.[18] He was also an inspired political agitator, having launched his career as one of the leaders of the tragic 23 *de octubre* protest rally. In the aftermath of that shooting, González was arrested and sent into exile, where he remained until the February Revolution.

González was no mere rabble-rouser, however. Although he came from the interior and had little formal education, his father had been a wealthy farmer. Consequently, as a young man, González had traveled to Europe and around South America. He was a steady contributor to the Colorado newspaper, *Patria*, and eventually became its editor. He had a vigorous writing style that lent itself to polemics, but he also showed an aptitude for poetry. In short, González was an "engaged intellectual," who also had considerable leadership ability and a commanding personality which won him a fanatical following. At the age of thirty-nine he was elected president of the party, and on returning from exile he reassumed the editorship of *Patria*. He also accepted a commission from the Franco government to lead a cultural mission to Argentina and Uruguay, but resigned that position when the Colorados broke with the revolution. Once again he was arrested, and was sent to a concentration camp called Peña Hermosa, far up the Paraguay River. He soon escaped, however, and made his way to Argentina.

It was during this second exile that González's ideas took on more definite shape. He had always been a fervent nationalist, but now his contacts in Buenos Aires introduced him to a circle of Argentine youth from the Radical party, as well as many socialist intellectuals. He became friends with several leading figures of the nationalist left, including Raúl Scalabrini Ortiz, Gabriel del Mazo, Alfredo Palacios, and the famous Peruvian *aprista* Luís Alberto Sánchez. Such intellectual stimulation resulted in his publishing, in quick succession, two histories of the Chaco War, a couple of novels, some political essays, and a sociological study of Paraguay called *Proceso y formación de la cultura paraguaya*. This last work earned him a solid reputation among Latin American intellectuals.

But González's political essays are of most interest here. Gathered together in a journal called *Guaranía*, whose costs of publication he undertook himself, they elaborated a doctrine of national socialism that was opposed in every respect to the ideas of limited government and laissez-faire economics espoused by the Liberal party. For González, the so-called liberties of liberalism were false—they were only a facade behind which the rich were permitted to exploit the poor.

Only an interventionist government, working energetically to improve
the economic and cultural environment, could guarantee effective
freedom for the lower classes. Throughout all his writings, González
displayed an emotional, almost mystical, identification with the plight
of the poor Paraguayan peasant. His remedy for Paraguay's ills was
the establishment of a strong, unified state which would expropriate
the foreign imperialists and redistribute the wealth. In *Proceso y formación* he argued that such a socialist commonwealth was quite
within Paraguay's traditions and pointed to the authoritarian systems
of Francia and the Lópezes as the period in which Paraguay had attained her greatest independence and prosperity. Although they in-
furiated the Liberals, such writings established González as the Colorados' chief propagandist and won him the enthusiastic backing of
many young activists.[19]

González was not simply a socialist radical, however. In 1945, when
Morínigo was negotiating with the Colorados about joining his government, he offered González the ambassadorship to Uruguay, and
González accepted. Then, after the Colorados agreed to enter the
coalition cabinet, González was called back to Asunción to take up
the post of finance minister. By this time he and Morínigo had become close friends—so close that, before leaving Montevideo, González called a press conference at which he praised the Paraguayan
dictator and claimed that Morínigo "had never decreed oppressive
laws himself and was working to get rid of those which his predecessors had put in his hands."[20] Although it is surprising that a reputable
intellectual would speak such balderdash and, even more, that a man
of the left could embrace a dictator whose pro-Nazi sympathies were
so well known, it must be remembered that González was a nationalist
as well as a socialist. He wanted a revolution that would raise up the
workers and peasants, but it was to be a nationalist, hence an anti-
communist, revolution. In this respect he was like many of the radicals who supported the original Italian Fascist and German National
Socialist movements. That radicalism was suppressed later by Mussolini and Hitler when they decided to seek the support of big business,
but it flowed to the top in the Argentine variety of fascism which
Juan and Eva Perón led. In the late 1930s and early 1940s, González
and Perón had traveled in the same intellectual circles in Buenos
Aires. What is more, Morínigo, like González, was a populist from
the interior. As for his pro-Nazi leanings, many nationalists in Latin
America cheered for the Axis to smash Britain and the United
States. After all, the capitalist democracies were the leading imperialist powers in the region.

Shortly after returning to Paraguay, González began to disclose a political strategy for bringing the Colorados to power—a strategy that did not include either elections or a constitutional convention. He quarreled with Cháves, whom he accused of having "sold out" the party. According to González, he himself had negotiated a deal with Morínigo the previous year by which the Colorados were to have received six seats in the cabinet to only two for the military and one for the Febreristas. However, Cháves, either through treachery or ineptitude (so González alleged), had allowed the Febreristas parity in the cabinet. Worse yet, the Febreristas actually controlled more ministries, for Valdovinos held two portfolios. That gave the Febreristas four ministries to only three for the Colorados, and that was unacceptable. Either the Febreristas would have to give up one of their posts or else Morínigo should create a new ministry—perhaps a ministry of labor—and assign it to the Colorados. As might be expected, such demands soon caused relations within the cabinet to deteriorate.

Little did González care, for he was preparing to take power by force. What is more, he had Morínigo's secret backing for his plans. What sort of political deal the two men made is not known in detail, but whatever the understanding, it became clear that Morínigo's police were instructed not to interfere as González began a violent campaign to intimidate the other parties. The first step was to break the hold of the Febreristas and Communists on the labor movement. To do this, González organized squads of toughs who raided the union meetings and attacked the leaders; similar tactics were employed in the universities. Colorado hecklers shouted down Febrerista, Liberal, and Communist speakers at student gatherings and provoked fights. Little by little, González built up a storm trooper organization which he called the Guión Rojo (Red Banner) corps. The Guionists were a fanatical and well-drilled shock troops who could control the streets and disrupt the activities of the rival parties.

A good example of Guionist street tactics took place on 14 August, the day when many top Liberal party leaders, including former president Guggiari, returned from exile. Like Franco, they came by riverboat and found a throng of admirers at the docks to greet them. After disembarking, the Liberal chiefs were escorted in a big parade up the Calle Colón, which leads from the docks, and then down the Calle Palma, which runs directly into the heart of town. The Calle Palma, however, goes past the Pantheon of Heroes—the anti-Liberal monument where the bodies of Marshal Solano López and General Caballero lie in state. There the cheering Liberal crowd was met by a large gang of well-armed toughs who shouted insults at them and followed this up with a barrage of stones. Fistfights broke out as the two angry mobs surged together. Suddenly, there was a crackle of gunfire. The police, who had been standing by, moved in with tear gas and mounted troops. It was estimated later in official reports that over two hundred shots were fired. Miraculously, no one was killed.[21]

The police put the blame on the Liberals. The Guión Rojo was not even mentioned. Nor did the police investigate the Guionists after another incident, on 8 September, when a squad of thugs stormed into the offices of the Liberal newspaper, *El País*, while the next morning's edition was being prepared. The staff was beaten badly and the presses were damaged. It was known all over town that the Guión Rojo was responsible, yet Morínigo held up the investigation and even placed a month's ban on the political activities of the Liberals. He accused them of scurrilous attacks on his government. In fact, *El País* had called on the army to oust Morínigo, whom they accused of plotting to stay in power. When *El País* returned to circulation, it was attacked again in gangland style. On the evening of 13 December a carload of Guionists pulled up outside its offices and poured more than thirty rounds of pistol fire through the windows. Fortunately, no one was killed.[22]

Clearly, the political experiment was breaking down. General Rovira, whom everyone trusted as an honest and well-intentioned officer, resigned in mid-September as minister of interior. He was disgusted at having all his investigations frustrated by Morínigo and Natalicio González. His successor was General Amancio Pampliega, another military moderate. In the meantime, Paraguayans were learning to their increasing discomfort that freedom for one's own faction implied freedom for one's opponents as well. For instance, Catholic conservatives were outraged at the upsurge in Communist party activity. The Communists were tireless. Their leaders organized street demonstrations, harangued crowds, and sent their militants to plaster hammer and sickle posters all over the downtown buildings. The Communists already controlled the stevedores' union and were trying to organize the transport and communications workers. They claimed a membership of around four thousand and boasted that it would soon double. In mid-October the Catholic conservatives organized a massive march through the streets of Asunción, demanding that the Communist party be outlawed as the first step in a "grand, national, anticommunist crusade." Concerned to avoid a clash with the church in this very traditional and Catholic nation, Obdulio Barthe and Oscar Creydt, the country's two top Communists, met with Monseñor Juan Bogarín, the archbishop, to assure him that the Communist party would not attack religion.[23]

Meanwhile, the Febreristas were growing impatient. By late September no sign of the promised elections was visible, although Christmas Day had been set as the date for opening the constitutional convention. True, an electoral junta had been formed, but the Colorados soon entangled it in a dispute over which parties could supervise the balloting. One of the points on which the Febreristas had insisted as a condition for entering the cabinet was that a general political amnesty would be declared and all parties would be permitted to take part in the elections. Morínigo was dragging his heels on this. Although the Liberals and Communists were being tolerated, neither an official amnesty nor a pronouncement that they could register to run for office had been made. Most disturbing of all was the growing violence of the Guión Rojo and the obvious indifference of the police to it. By now the Febreristas were convinced that Morínigo and González were planning a coup. So, to forestall it, they struck first. On 20 September a Febrerista army officer, Lieutenant Colonel Alfredo Galeano, attempted to seize the government. When the plot failed, its leaders were rounded up and sent to Peña Hermosa, and the abortive revolt was disavowed by the Febrerista executive committee.

The Febreristas' failure made the Guión Rojo even more arrogant. *El País* was attacked a third time. Guionists also started another drive to wrest the labor movement from the Febreristas and Communists and to take over the Febrerista-dominated Paraguayan University Student Federation (FUP). On the day following Colonel Galeano's arrest the FUP held a mass meeting to which all the political parties were invited. The federation intended by a free exchange of views to see if it were not possible to hurry up the calling of elections. Instead, Guionist agitators disrupted the meeting and caused the other groups to withdraw. Then, on 13 December, an FUP march around the city's main square was fired on by Guionist gunmen. At the sound of the firing the police moved in and began to arrest, not the attackers, but the marchers.

The final collapse of the coalition government came in early January 1947, the date for holding the constitutional convention having come and gone with no action. Natalicio González had carried his demand for the creation of a labor ministry to the Council of State where, over the protests of the Febreristas, he was upheld on an 8 to 7 vote. Now the question was who would get the new post. Whoever controlled the Labor Ministry would have the unions in his power, for the government had the right to give or withhold legal recognition. The Febreristas demanded the new ministry because, they argued, they were the country's leading labor party. The Colorados claimed it on the grounds that they had a right to an equal number of minis-

tries. Of course, Morínigo decided in favor of the Colorados. Therefore, on 10 January an all-night meeting of the Febrerista executive
committee hotly debated whether to stay in the government or pull
out. Valdovinos insisted that the party should not voluntarily give up
positions of power, and when he was finally voted down he stormed
angrily from the room. The majority faction then drew up a list of
demands, calling for the collective resignation of all Febrerista and
Colorado ministers. An all-military cabinet should take over, they
said, and guarantee the holding of elections.

As events were to show, the Febreristas were right in placing their
faith in the military. However, Morínigo and González had been carefully filling all subcabinet posts with trusted Guionists, and were not
prepared to surrender these crucial positions so easily. Morínigo's
answer to the Febreristas was to dissolve the coalition government on
14 January and declare a state of siege. He formed a new cabinet of
five Colorados and three military officers with close Colorado connections.[24] Meanwhile, the police began rounding up Febreristas, Liberals, and Communists. Colonel Franco and Liberal party president
Jerónimo Zubizarreta were arrested. So were Raimundo Careaga, the
Febreristas' FUP president, and Roque Gaona, the editor of the
Febreristas' newspaper, *El Pueblo*. Rafael Oddone, the editor of *El
País*, took refuge in the Brazilian embassy, while Arnaldo Valdovinos
received asylum from the Argentine embassy. Within a few days,
though, most of these men were allowed to go into exile.

The Civil War of 1947

Although Morínigo had clamped down again, the brief period of
freedom under the coalition government had unleashed expectations
of reform once more, and they were not to be so easily suppressed.
After almost six weeks of ominous calm the reaction finally came. On
the night of 7 March a gang of young Febreristas suddenly attacked
the central police station in downtown Asunción. Shouting "*Viva el
Coronel Franco!*" they stormed the building and took it after a heavy
exchange of gunfire. Police Chief Rogelio Benítez was severely
wounded in the fighting (his arm had to be amputated afterwards),
and his private secretary was killed. At the same time, another group
of Febreristas tried to invade the Military College, just across the
street. This attack failed, however. Then, Colonel Carlos Montanaro,
the head of the college, brought out his cadets and surrounded the
police station. Now the fighting began in earnest. For the next hour

or so the cadets directed a heavy barrage at the police building until finally the sixty or so Febreristas inside surrendered.

That revolt, however, was only the prelude to the real uprising. On the following day the military garrison in Concepción deposed its commander and pronounced itself against the government.[25] Major César Aguirre, who headed the mutiny, demanded Morínigo's resignation and called on the other military bases to join the revolt. Within a short time most of the troops in the Chaco came over to his side. In the meantime, Major Aguirre sent patrols up the river to liberate the prisoners at Peña Hermosa and extend the rebels' control over the other outposts to the north. Now that Colonel Galeano was free, Major Aguirre turned the leadership of the Concepción garrison over to him.

At this point the rebels could have marched on Asunción—and had they done so Morínigo might have fallen. Instead, they hesitated. Neither the Campo Grande garrison, nor the capital's infantry regiment, nor the artillery in Paraguarí had declared itself. Although the rebel forces had been considerably augmented by the support of the Chaco soldiers, they were uncertain of the reception they would get if they made a move toward the capital. So they waited for further defections. As events were to show, it was a fatal decision, for it caused the rebellion to lose momentum and allowed Morínigo time to prepare his defenses. At the time, however, it looked as though the revolt were gathering unchallengeable strength. Most of the officer corps deserted the government, and Febrerista, Liberal, and Communist irregulars hurried to Concepción to join the revolution. The most exciting news was that Colonel Franco had flown back from exile and was now in command of the antigovernment forces.

Morínigo's position was shaky, but he also had certain resources that were to prove crucial in the showdown. First, he had the Colorado party with its great mass of peasant followers, the *py nandí*, or "barefoot ones." Some fifteen thousand of these were hastily organized into a militia and sent out, with the few remaining weapons from the armory, to block the approaches to Asunción. Meanwhile, the Guión Rojo took up positions as an "urban guard" whose job it was to root out "fifth columnists." The Guionists were empowered to enter any home without a warrant to search for arms, propaganda, radio transmitters, or known rebel sympathizers. It was a reign of terror, with Colorado party members on every block spying on their neighbors and reporting their movements. More than a thousand Febreristas, Liberals, and Communists were arrested in the first few weeks, and many thousands more took refuge across the river in Argentina.

The second great asset that Morínigo enjoyed was his friendship with Juan Perón and the aid he received from the Argentine dictator. Although both governments denied that any aid was ever requested or sent, the weight of evidence suggests that guns, ammunition, and trucks were shipped to Paraguay. This was attested to not only by a Brazilian observer, General J. A. Flores, but also by Colonel Federico Weddell Smith, Morínigo's own commander in chief.[26] Otherwise, it is difficult to account for the firepower of the loyalist troops when, by the government's own estimate, the vast bulk of the country's arms and munitions was in rebel hands at the beginning of the war. Perón also helped Morínigo when he held up the departure of two Paraguayan gunboats, the *Humaitá* and the *Paraguay*, from Buenos Aires after their crews had removed their officers and declared themselves for the revolution.

Up to the end of April the civil war consisted of only minor skirmishes between the rebels and the *py nandí* militia. It soon became obvious that the rebels' waiting game was adding little to their original strength, while it was giving Morínigo time to train and equip a new army. When the rebels finally decided on action, though, a week of heavy rains set in which caused the Paraguay River to rise and flood the low-lying areas between Concepción and the capital. Unfortunately, at this moment the navy suddenly decided to declare its support for the revolution.[27] Centered in the harbor of Asunción, the navy revolt was the most dangerous moment yet for Morínigo. What is more, the naval base borders a large working-class quarter. Mobilized by the underground Febrerista Resistance Committee, large numbers of workingmen joined the revolt. Within a few hours a sizable part of the city was in rebel hands. If this had been coordinated with a land attack, Morínigo would surely have fallen. As it was, though, the rebel forces in Concepción were unable to move. The *py nandí*, the police, and the Campo Grande cavalry—which now sided with the government—soon bottled up the revolt in Asunción. Eventually the artillery regiment from nearby Paraguarí joined the loyalists, which decided the issue in favor of Morínigo. But the fighting was fierce and bloody, and the rebels held out for days. During a brief truce in the battle, Colonel Federico Weddell Smith, the commander of the government's army suddenly defected and fled the country. Once on Argentine soil he attacked the Morínigo regime for its brutality. In reply, Morínigo accused his former officer of having collaborated secretly with the rebels.

Under a protective artillery bombardment that reduced the navy yard and the surrounding houses to ruins, the government troops retook the workers' quarter block by block. Still, the rebels fought on amid the rubble until, after four days of defending their ground, they were overwhelmed by swarms of *py nandí*. The survivors received no mercy; many were gunned down as they tried to escape across the river.

After that the war began to turn in Morínigo's favor. By July his armies had taken the offensive and, after a series of bloody, seesaw battles, Concepción finally fell on 31 July. When the news reached Asunción, bells began to ring all over the city to celebrate the end of the fighting. The Colorados were jubilant.

But it was a trap. Colonel Franco had abandoned Concepción the previous night, leaving behind only a skeleton force of the sick and wounded to give the appearance of resistance. At that very moment the rebel army was heading downstream for an attack on Asunción. Its fleet consisted of a motley assortment of commandeered riverboats: launches, tugs, fishing boats, and other small craft. The rebel command itself was housed in an old paddle-wheeler. Meanwhile, Morínigo's army was stranded. More than 190 miles of marshy woods lay between it and the capital, with no good connecting roads. It would take days to double back and march to Morínigo's relief.

The siege of Asunción began on 3 August, when Franco's forces disembarked just north of the city and began an encircling movement. Once again a hastily assembled defense, consisting of Campo Grande troops, Guionists, and *py nandí*, was thrown up to hold back the invasion. The fighting was tremendous, and at one point the rebels penetrated into the suburbs as far as the Botanical Gardens. But the defenders held on tenaciously, aided—so Franco claimed later—by new airborne shipments of Argentine weapons. Morínigo himself stayed at the battle line, exhorting his soldiers to stand firm. In the end the rebels were unable to overpower the city's defenses. By 14 August they were caught in a crossfire between the troops defending the city and Morínigo's main forces, who managed to catch up with the rebels from behind. Unwilling to give up while they were so near their prize, Franco's soldiers fought on for another five days. But by 19 August they had spent themselves. The siege collapsed, and both officers and men scrambled to save themselves as best they could. Many of them fell prisoner, but most escaped to Argentina. With them went the last hopes of democracy.

Chapter 3. Colorado Rule and Misrule

The Guión Rojo in Power

The end of the civil war left the Colorados the undisputed masters of
the state. The defection of nearly 80 percent of the officer corps to the
rebel side meant that only Colorado military men remained in positions of command, and the rank and file of the new loyalist army was
made up of Colorado recruits. What is more, the party not only controlled the army but was also in a position to monopolize all of the
government jobs.

The opposition was completely demoralized. The victors rooted out
any remnants of it with savage relentlessness. Passions built up during the civil war were unleashed in the "Colorado Terror," a block by
block search by Guión Rojo thugs for any suspected opponents. So
oppressive was the atmosphere that tens of thousands of Paraguayans
streamed into Argentina over the next several months. Although it is
difficult to judge accurately just how many people emigrated during
the civil war and immediately afterward, estimates range from two
hundred thousand to four hundred thousand and upwards. That
represented about one-third of the country's population.[1]

Some, of course, could not leave even if they wished to. At least
four thousand prisoners were being held at the war's end. They had
been captured in the drive on Concepción, during the naval revolt, in
the final retreat of the rebel army, or in the roundup of suspects
afterwards, and their numbers included both military and civilians.
Although many were later sentenced to exile and others were sent to
prison camps, some, such as the Febrerista general secretary, Humberto Garcete, were executed.[2]

Paradoxically, the mood of suspicion and fear penetrated even the
Colorado party itself. Instead of bringing unity to the party, victory

deepened even further the split between Natalicio González and Federico Cháves. Doctor Mallorquín had died during the war, and these two rivals struggled to decide who would succeed him as head of the party. The winner would control not only the Colorado organization but also the future government. Cháves seemed to have the advantage, for he had the support of a majority of the party's executive committee, the Junta de Gobierno. On the other hand, González had the backing of his Guión Rojo, whose violent tactics shocked the "democratic" faction. He also counted on the support of President Morínigo, who declared himself in favor of González as his successor in the presidential elections scheduled for early 1948.

The confrontation between these two Colorado leaders finally occurred in November 1947 at the party convention to nominate its slate for the forthcoming elections.[3] The atmosphere was tense in the Municipal Theater when the convention opened there on 16 November. Long before the official opening time the galleries were packed with party notables, government leaders, and foreign diplomats. The first day gave no hint, however, of what was to come. Eulógio Estigarribia, the acting party president, opened the convention by asking everyone to stand for a moment of silence in memory of Doctor Mallorquín. After that the party's vice-president, José Zacarias Arza, read a long speech to the delegates in which he called on them to deliberate calmly and to maintain party unity, whatever the outcome of the convention might be. Then Estigarribia appointed the Commission of Powers to pronounce on the validity of the delegates' credentials. As the first session adjourned, all seemed in order, but those in the know were aware that the Cháves forces were busy packing the convention for their candidate. Both Estigarribia and Zacarias Arza were in that camp already.

Each side was busy that night. Relying on their control of the party apparatus, the *democráticos* were determined to prevent any slipups on the floor. In the previous party elections for delegates to the convention the voting had been very close and charges of fraud had been hurled back and forth between the two factions. Therefore, it was certain that many of the delegates' credentials would be challenged before the Commission of Powers. Cháves's followers had claimed a majority of the elected delegates, but the Guionists would certainly dispute the legality of some of those victories. However, since the *democráticos* still controlled a majority of the incumbent party executive committee, they were in a position to appoint the Commission of Powers. When the commission met that night to review the delegates' credentials, the Guionists discovered, to their chagrin, that the *democrático* majority refused to entertain any of their complaints of fraud.

Worse still, the commission went on to impugn the credentials of some of the Guionist delegates and to issue new credentials to their *democrático* rivals.

Nevertheless, the Guionists had a battle plan of their own. Posters of Natalicio González had already been plastered all over Asunción. Now, throughout the night, squads of chanting Guionist militants marched up and down the streets. They surrounded the Municipal Theater and even got inside, where they occupied the galleries. When the convention opened the next day, all the seats above the main floor, including the aisles, were jammed with Guionists. As the delegates filed in the air was filled with rhythmic chants for González.

Some Cháves supporters who had managed to squeeze in shouted back. Surrounded by his Guionist toughs, González watched the proceedings from one of the balconies, while Cháves stayed on the floor with the other members of the Junta de Gobierno. The first order of the day was the vote for a convention chairman. Despite the growing unruliness of the audience, Estigarribia called for the balloting to begin. As each delegate announced his vote, the two factions shouted cheers or whistled disapproval, and emotions began to mount dangerously. In the end the Guionist candidate, Manuel Talavera, lost by 2 votes, 77 to 75.

When the verdict was announced, the galleries exploded into an uproar. Bricks and stones showered onto the convention floor. Some Guionists even pulled down the glass lampshades from the gallery walls and threw them at the scrambling delegates. Fights broke out in the aisles, and everything was in pandemonium. Suddenly, squads of Guión Rojo thugs broke into the hall and, shouting "González to the presidency!" began flailing about with clubs. Dazed and frightened, the *democráticos* retreated from the theater in disorder leaving the Guionists in complete control.

On the following day, Manuel Talavera steered through the nomination of González as the Colorado party's presidential candidate, along with a list of forty congressional nominees. There was no opposition. The Guión Rojo saw to that. González himself was not present for the final vote; modesty forbade it. But a commission was sent to inform him of the result and to bring him back to the convention. As he entered the theater and walked to the podium, a resounding applause went up from his supporters. Cheers continually interrupted his acceptance speech, during which he outlined his political program. Finally, the convention wound up its session by approving the Guionist slate of candidates and purging the local party committees of any remaining *democrático* leaders.

Meanwhile, President Morínigo was busily foiling any possibility of a *democrático* counterattack. He removed Federico Cháves and his friend Bernardo Ocampos from the cabinet and kept the *democrático* leader under house arrest at his summer home in the lakeside resort town of San Bernardino, about forty miles from the capital. Another supporter of Cháves, Major Vicente González, who commanded a cavalry regiment at Campo Grande, was not so fortunate. His chief, Colonel Enrique Giménez, had him arrested and kept under close guard until the following April. Then, he was executed along with a number of rebel prisoners.[4] The editorial staff of *La Razón*, the party newspaper, was purged, and the paper was turned over to Sabino Montanaro, a Guión Rojo polemicist. Knowing well the Guionist penchant for violence, many prudent *democráticos* joined the stream of exiles to Argentina, Uruguay, and Brazil.

Others, however, were determined to fight back. One young militant named Epifanio Méndez Fleitas had been plotting ever since the convention to win over the heavily armed Battalion 40 of the police to the idea of a coup. Some of the officers were willing, and they set the target date for sometime during the Christmas season, so as to profit from the holiday distractions. But the plot was discovered at the last moment, and Méndez Fleitas was arrested. In early January another young activist, J. Bernardino Gorostiaga, tried to subvert the Campo Grande troops. That attempt failed too, because of the ever-vigilant Colonel Giménez. Evidence gathered by the police linked influential *democráticos* to these two conspiracies, and the Guionist-dominated Junta de Gobierno took the opportunity to expel several of their more prominent opponents from the party—men such as J. Eulógio Estigarribia and José Zacarias Arza. The government also announced the arrest of generals Rovira and Pampliega, who were accused of having acted the part of go-betweens in the Campo Grande plot.[5]

Despite these disturbances, the electoral process went ahead. Although it was legally possible for other parties to enter the race, none presented itself. Even so, Natalicio González campaigned throughout the country as though he were in a neck-and-neck contest. Meanwhile, both the *democráticos* and the opposition parties urged their supporters either to abstain from voting or to cast blank ballots. Abstention was difficult, however, because voting is obligatory in Paraguay and failure to go to the polls can result in a fine. Every voter carries a registration booklet, which is stamped when he votes. When an individual goes to obtain an official document—such as a marriage license, a driver's license, or a passport—he must present his booklet for identification. If he does not have the correct stamps in his booklet, he is liable to arrest. Therefore, most eligible voters went to the polls on 14 February 1948, at which time they were handed a slip of paper with Natalicio González's name on it, along with the names of the congressional slate. No other names were on the ballot, and any attempt to alter the ballot automatically voided it. This procedure prevented even the casting of a blank vote, as the elector could do nothing except dutifully drop the slip of paper into the ballot box. Not surprisingly, González and his ticket won.[6]

The new administration was scheduled to take office on 15 August. Morínigo declared himself to be pleased with the results. He had endorsed González all along, and now he claimed that he was looking forward to stepping down and returning to military life. Rumor had it that González had agreed to name him the army's commander in chief, a prospect that did not please some Guionists. Instead of unifying them more, it seems their sudden rise to power had weakened the discipline in their ranks. Other men just below Natalicio González were becoming ambitious, and they did not approve of the close collaboration between Morínigo and their leader. After all, as army commander in chief, Morínigo might stage a coup and return to power. He had turned on his friends before, and at fifty-one he was still young for a politician. They doubted that he would accept the termination of his career at that age. On the other hand, if Morínigo's friendship for Natalicio González was sincere, he might use the army to perpetuate him in power. Either likelihood was intolerable to those Guionist subordinates who were beginning to aspire to the presidency themselves.

Chief among these dissident Guionists was Felipe Molas López, a forty-eight-year-old dentist. Like Natalicio González, Molas López was a left-wing Colorado who had joined the party when very young, had served in the Franco government during the February Revolution, and had been strongly influenced by Peronism during a long exile in Argentina. He had had administrative experience, having served as *intendant* (mayor) of Asunción in 1936, until Franco purged the Colorados from his government. The most outstanding feature about Molas López's character, however, was his notorious thirst for power. He was an inveterate plotter and a master of the double cross. When he came to power the following February, people joked that he was now the unhappiest man in Paraguay, for he had no one else to conspire against. One biographer confides that,

> if we looked up his genealogy, no one would be surprised to find that his soul originated in that age when the angels rebelled. Because in fact Felipe Molas López had a restless temperament and a profoundly nonconformist philosophy that stirred his rebelliousness until it consumed his spirit. Consequently, he al-

ways lived in search of power, dreaming of command, fired by the spirit of adventure carried on in the emotional atmosphere of conspiracy. . . . If Curzio Malaparte wrote on the "Technique Of the Coup d' Etat," then Felipe Molas López might have written a small library on the subject, with expert examples drawn from his personal experience.[7]

Over the next several months Molas López played a masterful game of intrigue. His first step was to dislodge Morínigo, who was always dangerous, and to get Natalicio González safely into the presidency. The next step was to bump González out of the way and seize the office for himself.

Morínigo's fall came unexpectedly in a bloodless coup executed on 3 June. It had been preceded by a series of oblique moves that hid the motives of the Molas López faction, which now called itself La Pena. First, Molas succeeded in getting Natalicio González to pressure Morínigo into dropping Victor Boettner, the education minister, from the cabinet. Boettner was a Colorado moderate, so his sacrifice was acceptable to both the Guión Rojo and Morínigo. Next, Morínigo was persuaded by González to promote the police chief, Mario Ferrario, to the cabinet to fill the vacant education post. Ferrario had taken over the police back in March 1947, after Rogelio Benítez was severely wounded in the abortive Febrerista attack on the headquarters. Fiercely loyal to Morínigo, Ferrario had been thoroughly ruthless in suppressing the opposition in Asunción, and after the civil war he had been useful in wresting control of the Colorado party from the *democráticos*. Morínigo considered Ferrario's elevation to the cabinet a reward; as minister of education he could clamp down harder on his bête noire, the university.

But that left the office of police chief vacant. Maneuvering skillfully, Molas López had his brother-in-law Liberato Rodríguez appointed to the post. Immediately, Rodríguez joined the plot to oust Morínigo.[8] Other key men were soon recruited: Colonel Carlos Montanaro, the head of the Military College; Colonel Alfredo Stroessner, commander of the First Artillery Regiment at Paraguarí, about forty miles away; and Mario Mallorquín, the son of the former party president. In addition, Molas López could count on two of the four regimental commanders at Campo Grande: Major César Mallorquín, Mario's brother, and Major Adalberto Canata, a cynical opportunist who had a taste for the role of president maker.

With the police now in the hands of his enemies and the cavalry base at least neutralized, Morínigo was in great danger. Still, to make their position overwhelming the plotters sought more recruits.

Stroessner contacted his friend and former artillery superior General Raimundo Rolón, now head of the army, who agreed to back the coup. Stroessner also had friends in the air force who offered their support. But as the conspiracy widened, leaks occurred, and Morínigo's suspicions were aroused.

This time, however, he had realized the danger too late. At eleven o'clock on the morning of 2 June he ordered Rodríguez's dismissal as police chief and his arrest, thus spurring the plotters into action. Molas López quickly assembled a group of leading Colorado party and military leaders, among whom the conspirators were liberally represented—although this was not known to the rest—and charged that Morínigo's firing of Liberato Rodríguez was the prelude to a coup aimed at keeping himself in power. Given Morínigo's past, this was a plausible argument, and it won over those not previously committed. Among those were the two remaining regimental commanders at Campo Grande; Lieutenant Colonel Rogelio Benítez, the one-armed former police chief who now headed the capital's infantry regiment; Major Nelson Rolón, head of the Signal Corps, who promised to seize all communications; and the navy's two top-ranking officers.

Meanwhile, Morínigo was trying to contact his military chiefs too, but was unable to do so. In desperation he sent out his palace guard to arrest Molas López and Rodríguez, who had gone to the home of Natalicio González to inform him of what was happening. While they were talking to the astonished president-elect, who had not known of the conspiracy, the guardsmen arrived and began pounding on the door. Molas López and Rodríguez barely escaped by dashing through the cellar to an adjoining house.

Meanwhile Colonel Enrique Giménez, Morínigo's cavalry chief, was being held prisoner at Campo Grande. Shortly after five o'clock motorized troops and artillery forces began to move on the capital. Morínigo barricaded himself in the palace, but by two-thirty the next morning he realized the hopelessness of the situation. His formal resignation was handed to Molas López and Mario Mallorquín, who had been delegated by the rebels to receive it. Morínigo, Ferrario, and César Vasconcellos, the foreign minister, were placed under arrest. After eight years in office, Morínigo was finally beaten. The coup had cost no lives and had caused no damage.

Later in the day the leading military commanders issued a statement justifying their role in the revolt and promising an orderly transferral of power to the president-elect. At the same time, Juan Manuel Frutos, the chief justice of the Supreme Court, was appointed provisional president. His government included most of the leaders of the coup.[9]

Later the cabinet named for the provisional government became the basis for Natalicio González's administration too. After years of pursuing power he assumed the presidency in August with very little authority to select his ministers. According to reports, the military rejected two of his lists of nominees, and in the end he had to retain Molas López, Mario Mallorquín, and other *molaslopistas*, although he was allowed to shift the portfolios around. Colonel Montanaro's brother Domingo was also kept on as foreign minister, and General Rolón remained as defense minister. González also had very little power in military appointments. Major Adalberto Canata was promoted to lieutenant colonel and made commander of Campo Grande. Liberato Rodríguez was dropped as police chief, but another *molaslopista* was named in his place. González later wrote that, on taking office, he "could not count on a single regiment being faithful." The only men in his cabinet to whom he could turn were his old friend and cofounder of the Guión Rojo, Victor Morínigo (public works), and Leandro Prieto (finance).[10]

Obviously, Molas López's clique had managed to leave themselves in a good position to eliminate González at the first opportunity. They had Stroessner's artillery troops and Montanaro's cadets. In addition, Mario Mallorquín acted as liaison with Campo Grande, where his brother Colonel César Mallorquín and Colonel Canata were counted on to bring over the cavalry. General Raimundo Rolón and General Mushuito Villasboa, the new army commander in chief, were also in on the conspiracy—as was Nicolas Scorza Fuster, the new police chief. The plotters penetrated even González's own Guión Rojo: Enrique Volta Gaona, another of the Guión's original founders, was now backing Molas López.

The ring was not completely closed around González, however. The Colorado party's president, Manuel Talavera, was a good friend, and Colonel Rogelio Benítez, the commander of the Fourteenth Infantry Regiment, was at least uncommitted. Then, in mid-October, González made a bid to free his hands further by replacing Scorza Fuster as police chief with one of his own men.

As it had in the previous coup, this attempt to remove their hand-picked police chief prompted the conspirators into action.[11] In the early morning hours of 26 October, Colonel Montanaro led his cadets in a sudden attack on the police station. Though taken by surprise, the police fought back. Mortars and automatic weapons were brought into the fight, and heavy streams of fire were poured back and forth across the street. Within hours much of the police station was badly damaged, and a fire had broken out which spread to the adjacent buildings. In the meantime, Colonel Stroessner was moving his artillery regiment along the seventy-kilometer road to Asunción to back up the revolt.

Awakened in the middle of the night with the news that his government was about to be overthrown, President González quickly showed a fighting spirit that was to save the day for him. First he tried to call Campo Grande, but could not get through. Next he called Colonel Benítez at infantry headquarters. Inexplicably, the rebels had failed to cut all communications within the capital, a fatal oversight that would not be rectified until five in the morning, three hours too late. Thus, González reached Benítez, who was loyal to the president, and dispatched him to intercept Stroessner. Then, González drove to the Campo Grande base, some ten kilometers away. No troops had moved, so far, from Campo Grande. The officers there were undecided and arguing among themselves. Colonel Canata was having second thoughts about the revolt, while Colonel Mallorquín was insisting that the troops move. At this point, González walked in and exhorted the officers to remain loyal. His bold action in going straight into the lion's den appealed to the soldiers, and they swung over to his side. Colonel Mallorquín was arrested, and Campo Grande declared for the government. Before dawn troops were on their way to the capital to suppress the revolt.

Meanwhile, Colonel Montanaro was running into difficulties. His first assault on the police station having been repulsed, he ordered a heavy mortar bombardment. Also, an air force plane dropped a couple of bombs to aid the attack. But although their building had been reduced to rubble, the police fought back with heavy automatic weapons. Fierce fighting lasted past dawn and all through the morning. Montanaro's hopes dimmed even more, however, when Campo Grande troops began moving into the city and firing on his positions. Still, the arrival of the artillery might save the attack for the rebels.

However, Benítez had stopped Stroessner outside the capital. While the two forces faced each other, Generals Rolón and Villasboa arrived with the news that the Campo Grande garrison had deserted the coup. If Stroessner surrendered, they said, they would guarantee his escape. Hiding him in the trunk of a car, they drove Stroessner to the Brazilian embassy, where he was given asylum. At seven o'clock that evening, Montanaro received the news that Stroessner had fled, and he requested a truce. Finally, at seven-thirty, he gave up too.

Mario Mallorquín and Volta Gaona were rounded up soon afterward, along with six deputies—including Sabino Montanaro, a brother of the colonel's. The other brother, Domingo, who was then foreign minister, was out of the country attending an United Nations meeting. He was sent a telegram informing him that he was fired from his post and warning him about returning to Paraguay. Mallorquín and the Montanaro brothers were read out of the party by a dutiful Junta de Gobierno, and two more *democráticos* were purged at the same time: Osvaldo Cháves, a nephew of the former party chief, and Roberto L. Petit. Police reports alleged that those two had been gobetweens in lending the support of the *democráticos* for the coup. The military was purged too. Colonel Stroessner was in exile, and colonels Montanaro and Mallorquín were in jail. Thus, many of González's more dangerous enemies had been eliminated.

Nevertheless, the president's position was shaky. Molas López could not be directly implicated in the coup, and he was still too influential to be purged. So he not only went free but even retained his post in the cabinet. Similarly, generals Rolón and Villasboa kept their posts, and Colonel Canata continued as head of Campo Grande as a reward for his loyalty. González's weakness was emphasized even more the following month when Rolón and Villasboa pressured him into firing Major Narciso Campos as police chief. Campos, who had directed the heroic resistance of the police to Montanaro, was firmly loyal to González. His departure left the president vulnerable from that quarter. Worse, the two generals demanded and got the appointment of Liberato Rodríguez as minister of interior, a post which controls the police. Upon taking office, Rodríguez named Molas López's brother, Venancio, as the new police chief.

Although these were hard concessions for González, he agreed to them because he hoped to placate Colonel Canata and cement his support. The cavalry had saved him before, and with the loyal Colonel Benítez heading the Fourteenth Infantry Regiment, González thought he might have a chance when the inevitable coup came. Finally, González was trying to hem in the *molaslopistas* by seeking a rapproachement with the *democráticos*. He announced that it was time to pull the party together and that he would personally take the lead in doing so. Accordingly, he sent out peace feelers to his arch-rival, Cháves.

But it was too late for the olive branch. González's storm trooper tactics in the past had permanently alienated the *democráticos*, who now rebuffed his advances. At the same time he had taught the *molaslopistas* the efficacy of violence. Over the next few weeks the two dissident factions came to an agreement that the only way to pacify the country and restore party harmony was to get rid of Natalicio González. The move that touched off the coup was a public declaration by Manuel Talavera, the party president, calling for the dismissal of Venancio Molas López as police chief. Then Talavera himself proceeded to purge certain local party officers known to be *molaslopistas*. That was on 9 January 1949. On 13 January, Felipe Molas López and Liberato Rodríguez responded with their own manifesto, accusing the González faction of conspiring with antiparty elements—specifically, expresident Morínigo—to keep the Colorados divided.[12]

During the next two weeks the Molas López brothers, Rolón, Villasboa, and Rodríguez were busy preparing their coup. This time Colonel Canata would stand firm; the prospect of Morínigo's return (and revenge) had decided him. When it came, the coup was quiet and bloodless. It began unobtrusively about midday on 29 January, when police detachments began taking up positions around the Presidential Palace. Shortly afterwards all radio transmission was cut off.[13] It was not clear at first whether the palace was under protection or under siege, but by nightfall González was convinced that a coup was on.

A message was sent—it is not clear how—to the Campo Grande garrison, asking for help, but the answer came back that Colonel Canata was demanding the president's resignation. The infantry was also contacted, but Colonel Benítez lay violently ill, so no troops were ordered to move. González and his followers later charged that Benítez had been poisoned.[14] That left only the artillery; however, by this time all roads from the city had been cut. Abandoning the fight, González made a dash for the Brazilian embassy, where he and Manuel Talavera received asylum. They were lucky, for already many other top Guión Rojo men, including Victor Morínigo and Leandro Prieto, were under arrest.

Molas López was closer to the presidency, but it was not his yet. General Raimundo Rolón, the army's senior officer and defense minister, was next in line. At nine that evening the Congress met in special session to swear him in as provisional president. He made a brief speech, promising to call elections within sixty days. Next morning at ten o'clock, Rolón appeared again before Congress to get approval for his cabinet. General Villasboa moved up to defense minister, and Colonel Canata took his place as army commander in chief. Liberato Rodríguez stayed on as interior minister; Venancio Molas López remained as police chief; and Felipe Molas López continued as minister of education, but he was also named president of the Colorado party. Meanwhile, large crowds of *democrático* sympathizers assembled in the main square to cheer the overthrow of González. From there they went to the homes of Federico Cháves and Eulógio

Estigarribia, their two top leaders, to encourage them with a show of support.

True to his word, General Rolón announced a few days later that general elections would take place in April. Moreover, to pacify the country he announced that even the exiled opposition parties would be allowed to return and take part.[15] That was a blow to all Colorado factions. Worse yet, on 19 February the chiefs of all the armed services issued a joint statement calling on Rolón to run for president as a nonpartisan candidate dedicated to reconciling the country's political feuds. Although Rolón denied any intention to run, the Colorado politicians were afraid that the military might draft him.[16] Molas López and the *democráticos* began to close ranks against the common threat. The elderly Cháves designated José Zacarias Arza, a seasoned *político*, to act as liaison man for the *democráticos* in the planning of a coup.

Although still in exile, the pivotal man in this new plot was Colonel Alfredo Stroessner. Others who had taken part in the botched October 1948 coup had been pardoned by General Rolón, but the amnesty had not included his erstwhile friend and protege—possibly because he did not trust him. However, one of Stroessner's good friends, Colonel Hermínio Morínigo (no relation to the exdictator), had been appointed to head the presidential staff. Thus, Morínigo was in a position to intercept information and keep Rolón ignorant of what was happening. A second mistake was the appointment of Colonel Emilio Diáz de Vivar, a friend of Stroessner's, as the new commander of Campo Grande. A third mistake was keeping Liberato Rodríguez and Venancio Molas López in office, for they controlled a vast intelligence apparatus.

The plan of the coup was simple in the extreme. Stroessner was to sneak over the border, make his way to Paraguarí, and rally his old artillery regiment to march on Asunción. At the same time, Colonel Diáz de Vivar would move in with the cavalry, and the police would join in support. Colonel Morínigo would hold up any warning messages.

Then a fortuitous thing happened which gave the plotters an ideal opportunity. Monseñor Juan Bogarín, the much-beloved archbishop of Asunción, died. He had served for seventy-two years in the priesthood, the last nineteen as head of the Paraguayan church. Huge crowds attended his funeral in the National Cathedral, and all the top government and military leaders were there. Afterwards, Felipe Molas López had all the high clergy and government officials to his house for the wake. In the midst of this, Colonel Diáz de Vivar slipped away to join

his troops at Campo Grande. Stroessner had already appeared at the
artillery barracks, to the warm welcome of his men, who arrested
Rolón's appointee. Within a few hours, while General Rolón and
Colonel Canata were sitting down to a banquet at the wake, rebel
troops were entering the city. The honored guests were still unaware
that anything was wrong until the troops had surrounded the house
and Molas López, until then the perfect host, suddenly announced,
"Gentlemen, the jig is up!"[17]

Thus, the February coup brought Molas López to the presidency at
last, but he was not to be the chief gainer by it. True, his brother-in-
law Rodríguez still held the Interior Ministry. Also, an old friend,
Mario Mallorquín, returned from exile to join the cabinet. However,
of the nine ministerial portfolios, six went to the *democráticos* as the
price for their support.[18] They controlled the Defense Ministry, and
the new police chief, Epifanio Méndez Fleitas, was a young *chavista*
of exceptional energy and talent. General Diáz de Vivar, the new army
commander in chief, also seemed to favor Cháves. Finally, Cháves
himself now claimed the Colorado party presidency. Like Natalicio
González, Molas López came to the presidency with only a tenuous
hold on the office.

In reality the *democráticos* were in charge. Federico Cháves, who
in addition to heading the party was president of the Congress, was
running the country in fact, if not in name. The *democrático*-
controlled government initiated a thorough housecleaning of Guionists
from positions of power, which opened the way for liberalizing the
political system in other respects. At the end of March 344 political
prisoners were released from various concentration camps around the
country, where they had been held ever since the civil war. It was announced that this was a step toward normalizing the country's civic
life and that a general amnesty was to follow. Significantly, the cabinet at this time was composed entirely of civilians; a civilian, José
Zacarias Arza, controlled even the Defense Ministry—and that was
rare for Paraguay.

Molas López was by no means content with only apparent power.
To free himself from Cháves he planned still another coup, this one
to coincide with a trip to Brazil by Zacarias Arza and Colonel Diáz de
Vivar. Molas López had been doing some fence mending with Natalicio González's faction. Those Guionists, now in exile, were willing to
forget their grudges for the time being in order to keep the even more
hated Federico Cháves out of power. According to the plan they agreed
on, a party of armed exiles led by Colonel Enrique Giménez, ex-
President Morínigo's cavalry commander, was to form just across the
border and wait for the signal to strike.[19] The attack would be coordi-

nated with a *cuartelazo* involving the air force and the Campo Grande cavalry. The latter could be counted on because they were now under the command of Mario Mallorquín's brother Colonel César Mallorquín.

However, since too much contact between the brothers at the cavalry base might cause suspicion, the plotters looked for someone else to act as a liaison. They found an unlikely candidate in Eulógio Estigarribia, a high-ranking *democrático* whom few would suspect of plotting against his colleagues. Estigarribia had become disaffected with the *democráticos*, however. He and Cháves had quarreled recently because Cháves insisted on presiding over both the Congress and the Colorado party. Estigarribia felt that one of those posts should go to him, but Cháves wanted to keep as many levers of power in his own hands as possible. When the *molaslopistas* learned of the dispute, Molas López and Mario Mallorquín invited Estigarribia to a private dinner, at which they expressed their opinion that he was the only leader sufficiently respected by all to unite the badly fragmented party. The presidency was his if he would join the revolt. Although he modestly refused the presidency, Estigarribia did agree to act as an information link between Campo Grande, the air force, and the civilian conspirators.[20]

Then the plotters tried to enlist General Stroessner. They expected his cooperation because in the past he had always thrown his artillery behind Molas López, but this time he went to General Diáz de Vivar and told him of the plot. Perhaps Colonel Giménez's role in the plan turned him against it, for the two men had long been enemies. Or perhaps he simply calculated that the *democráticos* were the stronger faction. Whatever his reasons, his action set in motion a hurried countercoup. Méndez Fleitas was ordered to arrest all the civilian conspirators, except the president. Then General Diáz de Vivar contacted one of his proteges, Major Nestor Ferreira, who was a regimental commander at Campo Grande. When the army commander in chief arrived at cavalry headquarters, he found Colonel Mallorquín at bay, blocked from moving his troops by Major Ferreira's regiment. Upon the arrival of their superior officer the revolt collapsed and Colonel Mallorquín was arrested. Also taken at the First Cavalry Regiment headquarters was Eulógio Estigarribia, caught red-handed.

That evening the Colorado party's executive committee met, and after studying reports submitted by police chief Méndez Fleitas—who had been efficient in rounding up the plotters—it called for the immediate removal of Molas López, Mario Mallorquín, and Liberato Rodríguez from office. Lacking any military or party support, Molas López had no choice but to surrender peacefully to the delegation that came to the Presidential Palace to demand his resignation. That same night, Federico Cháves was sworn in as provisional president. The Guionist era was over.

The Democráticos in Power

Despite his reputation as a democrat, Federico Cháves found it necessary, after only three weeks in power, to reimpose the state of siege that had been in effect, with only brief interruptions, since early 1947. That allowed him to suspend habeas corpus, censor the press, and break up suspicious meetings. The reason for all this was that both Natalicio González and Molas López were busy in Argentina with plots to overthrow him. The Guión Rojo still had many supporters inside Paraguay, as attested to by the red painted signs reading "Natalicio" that appeared every morning on the walls of Asunción. Cháves, for his part, was trying to have González extradited from Argentina on the charge that he had embezzled large sums from the public treasury while he was Morínigo's finance minister. As relations between Paraguay and Argentina were friendly at the time, González feared that Perón might sacrifice him for some diplomatic advantage. He moved to Uruguay, but the Uruguayans considered him an embarrassment, so he went to Cuba. Finally he settled permanently in Mexico.

Meanwhile, Cháves scheduled elections for July 1950. As usual, it was to be a one-candidate race. In May the Colorado party nominated him as its standard-bearer. At the same time, the convention published a long list of Guionists who were to be read out of the party. When the Liberals, counting on Cháves's reputation for tolerance, asked for permission to hold their own convention and enter candidates in the elections, they found that democracy was little more than a slogan for the Colorado leader. Cháves ordered the Liberal chiefs to leave the country at once, and when they refused, he had them rounded up and put in *confino*, a form of house arrest in which the prisoner is sent to a small village in the interior and kept under police surveillance.

But political dissidents were only one of Cháves's problems as he began his first regular term. The country at that time was suffering a period of inflation that pushed food prices up by 14 percent a year, clothing by 15 percent, and rents by 100 percent.[21] Between 1948 and 1949 the value of the *guaraní*, Paraguay's unit of currency, had dropped from 6.0 to 8.9 to the dollar on the free market. Over the next two years it was to fall even further, until it reached a free market rate of 50 to the dollar.[22] The official exchange rate was revised from 3.1 to 15 to the dollar, but the discrepancy was so great between the fixed government price and the real value of the *guaraní* that the black market trade in currency was brisk and widespread. By March 1951 the situation was so serious that the government had to declare a moratorium on the payment of its debts.

The spiraling cost of living was undermining wages, causing labor unrest. The Paraguayan Workers' Confederation (CPT) held its second congress in July 1951, at which time the leadership made it clear to the government that unless wage increases were granted a general strike was likely. Cháves and his ministers attended these sessions and agreed to the workers' demands. The government decreed a 50 percent boost in wages. However, that action gave another spur to inflation, and the rise in prices practically wiped out the gain in wages. Turning its attention to prices, the government published a list of official prices, covering a wide range of goods, and passed a law requiring merchants to keep strict records on their stock and sales. Police kept a close check to try to prevent black market activity.

No amount of government regulation seemed to work. As early as January 1950 the administration had issued a far-reaching decree, the Law for the Defense of the National Economy, which gave the Ministry of Economy the power to regulate the sale, transfer, and storage of articles of prime necessity.[23] All this act had accomplished was to drive such goods onto the black market. The government's subsequent attempts to uproot the black market had simply opened up new opportunities for payoffs and corruption; it had had no effect on stabilizing the cost of living. Now the government tried to drive the black market out of business by purchasing necessary goods and selling them to the public at cost. But even this extreme measure failed. Since the program could not possibly satisfy demand, it only further depleted the treasury, while enriching a few producers.

Most economic crises have complex causes, but for the sake of clarity three main factors can be identified here to explain Paraguay's woes. First, the civil war had disrupted the economy and destroyed much capital. The massive flight of people during and after the war had had a strong dislocating effect. Government instability and political terror had frightened off even more capital and certainly prevented any coherent rebuilding program. Official statistics published in 1952 showed that production was down and that national income was lower in 1950 than it had been in 1946. Total annual income had declined from around $150 million to only $118 million, while per capita income went down from $125 a year to a mere $85.[24] Second, the amount of money in circulation had increased enormously—by

40 percent in the first half of 1952 alone. That would have been inflationary by itself. The causes of this increase were largely political: Central Bank funds were used to reward faithful Colorados. Ostensibly, these were development loans to businessmen and farmers, but in reality they were a method of greasing the party machinery.[25] Third, the Paraguayan economy was closely tied to that of Argentina, and the Peronist economy had recently entered a period of falling production and rising prices. That had several effects in Paraguay. For example, Argentina traditionally traded its beef for Paraguayan lumber; but with the drastic slump in beef production, imports in lumber had to be cut in order to save on foreign exchange. Further, the Paraguayan canning industry, which canned and reexported Argentine beef to pay for wheat imports, could not get enough meat to maintain production. The cutback in canned meat exports caused lowered wheat imports, which raised the price of bread—and so on.[26]

The Paraguayan government received some help in late 1952, when it secured an emergency loan from the International Monetary Fund. The price for this relief was that the government had to pledge to hold wages steady and reduce its budget. However, it soon proved impossible to enforce the antiinflationary program. The tightening of credit brought loud protests from businessmen, many of whom were important Colorados. Price controls were evaded by the black market and by smuggling, which now increased enormously. Cattle, which fetched higher prices in neighboring countries, were simply driven across the border, whose thousands of miles of forest and swamp were impossible to patrol. Workers, especially government workers, who were also the rank and file of the Colorado party, were effective in pressuring for wage increases. Thus, in mid-1952 civil servants were granted a 40 percent salary increase, and by the end of the year they had demanded and gotten another 80 percent hike. Nongovernment workers fared almost as well. In 1953 they received a 30 percent raise at midyear and another 20 percent raise a few months later. In short, political necessity made the government unwilling to apply the brakes to inflation.

Despite the economic crisis and his own advanced age (he was seventy-three), Federico Cháves engineered his renomination for a second term on 30 June 1952, and he was duly reelected the following February. Although he did this with apparent ease, Cháves's decision to hold on to power as long as possible was making his ambitious followers restive. Little did Cháves know or care, for his position seemed unchallengeable. During 1952 his police snuffed out plots by Eulógio Estigarribia and expresident Rolón before they ever got beyond the initial stages. As usual, a number of civilian and military conspirators were sent packing to Argentina, but those affairs could not be said to have caused the government great concern.

Still, the economy was a nagging problem. So, in September 1952, Cháves changed his economic team. Guillermo Enciso Velloso became the new minister of finance; J. Bernardino Gorostiaga became minister of industry and commerce; Juan Ramón Cháves took over the Justice Ministry, which handled labor problems; and Epifanio Méndez Fleitas left the police to head the Central Bank. The first three men were little more than loyal *chavista* hacks, but Méndez Fleitas was a much different sort. He was a truly dominating personality, and was to occupy the center of the political stage for the next few years.

The former police chief had all the makings of a successful Latin American *caudillo*. He was tall, burly, and had a commanding presence. He sported a small, black moustache on his thick-boned face, and his nervous intense eyes revealed a quick intelligence. Like Natalicio González, Méndez Fleitas was a self-taught country boy who was fluent in Guaraní and adept at handling crowds of peasants and workers. Like González, too, he was something of an intellectual, having composed Guaraní music and written some political works— although the latter were more polemical than philosophical. His rapid rise through the party ranks was based largely on his outstanding organizational talents and his tireless energy. Starting out as a protege of Enciso Velloso, he was put on the original executive committee of the Colorado Youth in 1942. From there he went to work for the police during the Morínigo years. Later, in 1948, he tried to use his police contacts to overthrow Natalicio González. Although the attempt failed, his boldness brought him to the attention of the *democrático* leaders, who included him in the successful coup of January 1949. Molas López made him his chief of police, an action he regretted later when Méndez Fleitas played a key role in his ouster.

When Cháves came to power, he retained Méndez Fleitas as head of the police because of his proven skill. It was a good choice, for Méndez Fleitas subsequently handled conspiracies by Rolón, Estigarribia, and various Guionist factions so efficiently that they never got beyond the talking stage. In fact, it was largely owing to him that Cháves had no serious opposition. The president rewarded Méndez Fleitas well for his service: in addition to his police duties, Méndez Fleitas attained the directorate of the Institute of Agrarian Reform, was made a member of the Colorado party executive committee, and was elected to the Congress.[27] In short, Méndez Fleitas was recog-

nized as an all-purpose troubleshooter. When he came to the Central
Bank, he already had a reputation as a future leader and was gathering around himself a large personal following.

At the same time, he was controversial. As a youth in the 1940s,
Méndez Fleitas had flirted with the Febrerista movement. Although
he had switched to the Colorado party soon after, he remained very
much a populist. His hero was Perón, whose anti-American and pro-
labor program appealed to Méndez Fleitas's plebeian sympathies. Thus,
the new Central Bank president was no mere party time-server. He
was as opposed to the old landowner-importer "oligarchy" inside
Paraguay as he was to the foreign "imperialists." Although the Colorado party had by no means adopted socialism as its official ideology,
Méndez Fleitas's views fit well with the socialistic tendencies of the
Cháves administration. His influence on the government's economic
policies was soon felt. Perhaps the clearest example of this was the
signing, in August 1953, of a treaty with the Perón administration that
established an "economic union" between Paraguay and Argentina.
Among other things, this agreement provided for a free trade zone,
reciprocal industrial investments, the merging of river fleets, and the
combining of mineral resources.[28] Since Paraguay had relatively little
trade or capital to contribute to such a merger, most observers saw it
as an Argentine economic takeover.

Such maneuvering earned Méndez Fleitas the enmity of the party's
conservative wing. These men looked with alarm on the increasing
influence in Paraguay of Peronism, which they saw as the worst sort
of populist demagoguery. Furthermore, they were uncomfortable
about the spreading network of government economic controls, for
although these merchants and *latifundistas* managed to evade most
restrictions they were a constant irritation. Finally, their influence in
official circles seemed to be on the decline. While Méndez Fleitas continued to gain influence, the principal conservative Colorado, Rigoberto Caballero, was dropped from the cabinet. Caballero's mistake
had been to aspire too openly to succeed Cháves. Indeed, he had even
contacted the military chiefs in 1952 to seek their support for his
candidacy on the assumption that Cháves would not run again. "El
Reeligido" resented his subordinate's talking to army men behind his
back, however, and he did not reappoint Caballero when the new
cabinet was formed.[29]

In previous party struggles the Guionist and *molaslopista* Colorados
had used Méndez Fleitas's well-known working-class sympathies to
label him a communist. Now this theme was taken up again by the
conservative *democráticos*, for whom *epifanismo* became synonymous
with Bolshevik infiltration of the party. Going further, Méndez

Fleitas's opponents even accused him of using Central Bank funds to build up his own personal following and to subvert the economy.[30] A showdown finally came in June 1953, when the Sociedad Rural, a powerful cattlemen's association, held its convention in Asunción. The ranchers' chief complaint was the government's fixing of low beef prices at a time when the economy was suffering from runaway inflation. This policy was ruining them, they claimed, and they accused Méndez Fleitas of being behind the current policies. They were especially angry at the government's intransigence on beef prices, for it had also decreed two large wage increases in recent months which totaled a 50 percent raise for the workers. Now the cattlemen demanded no less than a 100 percent hike in beef prices to offset their increased costs. Méndez Fleitas, who had been invited to attend the sessions and participate in the discussions, came out strongly against this. He pointed out that such an increase would only give another spur to inflation and, moreover, would bear down heavily on the poor. This reply was greeted by a noisy protest from the cattlemen. They went to the Presidential Palace and appealed to Cháves. After applying much pressure they got their way.[31]

The charge that Méndez Fleitas was building a personal following was no empty one. Within the cabinet itself he could count on the support of Enciso Velloso, his former patron, and Tomás Romero Pereira, a former president of the Colorado party who was now the interior minister. Outside the cabinet, Méndez had cultivated the friendship of Major Mario Ortega, who had succeeded him as head of the police, and General Stroessner, who had recently been promoted to army commander in chief. This was a formidable coterie and one which posed a potential challenge to Cháves, a situation to which the president was certainly not blind. A rift had developed within the cabinet over his concessions to the ranchers, and Cháves used this as an excuse to remove Méndez Fleitas, Enciso Velloso, and Romero Pereira from their posts on 7 January 1954 and to replace Major Ortega as police chief with Roberto L. Petit. He did not get rid of General Stroessner, though, and that was to prove his undoing.

For the moment, however, Cháves's hold on the presidency seemed firmer than ever. Luck seemed to be with him too, for on 2 March, Felipe Molas López, one of his most noxious rivals, died suddenly of a heart attack. With Molas López dead and Natalicio González in retirement far away in Mexico, no Colorado leader of the first rank remained to challenge him. True, General Stroessner was still a worry, but he had no base in the Colorado party. Moreover, the new police chief had a plan for dealing with him.

Like Méndez Fleitas, Roberto L. Petit was a young, up-and-coming personality in the party. Known as a reformist *democrático*—but more moderate than Méndez Fleitas—he was a member of the party executive committee, president of the most important Colorado cultural organization, the Blás Garay Cultural Center, and president of the Agrarian Reform Institute. Just before taking over as head of the police he had also been president of the Colorado Youth.[32] He was considered to be completely loyal to Cháves and the one most likely to succeed him as the party's head. Determined to place the power of the Colorado party on a footing that would be independent even of the military, Petit convinced the president to increase the fighting strength of the police. One police unit, Battalion 40, was already heavily armed. Under Petit's plan it would be strengthened in size and armament to the extent that it could serve as an effective counterweight to the army.[33]

The army leaders viewed this new policy with misgivings, of course, and no one more so than General Stroessner. A plot began to form, involving Stroessner, Méndez Fleitas, and Romero Pereira. It was not clear who would win in a showdown. Cháves controlled the police, and the commander of Campo Grande, Lieutenant Colonel Nestor Ferreira, was firmly loyal. On the other hand, Stroessner could count on the artillery, the navy, the Military College, and the capital's Fourteenth Infantry Regiment. Also, Major Virgilio Candia, one of the regimental commanders at Campo Grande, was a good friend of Méndez Fleitas.

Méndez Fleitas formulated the original strategy. As he planned it, the coup would take place on Sunday, 8 May, when Argentine President Juan Perón was to arrive in Paraguay on a grand state visit. Military units would be called out anyway for reviews, and at that time Major Candia was to seize Colonel Ferreira. Naval infantry units, led by Captain Gabriel Patiño, would then take over the downtown. Stroessner, as commander in chief, would order all other units to stay in the barracks.

The coup was moved up suddenly to 4 May, however, when Colonel Ferreira unexpectedly left the capital on an inspection tour. Immediately, Stroessner appointed himself the interim commander of Campo Grande. What happened after that is not entirely clear. Apparently, Cháves and Colonel Ferreira learned of the plot. Cháves ordered Major Candia's arrest, and Ferreira hurried back to resume his command. Stroessner, who had not been consulted about Candia's arrest, claimed that Cháves's order was an "insult to the military's honor" and called out the troops. A brief struggle then ensued inside Campo Grande, ending with Ferreira's arrest.[34]

Soon the cavalry forces were entering Asunción, while the marines seized the telecommunications. Cháves had only the police to defend him, but Battalion 40 was so well armed that it held off rebel assaults all through the night of 4 May and during most of the next day. The fighting was the most bitter of any revolt since the civil war. In the end the police were overwhelmed. Petit and twenty-four others were killed, and over one hundred persons were wounded. Cháves resigned and was placed under guard.

Tomás Romero Pereira, a sixty-five-year-old Colorado party leader, took over as provisional president. He was an architect by profession, having studied at the University of Buenos Aires and the Sorbonne, but his past was rather checkered. He had originally pursued a military career in the cavalry, but was dismissed from the service in 1908 for taking part in a plot against the government. That was when he began his travels and studies abroad, which took him all over South America, Europe, and the United States. At last he returned to Paraguay, got a job as a planner of public works, and became active in Colorado party affairs. He served his first term as president of the party from 1926 to 1930. Then, when the Chaco War broke out, he returned to the army as a lieutenant colonel. Romero Pereira had been in Cháves's government since 1950, first as minister of public works (1950–52) and then as minister of interior (1952–54). An avid *político*, he enjoyed the plotting involved in Paraguay's Byzantine struggles, and he could be coldly calculating and ruthless in a fight. But, despite his varied background and experience, he was seldom the real leader in the plotting. Rather, the new provisional president was more of a useful, well-honed weapon which more talented *caudillos* might seek to use for their own ends.[35]

The other leading plotters also returned to the government. Epifanio Méndez Fleitas resumed his old post as head of the Central Bank, and Major Ortega took over again as chief of police. Enciso Velloso, who was becoming too old for the rough-and-tumble, became ambassador to the United States—a political prize. Another one of Cháves's former associates, Angel Florentín Peña, the former minister of agriculture, became president of the Colorado party. But the real strongman of the situation was General Stroessner. With the armed forces behind him, he was a power to be reckoned with. On 14 June the Colorado party convention accorded him its official nomination for president in the forthcoming elections. In typical Paraguayan fashion, he won unopposed on 11 July and took the presidential oath on 15 August, Asunción Founders' Day.

So began the long period of Stroessner's rule, the so-called *stronato*. None of the power-hungry Colorado *caudillos* were aware at the time, of course, of what was about to happen to them. They had become completely absorbed in their petty personal and factional feuds and were so used to making and breaking presidents from within their ranks without any serious challenge from other groups that they considered Stroessner's presidency only a temporary interlude. In reality, though, the Colorados had mismanaged the country and thrown away their opportunities to solidify their hold on political power through unity and discipline. Having created chaos and division within their ranks and within the nation, they were vulnerable to a leader who could enforce unity and discipline, as Stroessner was to teach them in the coming years.

PART 2. THE CAUDILLO

Chapter 4. The Rise to Power

Considering that his is one of the world's oldest dictatorships, it is surprising that there is no full-length biography of Alfredo Stroessner. No friend has written an official *apologia*, and no enemy has bothered to debunk him. All that exists are a few booklets that give only the rawest information about his army career, a scattering of newspaper articles, and a chapter by Richard Bourne in his book *Political Leaders of Latin America*, which in turn is dependent on the same sources.[1] Thus the biographer must recreate Stroessner's character and career from bits and pieces taken from news stories, political narratives, and the record of his deeds in office.

From another point of view, however, it is perhaps not so surprising that Paraguay's dictator is so little known despite his long tenure in power. To a great extent his "low profile" is deliberate. Like many poor countries, Paraguay needs foreign aid, and that is harder to obtain if one's government is branded a pariah by world public opinion. The less attention that is drawn to the fact that Stroessner is a strong, successful dictator, the better.

Thus, unlike more flamboyant Latin tyrants such as Perón, Trujillo, Somoza, or Castro, Stroessner has been content to appear before his countrymen as a solid, sober, churchgoing family man. That has not been very hard for him because in reality his personality is anything but colorful. Bourne describes him as "heavy and ponderous in his movements . . . a taciturn man with wary eyes."[2] He is strongly built, with Germanic features, and wears a thin moustache. In contrast to the usual supermacho image of Latin dictators, there has never been any scandal attached to his private life. He and his matronly wife, Doña Eligia, live unostentatiously. A kindly and pleasant exschoolteacher, she accompanies him on many of his political trips and often stands in for him on minor ceremonial occasions. His daughter, Graciela, also used to go with him on his frequent tours of the interior before she got married. The elder son, Gustavo, is an air force officer. He is said to be serious, competent, and a possible successor to his father. Hugo, the younger son, has the reputation of being a playboy. Otherwise, the Stroessners are not a remarkable family. Unlike the Trujillos, for example, they neither flaunt great wealth nor hoard the top governmental positions.

Stroessner's rise to power had nothing to do with charisma. On the contrary, his rivals often overlooked him and underestimated him because he seemed so dull and plodding. Nor is his success at staying in power due to any ability to electrify the masses, despite all the sycophantic adulation that amounts practically to a cult of personality surrounding him. He is an uninspiring speaker in public, given to patriotic platitudes and boring recitations of his regime's material achievements. On the other hand, the key to Stroessner's success may be found in certain other of his personality traits: self-discipline, an unusual capacity for work, a liking for details, and an undoubted administrative ability. True to his military background, he starts each day at four-thirty and often works until past midnight. As we shall see, he keeps in close personal touch with all the governmental departments, with his party chiefs, and above all with the army. Although he knows how to delegate authority and has built up over time a reliable team of subordinates, he keeps constant tabs on all of them, preferring to meet with his ministers individually rather than collectively. In short, Stroessner dominates Paraguayan politics because he works harder, does his political homework better, and is a first-rate strategist. This slow and steady competence has enabled him to outlast many a brilliant but incautious opponent.

Stroessner's Early Career

Alfredo Stroessner entered the Military College in 1929, at the age of sixteen. We know little about him before then, except that his father was a German immigrant who came to Paraguay in the 1890s, settled in Encarnación, married a Paraguayan woman, and opened a beer factory. The young cadet entered his career at a propitious time, for three years later the Chaco War broke out. Even before his studies were completed, Stroessner was sent to fight at the battle of Boquerón. He earned a medal for bravery there and a month later received his second lieutenant's commission. Trained as an artillery officer, by the end of the year he had been given command, in succession, of a field gun battery and a mortar group.

Stroessner was a good and brave officer. He distinguished himself at the bloody battles of Nanawa and El Carmen. An official citation after El Carmen describes him as an "excellent" and "brilliant" commander whose artillery forces "heroically" resisted the attacks of four Bolivian regiments, leaving one hundred and fifty of the enemy dead on the battlefield. He later received the Chaco Cross medal for that action. In March 1934 he was promoted to first lieutenant.

His superiors' reports—which are consistent with others throughout his career—described him as a good leader of troops. He was considered to be a careful organizer: not exceptionally brilliant, but hardworking and tireless. He instructed his men carefully and won their respect through his concern for them. More than once he was described as a good comrade and a cheerful (*alegre*) type. It was noted especially that he enjoyed taking on responsibilities.[3]

Stroessner continued to rise in the military hierarchy after the war. The Febrerista government promoted him to captain in 1936, and soon after Morínigo became president in 1940, Stroessner attained the rank of major. Adapting himself quickly to peacetime routine, he married and began to raise a family. He also continued to receive favorable notice from his superior officers at the General Brúgez Regiment artillery barracks in Paraguarí for his spit and polish during military reviews and for his good showing in the advanced training courses. He excelled especially in mathematics, in which he placed first out of a class of twenty-five—a small fact which nevertheless helps illuminate his methodical character. His commanding officer, Lieutenant Colonel Amancio Pampliega, concluded in one of his reports that Major Stroessner was "a complete officer with a great future in the army." Stroessner also received a personal commendation from Pampliega's successor, Lieutenant Colonel Raimundo Rolón.

All of this was important for young Major Stroessner, for Pampliega and Rolón were on the way to becoming important personages. Pampliega was to be named minister of defense and, later, minister of interior in Morínigo's coalition government. Rolón was Natalicio González's minister of defense and, as mentioned above, eventually succeeded him to the presidency. To be regarded highly by such influential officers meant that Stroessner's career was likely to be encouraged too, and his opportunity was not long in coming. In October 1940 he was selected as one of a group of junior officers to go to Brazil for special artillery training.

The reports filed by Stroessner's Brazilian instructors are also revealing for their impressions of his character and behavior. Despite the language differences and (according to the Brazilians) his poor previous training in gunnery, Stroessner proved, as usual, to be a good pupil. He showed intelligence and an ability to learn quickly. Like his Paraguayan commanders, the Brazilians were impressed by his enormous capacity for work and his persistence, which they ascribed to his unusual physical strength, and they noted his "spirit of initiative," his seeking out of responsibilities, and his natural abilities as a leader. He earned the esteem of his Brazilian instructors and his own colleagues, one report noted, "by his gentlemanly attitude and his military bearing." On the other hand, Major Stroessner seems no longer to have been the outgoing, *alegre* type of before. Instead, he had become, according to the Brazilians, "discreet and very circumspect." [4] Perhaps Alfredo Stroessner was already acquiring ambitions, for this discreet and circumspect side of his character was to become increasingly dominant—and was to serve him well in future political intrigues.

Stroessner returned from Brazil in January 1941 to take up his new duties in the General Brúgez Regiment as an artillery instructor. As usual, his superiors wrote highly of him as a serious, diligent officer. His circumspection, which amounted to an acute political sensitivity, placed him on the right side of an abortive military plot against Morínigo in September 1943. As a result, he was not only cited officially for his "correct attitude" but was also rewarded with a nomination to the Superior War School. This was a crucial opportunity for Stroessner, and he did not waste it. Colonel Eulalio Fascetti, the school's director, was so impressed with him that he kept Stroessner on for more advanced work after the end of the regular course.

Stroessner's success at the Superior War School was followed immediately by signal honors. In November 1945, just a week after receiving his diploma, he was made commander of the General Brúgez Regiment, Paraguay's chief artillery unit. A month later he was promoted to lieutenant colonel. At thirty-three years of age, Stroessner was the army's key artillery officer.

Colonel Fascetti must indeed have been exceptionally impressed by his former pupil, for it was largely on his recommendation that Stroessner was assigned to the army's General Staff in June 1946. This appointment plunged Stroessner into the center of military politics, for Paraguay was entering the period of coalition government. Headquarters were rife with plots, and top officers were beginning to choose sides for the coming partisan struggle. This was a tricky situation, and Stroessner needed all of his customary caution and discretion to avoid a misstep that would cost him his career.

Apparently he steered a neutral course for as long as it was possible to do so. There is no evidence that Stroessner had ever expressed any political preferences up to this time. Certainly he had never joined any party. Bourne may be right in supposing that the Communists' par-

ticipation on the side of the rebels may have made him more sympathetic to Morínigo's cause, for his whole background and demeanor
were those of a conservative, bourgeois officer. On the other hand, he
may have based his final decision on calculated advantage and his
personal relations with top commanders. Two of Morínigo's key military supporters were friends of his: Colonels Emilio Díáz de Vivar and
Raimundo Rolón. Rolón was more or less Stroessner's *patrón*,
having preceded him as head of the General Brúgez Regiment, and it
is quite possible that his influence brought Stroessner over to the government's side. But the decision probably was not easy, for Stroessner
must have had other pressures. Generals Amancio Pampliega and
Vincente Machuca, who favored the opposition, were also friends. Also,
Colonel Enrique Giménez, Morínigo's commander at Campo Grande,
was a personal enemy. Stroessner put off choosing sides until the open
rebellion at Concepción made any further vacillating impossible.

The Southern Front

Stroessner did not figure prominently in the early stages of the civil
war. His first opportunity to distinguish himself came during the
naval revolt of 25–29 April. For three days rebel sailors, aided by
armed workers, had occupied the harbor and several city blocks in
the capital and had thrown back repeated assaults by cavalry and
heavily armed police units. Unable to dislodge them, Morínigo decided
as a last resort to destroy the navy yard and called in the artillery.
Under Stroessner's command, the General Brúgez Regiment occupied
a hill known as "La Tablada," which overlooked the naval base. They
set up their guns under the cover of night, and a few hours before
the dawn of the fourth day they began their terrible bombardment.
Stroessner had learned his lessons well in Brazil, for the barrage was
so accurate and devastating that the rebels were soon in headlong
retreat. By dawn, Lieutenant Patricio Colmán of Battalion 40 had re-
taken all the streets surrounding the base and had even penetrated the
naval yard itself. When the last rebel redoubt fell that afternoon, the
General Brúgez Regiment came in for a large share of Morínigo's
praise.[5] The president not only thanked Stroessner personally for his
"brilliant action" but also entrusted him henceforth with the defense
of the Southern Front.

The Southern Front lay in the territory of Misiones, the region
which lies across the Paraná River from Argentina. Since the main
rebel army was based in Concepción, to the north of Asunción, the
Southern Front was not the primary theater of war. Nevertheless, a

rebel breakthrough there would have threatened the capital with a pincers movement. Moreover, the area was threatened with an attack from two heavy Paraguayan gunboats that had defected to the rebel side. The two ships had been sent to Argentina for supplies, but while docked in the Buenos Aires harbor their crews had mutinied and taken them over in the name of the revolution. After some delay, the Argentine government reluctantly gave them permission to sail. Their first stop was Uruguay, whose government was more sympathetic to the revolution. There they loaded provisions, including mortar shells. In the first week of July the two gunboats, the *Paraguay* and the *Humaitá*, were finally ready, and their crews headed them up the Paraná, intending to bombard Asunción. In the meantime, rebel troops under the command of Colonel Carlos Ramírez were gathering in the south. The plan was to reinforce them with antigovernment exiles, who would be picked up by the gunboats on their way upriver.

Stroessner's job was to keep the rebel army in the south isolated from the main revolutionary force and to block the gunboats from going up the Paraguay River to attack Asunción. If he failed, the capital would be exposed to a three-pronged attack: by land from the north and south, and from the river. His first move was to occupy the strategic town of Humaitá, whose fort stands atop some high bluffs commanding the confluence of the Paraguay and Paraná rivers. This turned out to be a harder job than he had expected, however, because part of the local garrison and police had defected to the rebels. For a brief time Stroessner found himself besieged, but he soon managed to dominate the revolt by calling in air support and drawing on the Colorado militia—mostly *py nandí* irregulars. Many of the disloyal troops escaped, though, and joined with the rebel army. Back in the capital excited rumors began to circulate of a rebel breakthrough in the south.[6]

On 11 July, the day following the local garrison's mutiny, the *Paraguay* and *Humaitá* appeared on the river and prepared to run Stroessner's hastily constructed blockade. The battle that followed was one of the pivotal events of the war. Stroessner's batteries poured a steady barrage of fire down into the river, and the gunboats answered by shelling the fort. In the end, the ships decided to retreat. Instead of proceeding north up the Paraguay River, they turned east and headed up the Alto Paraná.

Although they had lost the first round, the *Paraguay* and *Humaitá* were still dangerous. Continuing to pick up bands of rebels along the riverbanks, they headed for Encarnación, Paraguay's second port. On 13 July they anchored near there and dropped off some one hundred and fifty men to reinforce the local guerrilla units. Government airplanes tried to disrupt the operation, but the sailors managed to drive them off with the boats' antiaircraft guns. Later another two hundred men disembarked at Puerto Ayolas, a little town east of Encarnación that was already in rebel hands. The port was being encircled. Encarnación's defenses consisted of only about two hundred men, most of whom were untrained *py nandi*. The rebels received another psychological boost when two cargo ships carrying war materiel to Humaitá defected to the revolution.

Nevertheless, both sides knew that the war would be won or lost around Asunción. Consequently, the *Paraguay* and *Humaitá* began to move back downstream for another run at Stroessner's blockade. What they did not know, however, was that he had been busy in the meantime. He had moved his troops around the point at Humaitá, so that now they commanded the exit of the Alto Paraná. What is more, he had chosen a spot where the channel narrowed between the mainland and an island. Both the densely wooded shore and the island were heavily fortified, so that the passing ships would be caught in a deadly cross fire. Indeed, his position was more formidable than previously, for Morínigo had sent down more artillery pieces and a sizable contingent of infantry.

On 5 August the rebel gunboats opened up the second battle to break through Stroessner's defenses. On that same day, Colonel Rafael Franco's troops were starting downstream from Concepción in their final assault on the capital. It was a critical moment for both sides, and the fighting along the Alto Paraná was so furious that the inhabitants of the nearby Argentine town of Yahapé decided to evacuate. Had the *Paraguay* and *Humaitá* managed to smash through, they would have joined forces with Franco to surround Asunción, and the rebels probably would have won. Instead, they were forced once more to back off. The rebel crews put their casualties ashore on the Argentine side and waited for night to fall before trying the blockade again.

Since Asunción was by now under siege, any news from outside got through only with difficulty. While Colonel Franco's men were pushing into the suburbs as far as the Botanical Gardens, reports reached Morínigo that the *Paraguay* and *Humaitá* had broken through at last and were hurrying to join the siege. It was the lowest point so far in the government's morale. Panic broke out in the city, and floods of people, including some government officials, boarded any sort of small craft they could find to escape across the river to Argentina.

The rumors were false. Reinforced by another fifteen artillery pieces and still more infantry, Stroessner's defenses had held. The *Humaitá* was put out of action when a mortar shell hit her fuel tank. The *Paraguay* was so badly crippled that her officers steered her to the Argentine shore and requested the authorities there to intern her to prevent her from falling into Morínigo's hands. Although the crew rose up and forced the officers to rescind the request, neither ship was fit to continue the fight.

The rebel gunboats were bottled up until 20 August, when Colonel Franco's army was forced to lift its siege and run for safety into exile. The war was over, and the rebel crews gave up and asked for asylum as well. Stroessner had the two ships seized and brought them to Asunción. They entered the harbor, white flags of surrender flying in the breeze, to a twenty-one-gun salute, while President Morínigo and a multitude of grateful Colorados greeted their hero. A general order on 26 August cited him as "outstanding" for his "brilliant action against the attempts of the rebels to organize the Southern Front and force a passage to the capital."

The Machiavellian

Morínigo's victory catapulted Stroessner into a position of primary influence. More than three-fourths of the regular officer corps had gone over to the rebel side at the beginning of the war. Stroessner was one of the few who had stayed loyal, and now he was one of a small group of active professional officers. Each man knew the others well, their strong points as well as their weak ones. The situation was full of opportunity for a careful, ambitious strategist. Stroessner, the man who excelled at mathematics and was an avid chess player in his leisure hours, soon showed himself to be an adept political schemer as well. Ambitious and ruthless, he plotted against every president he served under, from Morínigo right up through Cháves.

As usual, Stroessner appeared not to take a side among the various Colorado factions that were jockeying for power. He took part in the coup of 3 June 1948, which toppled Morínigo, but he did that in the name of the Colorado party generally rather than of any particular faction. That coup also rid him of his chief enemy, Colonel Enrique Giménez, who was ousted as head of Campo Grande at the same time. Even a careful man can make mistakes, however. In the botched coup against Natalicio González in November of that year, Stroessner joined the *molaslopistas*. When Colonel Canata, Giménez's successor at Campo Grande, switched sides at the last moment, Stroessner was forced to take refuge in the Brazilian embassy and, more humiliating still, had to make his escape by hiding in the trunk of a car.

The next few months were the low-water mark of Stroessner's political career. Even the ouster of Natalicio González in January 1949 failed to change his fortunes, for General Rolón neglected to pardon him. Apparently, Stroessner's ambition was beginning to show, and his former patrón did not trust him. However, General Rolón's tenure in power was to be a brief one. Molas López and Federico Cháves plotted his overthrow, and both factions considered Stroessner a friendly officer. His popularity with his soldiers made him a valuable member of the conspiracy. His role was to slip back into the country, go to Paraguarí, and retake command of the General Brúgez Regiment. In the actual coup, Stroessner's troops rallied around their former commander and were instrumental in overthrowing Rolón.

Molas López promoted Stroessner to brigadier general as a reward, but that was not enough to secure his loyalty. During the crisis of 9 September, when the *molaslopistas* planned to purge the *democráticos*, it was Stroessner's timely tip-off to the army commander in chief which allowed the *democráticos* to turn the tables. Once again, Stroessner was rewarded. Indeed, no president ever tried to cultivate his friendship as much as Federico Cháves. He gave Stroessner command of all the nation's artillery forces and, in April 1951, made him head of the crucial First Military Region, which includes the capital. Soon after that he reached the pinnacle of his army career when Cháves named him commander in chief of the armed forces.

At this time, too, Stroessner began to attract the attention of foreign governments with important interests in Paraguay. Perón invited him to visit Argentina in January 1951, after which he attended the presidential inauguration in Uruguay as his government's representative. He also represented Paraguay that September during Brazilian Independence Day ceremonies in Rio de Janeiro, and two years later he made another visit to Brazil as an official guest. Also in 1953 the State Department brought him to the United States. Finally, in that same year, the Argentine Order of Military Merit and the Brazilian Order of Military Merit were added to his already well-decorated uniform in ceremonies held only one day apart.[7]

In short, Alfredo Stroessner was becoming a politician to be reckoned with. Perhaps those foreign governments were aware of his part in the growing conspiracy against Cháves. Or maybe they were only playing it safe, knowing well the political value of an army commander in chief in Paraguay. Whatever their motives, they were right to court him. Less than six months later, Stroessner deposed Cháves and made himself head of the government.

In Paraguay, of course, achieving power is one thing, holding on to it is another. Alfredo Stroessner was only forty-one years old when he came to the presidency. The record of his predecessors suggested that he would be lucky to last the full five-year term to which he was "elected" after the coup. Indeed, the record hinted that Paraguay might really be ungovernable. To begin with, those old hatreds between the parties made any president's claim to legitimacy unacceptable to a sizable element of the citizenry. By 1954 the Liberals and Febreristas had recovered from the shock of losing the civil war and were talking of invading the country. In addition, the problem of factionalism among the Colorados made that party an uncertain prop at best. Also, by their quick ouster of General Rolón, the Colorados had shown that however much they might quarrel among themselves they would never accept a non-Colorado at the head of the government. An all-military regime was as intolerable to them as one headed by another party. Since Stroessner had never been known as a "party man," he could not expect their support. Yet he could not govern without the Colorados, because they provided all of the administrative personnel—what might loosely be called the civil service—and the army did not have the trained clerical staff to replace them.

Then there was the army itself. Some of the officers were fanatical Colorados, and they would resist any attempt by Stroessner to become independent of the party. Other officers were ambitious schemers; they would have to be watched and weeded out at the first opportunity. Finally, the Cháves administration had left him with an economic mess and a customs union arrangement with Argentina that compromised the country's economic independence.

Stroessner was now, in his turn, to appreciate the paradox of executive power in Paraguay that his predecessors had faced: after plotting for years to achieve the presidency, he found that high office did not automatically mean great power. Balanced against his broad constitutional prerogatives was the all-pervading disrespect for law that was bred of Paraguay's authoritarian tradition. The president commanded, but others obeyed only so far as they had to. Having helped to overthrow five presidents, Stroessner now found that to keep power he had to be constantly alert to attempts to undermine him.

Unlike his predecessors, however, Stroessner found the proper levers of power and got a firm grip on them. Those levers were the army and the Colorado party. At the beginning, he had no real support in the party, and although he was the commander in chief of the army, he could by no means count on the loyalty of all the officers beneath him. Thus, Stroessner started out from a relatively isolated position with only a few loyal military friends around him. However, he was soon to conquer both army and party in a series of skillful and complicated maneuvers.

Chapter 5. The Consolidation of Power

The Original Lineup of Forces

The overthrow of Federico Cháves on 5 May 1954 did not bring Stroessner immediately to the presidency. Important elements within the Colorado party and the army were either opposed or indifferent to him. Somehow they had to be propitiated, for if they combined against him they might be strong enough to upset his plans. To begin with, Cháves's *democrático* following was still entrenched in the government, and to dislodge them would cause wholesale disruption of the entire bureaucracy. Moreover, they still controlled the party apparatus and could count on support inside the military.

Epifanio Méndez Fleitas and his faction also controlled some key political posts. General Ceferino Vega Gaona, head of the Battalion 40 of the police, was a close friend, as was Colonel Mario Ortega, the new police chief. Méndez Fleitas also had powerful contacts in the army. Major Virgilio Candia, the new leader of the Campo Grande cavalry, and Captain Gerardo Osta, the artillery chief at Paraguarí, were *epifanistas*. If Méndez Fleitas had been able to count on the solid backing of the Colorado party, nothing could have stopped him from seizing the presidency for himself.

Unfortunately for him the party, as usual, was divided. The *democráticos* nursed deep grievances against the *epifanistas*. Not only had Cháves, their "grand old man," been betrayed by Méndez Fleitas but one of their most promising young men, Roberto Petit, had been killed in the May coup. Those who had once formed Cháves's inner circle— such as José Zacarias Arza and Osvaldo Cháves, his nephew—would neither forgive nor forget. Neither side wanted to see Stroessner as president, but each planned to use him temporarily to eliminate the other. For his part, Stroessner was ready for a truce with the *demo-*

cráticos, for they were a counterweight to Méndez Fleitas. The new regime thus began with a three-cornered struggle for power in which none of the sides had a clear-cut advantage.

The *democráticos* agreed to the truce with Stroessner only grudgingly. Indeed, Angel Florentín Peña, who succeeded to the party presidency, wanted the Colorados to retire from the government to show their displeasure. That would be a signal to their army followers to launch a coup. He was overruled by other members of the Junta de Gobierno, however. Such an action would only drive Stroessner and Méndez Fleitas closer together, and their combined forces would be more than a match for the *democráticos*. The wiser course, the Junta decided, would be to go along for the moment and wait for Stroessner and Méndez Fleitas to quarrel—as they certainly would, since both were ambitious men. When that happened, the *democráticos* could eliminate them one at a time. Meanwhile, the *democráticos* planned to continue enjoying the privileges that came with holding government jobs.[1]

The three factions agreed to set up a provisional government to rule the country until elections could be held. Tomás Romero Pereira took office as president, and he chose his cabinet carefully to give each faction some representation. Romero Pereira himself was an *epifanista*. There was some speculation that General Herminio Morínigo, the new defense minister, might be in that camp too, since he shared Méndez Fleitas's enthusiasm for the Peronist regime in Argentina. On the other hand, Morínigo was an old army buddy of Stroessner's, and personal ties weigh heavily in Paraguayan politics. Gustavo Storm, the interior minister, was a longtime supporter of the *democrático* faction, but he was also a close personal friend of Stroessner's. The *democráticos* were certain of the loyalty of Enrique Zacarias Arza, Fabio da Silva, and Hipólito Sánchez Quell—the ministers of health, justice, and foreign affairs, respectively. Stroessner could count on his friends General Marcial Samaniego, the public works minister, and Colonel César Barrientos, the minister of industry.

It was also understood that Stroessner would be the Colorados' nominee for president in the elections. The *democráticos* were in no position to impose a candidate of their own, and Méndez Fleitas, the only other major party figure, was completely unacceptable to them. Méndez Fleitas himself still pretended to be Stroessner's ally. He neither controlled the party's nominating machinery nor felt secure enough to try a coup, and he could expect nothing from the *democráticos*, who longed to be revenged on him. Therefore his best strategy was to help Stroessner into office and then work to undermine him.

Thus, General Stroessner was the only possible candidate. Nominated by acclamation at the Colorado convention of 14 June 1954, he was elected without opposition less than a month later on July 11 and took office on August 15.

Continuing the delicately balanced compromise, every faction got something under the new government. Méndez Fleitas returned as president of the Central Bank, which gave him access to government funds. Romero Pereira became interior minister, which allowed him to control the police, and also the new president of the Colorado party—an important concession to the *epifanistas*.[2] Guillermo Enciso Velloso, Méndez Fleitas's former *patrón*, was made ambassador to the United States. Thus, even though General Morínigo, the new defense minister, seemed to favor Stroessner, in spite of his Peronist sympathies, the *epifanistas* were satisfied for the moment. Two of Stroessner's friends, General Samaniego and Colonel Barrientos, stayed on in the new cabinet, but he lost control over another influential post when his friend Gustavo Storm stepped down as minister of interior. This loss was only partly compensated by the appointment of General Mario Coscia Tavarossi to head the army General Staff. Coscia, along with General Herminio Morínigo, had supported Stroessner in the abortive revolt against Natalicio González in 1948 and had gone into exile with him. Later his career had prospered as Stroessner became more powerful, and he could be expected to back the president in any crisis. Finally, the *democráticos* got their share of high government posts too. Zacarias Arza, Sánchez Quell, and da Silva all retained their portfolios. Juan Ramón Cháves, another nephew of the former president, was made ambassador to Argentina.

Not everybody was happy, though. Eulógio Estigarribia, a party maverick, had ambitions of his own. Until 1949 he had been second only to Federico Cháves in the *democrático* faction, but he broke with Cháves and supported Molas López. When Molas López's coup failed in September, Estigarribia found himself politically isolated. He and his few remaining followers attempted another revolt in 1952, but that was squelched before it ever got to the serious stage. Now, in January 1955, Estigarribia hoped to take advantage of the unsettled situation to make a third try for power.

In reality, Estigarribia's plans were unrealistic. Although he had the support of a few Colorado exministers like Ramón and Evaristo Méndez Paiva and Crispín Insaurralde, he lacked an adequate base in the military. A couple of retired cavalry generals agreed to line up support inside Campo Grande, and they managed to get a few junior officers to join the plot. Also, some lieutenants fresh from the Military College's graduating class promised to bring over the Fourteenth In-

fantry Regiment, based just outside the capital in the suburb of Tacumbú. Their friends in the college were supposed to take over that
building as well and rally the cadets in support of the revolt. The
target day was 25 January when General Stroessner was to visit the
Military College on an inspection tour. The cadets were to seize the
general, and the coup would begin. The whole thing was an ama-
teurish, long-shot gamble, to say the least.

The plan never got off the ground. Word of the intended coup
leaked out before the plotters were ready, and the police quickly
rounded them up. On 25 January the Junta de Gobierno met in a special session and passed a motion disassociating itself from the attempt. Drafted by Méndez Fleitas, it read: "In view of the commu-
nique from the interior minister . . . and other facts presented for the
Junta's consideration, we resolve to express our complete solidarity
with the government of our President, General Alfredo Stroessner, in
the present emergency, and to repudiate this attempt to subvert the
legal order and the public peace."[3]

The Argentine Factor

Méndez Fleitas could well afford to express his support for Stroessner
"in the present emergency." With Estigarribia's fall a minor, but
bothersome, rival was eliminated. Moreover, it seemed unlikely that
Stroessner would last much longer. The example of General Rolón,
who had tried to base a government on the military alone, was too
obvious. Stroessner had no real support in the party, and the cavalry,
artillery, and police were all on Méndez Fleitas's side. Besides, Méndez
Fleitas had wide popular backing, which Stroessner lacked. As the
leading Paraguayan spokesman for Peronism and a dynamic orator
whose humble background and command of Guaraní endeared him
to workers and students, Méndez Fleitas was a symbol of reform-
minded nationalism. Like Perón, he was trying to forge a powerful
coalition of labor unions, populist army officers, and nationalistic intellectuals. Moreover, his control of development loans as head of the
Central Bank was winning him backing from businessmen. Even
foreign writers were impressed by him. George Pendle, a British expert on Paraguay, described him as "an enlightened nationalist, a
composer of Guaraní music [and] an able administrator at the Bank."
According to Pendle, Méndez Fleitas was making progress in securing
financial and technical aid from Europe and the United States, and
"seemed to possess the diverse qualities that Paraguay needed in a
ruler."[4]

Méndez Fleitas's fortunes continued to improve until late 1955. Then something unexpected happened. In Argentina a violently anti-Peronist military faction succeeded in overthrowing Perón. In his flight from Buenos Aires, he took refuge aboard a Paraguayan gunboat anchored in the harbor and claimed diplomatic asylum. Although the Argentine authorities were tempted to storm the ship and take him prisoner, in the end they grudgingly agreed to respect a long-established custom in Latin American politics and to let him go. Nevertheless, Perón's settling in Paraguay caused a chill in relations between the two countries. The Argentines feared that Perón would try to regroup his followers there and use the neighboring country as a beachhead from which to mount a counterrevolution.

Those fears became certainties in the next few weeks as scores of other Peronist leaders managed to evade the Argentine border patrols and escape into Paraguay. Immediately they began to organize a resistance movement to encourage the Peronist masses in Argentina to revolt. They set up a radio station to broadcast political messages across the border, and Perón himself made pronouncements to the press that he would return shortly to Argentina to overthrow the military usurpers and that his party would sweep the next elections with at least 70 percent of the vote. What is more, under Méndez Fleitas's urging the Stroessner government was showing the refugees far more hospitality than was strictly necessary or diplomatically sensible. For example, former Peronist police agents joined the internal security division of the Paraguayan police as special advisers, and there they were able to use their positions to gather intelligence on the Argentine government.[5]

On 6 October the Argentine authorities sent Stroessner a harsh note demanding that Perón be expelled from the country. He had been allowed to take diplomatic asylum aboard the Paraguayan vessel, the note claimed, only after assurances from the ambassador that he would refrain from all political activity in Paraguay and retire to private life. It was clear that Perón had violated those conditions, and the Paraguayan government was at fault for not holding him to them. Since he was obviously unreliable, he should be sent away to some country outside the Western Hemisphere. Otherwise, the note hinted darkly, his continued presence in Paraguay would be "incompatible with the maintenance of harmonious relations between the two countries." To give added point to this veiled threat, Argentine ships suddenly found that the water level of the Paraná River had mysteriously dropped, and they were unable to go all the way upstream to Asunción.[6]

Perón was becoming an embarrassment to Stroessner. He had already embroiled himself in a conflict with the Catholic church in Paraguay when he made a statement to the press excoriating the Argentine clergy for their part in his overthrow. Then students at the National University began to protest his presence in the country. On 17 October, the anniversary of Perón's rise to power, some three thousand students tried to march through downtown Asunción to demand his expulsion. Although the police broke up the demonstration, Stroessner was learning that his guest was a political liability. The most decisive pressure came from Argentina, however. There was already an informal boycott of Paraguayan ports. The next step would be to close off the river to Paraguayan ships heading south, or to seal off the frontier altogether, including the roads and all train service. Moreover, evidence indicated that the Argentine army was supplying weapons to the thousands of Paraguayan exiles just across the border.

Personally, Stroessner liked Perón, and this added to his dilemma. The two dictators had become friends the previous year when Perón had visited Asunción to return captured trophies from the War of the Triple Alliance. Furthermore, Perón was under the special protection of Méndez Fleitas. If he sent him out of the country, Stroessner would be provoking an open quarrel with the *epifanistas*. On the other hand, if Stroessner didn't get rid of Perón, the government in Buenos Aires could threaten his whole administration.

In the end, Stroessner decided to give in to the pressure. But he did so in such a way as to save face. Waiting until Méndez Fleitas was out of the country on a mission to secure financial and technical aid, Stroessner replied to the Argentine note. He rejected the demand to expel Perón as an unacceptable interference in Paraguay's domestic affairs. Any sovereign nation, he insisted, had the right to grant political asylum. At the same time, he offered to intern Perón in some small town in the interior and to keep him from communicating with the press, if Argentina requested it. The offer was taken. On 13 October, Perón was sent to Villarica, where he was restricted in his movements. That, however, was unacceptable to Perón, who had no intention of retiring from politics, especially under such humiliating conditions. The former Argentine dictator asked permission to leave Paraguay, and on 2 November, Stroessner furnished him an army plane which would carry him to Panama. Almost immediately the Paraná River rose, again mysteriously, enough to let Argentine ships make it to Asunción.

But renewed good relations between Argentina and Paraguay did not last long. Another change of leaders in Buenos Aires that November brought an even more radically anti-Peronist government to power. Although Perón was gone, the other Peronist exiles were still conspiring in the name of their absent leader, and the pro-Peronist elements in Stroessner's government were protecting and encouraging them. The new government demanded that the exiles be expelled and began to apply pressure.

The Fall of Méndez Fleitas

It was no longer possible to avoid a showdown with Méndez Fleitas. Actually, he and Stroessner had grown cool toward each other ever since Méndez Fleitas had returned from his trip abroad to find Perón interned in the interior. By now, however, the lineup of factions inside the Colorado party had grown even more complicated, making the outcome of any clash extremely uncertain. The so-called *Re-encuentro* (reencounter) of 27 October 1955 was a general amnesty proclaimed by the Junta de Gobierno to reincorporate all previously expelled Colorado factions. Under it, Eulógio Estigarribia and his followers were allowed to return to Paraguay and participate in the party's affairs. More important still, the junta extended the olive branch even to the Guión Rojo. As a result, the Guión's cofounder Victor Morínigo came back from exile, even though Natalicio González preferred to remain in Mexico. Colonel Enrique Giménez, Morínigo's cavalry commander and Stroessner's old enemy, also returned, as did Edgar Ynsfran, an ambitious and violent young man who had been Natalicio González's protege.

The *Re-encuentro* was supported by *epifanistas* and *democráticos* alike.[7] But it was not generosity that prompted this act of reconciliation. The vicious party feuds of the recent past could not have been forgotten so soon. Possibly the Colorados were hoping to close ranks against a possible attempt by Stroessner to form an all-military government. Or, still more likely, each of the dominant factions hoped to gain the support of the reincorporated Colorados and thus become the most powerful.

In the meantime, Stroessner continued to seem eager to please everyone. He was deferential to the Junta de Gobierno and consulted party leaders on every appointment he made. Nevertheless, a political crisis was approaching, and the more astute Colorados were beginning to align themselves. No one was more sensitive to the changing atmosphere than the lean, ascetic-looking Edgar Ynsfran. Despite his relative youth and lack of experience, he possessed qualities that almost guarantee success in Paraguayan politics: discretion, a facility with words, and a restless enthusiasm for work. He combined the amoral instincts of a natural-born conspirator with the self-righteous temperament of a fanatic. Fittingly enough, he was to become Paraguay's "Grand Inquisitor." Because of his intelligence and drive, Ynsfran became the unofficial leader of the revived Guionist faction.

Almost as soon as he joined the party during the civil war, Ynsfran attracted the favorable attention of Natalicio González. Asked to write a piece for the 1947 edition of González's journal, *Guarania*, Ynsfran responded with an article extolling the violence of the *py nandí*. Let our opponents call us barbarians, he wrote, because we have a right to be proud of the Colorado peasant. His barbarism is a sign of the party's vitality—a sign that Coloradoism is a true movement of the people, and not just a clique of café society intellectuals.[8] Ynsfran had been a party member for less than a year when González put him on the Junta de Gobierno. It was a lightning start for his political career, but he suffered a setback when González fell from power. For a while, Ynsfran practiced law in Argentina, living in the town of Formosa, just across the river. On his return to Paraguay, he found a new *patrón* in Tomás Romero Pereira. Romero Pereira recognized his talent and introduced Ynsfran to Méndez Fleitas. Thinking to co-opt the young lawyer, Méndez Fleitas got him a job in the police force as chief of the investigative division, which handles political matters. From that sensitive spot, Ynsfran was able to follow the shadowy processes of plot and counterplot that were beginning to take shape. Though he was supposed to be a pipeline of information to Méndez Fleitas, he was also planning his own moves for the coming crisis.

Ynsfran knew, for instance, that the *epifanistas* were talking of a coup to be carried off sometime in late December—most likely on Christmas Day, to take advantage of the absence of many government officials during the holidays. He also knew that Stroessner suspected Méndez Fleitas's intentions and was preparing for a showdown. Considering later events, it is certain that Ynsfran got in touch with Stroessner too, without telling Méndez Fleitas. He had made his calculations and decided that the president would win the coming test of strength.

Even to this day, Méndez Fleitas denies having plotted against Stroessner. In *Diagnosis paraguaya*, a book he wrote to justify his actions, he describes a visit that Ynsfran paid him at home on the night of 20 December. According to his account, they discussed no politics; the two men simply spent the evening listening to music. Oddly enough, though, they decided to disconnect the telephone "in order to avoid inopportune calls."[9] Obviously, the story raises several questions. Whose idea was it to disconnect the telephone? Was it Méndez, who wanted to work on the details for the coming coup, or

Ynsfran, who wanted to isolate Méndez Fleitas from events that were already taking place outside?

Probably it was Ynsfran. As head of police investigations he must have known that on that very night General Stroessner was speeding along the highway to the General Brúgez Regiment artillery barracks in Paraguarí. Although Captain Osta, Méndez Fleitas's friend, was in charge there, Stroessner was preparing to take him by surprise. Upon arriving at the post the general made an unexpected appearance before the junior officers and appealed for their support. A former commander of the General Brúgez, Stroessner knew his men. They liked him, and what is more, they admired him for his courage in coming there alone. The artillery declared for Stroessner, and Captain Osta was put under arrest.

While the artillery prepared to move on the capital, Stroessner got back into his car and drove to the Fourteenth Infantry Cerro Corá barracks at Tacumbú. He was even more confident of their support because his good friend Major Patricio Colmán was in command there. Nevertheless, their loyalty had to be confirmed and the troops ordered to march. That being done, he had only the Campo Grande cavalry and the police to worry about.

At the same time that Méndez Fleitas and Ynsfran were "listening to music" and Stroessner was paying his evening calls, Major Virgilio Candia, the Campo Grande commander, was at the home of Romero Pereira, pleading with the Colorado president to use the party's influence to restore order at the base. It seems that Major Candia had overestimated his control over his troops. Stroessner had been commander in chief of the armed forces since 1951, and twice in the previous year he had assumed direct command of the Campo Grande division. As commander, Stroessner paid close attention to his subordinates' qualities and carefully screened their promotions. He also took care to keep in touch with his junior officers and to cultivate them. Now, Major Candia now found his authority challenged by three of his four regimental commanders.

Romero Pereira listened sympathetically, but remained noncommital. He agreed to talk with the Junta de Gobierno the next day and see what he could do. The deeply troubled Major Candia went away empty-handed. In retrospect it seems likely that Romero Pereira, like Ynsfran, had felt Stroessner's preventive coup coming and decided that the president was the likely winner. In any case, he did nothing to get in touch with Méndez Fleitas.

On the following morning, Méndez Fleitas received an urgent call from Colonel Ortega, the police chief, informing him that Candia's subordinates were in revolt against him. Soon afterwards, Ortega learned that Romero Pereira, as minister of interior, had ordered all police units including Battalion 40 to remain in their barracks.

Méndez Fleitas had to work fast to escape the quickly closing trap. With Colonel Enrique Giménez he went to "several military units" to "sound out their feelings." Apparently the two men found no support, for they next went to Victor Morínigo in order to bring him into town, where he was to support their cause before the Junta de Gobierno. By the time they returned to the capital, however, the junta had already met and agreed that Major Candia should resign his post at Campo Grande. At that, Major Candia accepted the inevitable and informed Méndez Fleitas by telephone that he was resigning, since he had support neither in the barracks nor in the party.

Méndez could do nothing now but try to brave it out. He still had many supporters in the army, although they were not in key positions at the moment. Also, the navy commander, Admiral Gabriel Patiño, was on his side, and General Vega Gaona still commanded Battalion 40. Finally, he thought that Romero Pereira and Ynsfran could be brought back into line if they could be made to see that all this was simply playing into the hands of the *democráticos.*

On the following day, Méndez Fleitas went, as usual, to the Central Bank. But he had not been in his office for more than five minutes when a soldier came in and ordered him to leave. Thereupon, Méndez Fleitas telephoned his friend Carlos Velilla, the finance minister. Velilla, who was more of a technocrat than a politician, was surprised by the news that Méndez Fleitas was out. He had had no idea that all these conspiracies had been going on around him.

Yet Méndez Fleitas still refused to accept defeat. On 28 December he appeared before the Junta de Gobierno to plead his case and ask for the party's support. Instead, the party issued a statement pledging its loyalty to Stroessner, and Romero Pereira's signature, as the party president, was right at the top, along with the signatures of the other junta members. More surprising, the document also contained the signatures of other Colorados who had little reason to applaud Stroessner—such men as Federico Cháves, Angel Florentín Peña, Victor Morínigo, and Eulógio Estigarribia. Most surprising of all, it seems that Méndez Fleitas decided to make one last attempt at salvaging his position and signed the document too.

Stroessner was hardly impressed by any such pledge from Méndez Fleitas, but he was too respectful of the latter's lingering support in the military to move abruptly. He preferred to unravel Méndez Fleitas's network of support slowly. First, he put Major Candia under arrest with Captain Osta and gave General Samaniego, the public works minister, temporary command of Campo Grande. Next, he "promoted" General Vega Gaona to division general and removed him as head of Battalion 40, "pending another assignment."

Cautious as usual, Stroessner sought to do his housecleaning quietly. Méndez Fleitas, Ortega, and General Morínigo—the three Peronists he had to get rid of—were called to the Presidential Palace and offered ambassadorships if they would leave the country. Morínigo, who had not been involved in any plot against Stroessner, agreed. But Méndez Fleitas and Ortega refused. Consequently, Ortega was fired as police chief on 5 January, and his place was taken by none other than Edgar Ynsfran. Immediately, Ynsfran began to compile an efficient dossier on his former benefactor, Méndez Fleitas, preparatory to having him expelled from the party. Though Méndez Fleitas was still at liberty, his every move was closely watched. Meanwhile, Ynsfran was moving his Guionist friends into key places. Major Ramón Duarte Vera, who headed the Police Academy, now became the assistant police chief as well. Saúl González, another Guionist colleague of Ynsfran's who was destined to rise high in the regime, became chief of investigations.

An atmosphere of suspense hung over Asunción throughout January 1956. Rumors abounded, and there were predictions of more purges to come and also predictions of a pro-Méndez counterattack in the making. It was said that a renewed struggle between the Guionists and the *democráticos* was tearing the party apart and would give Méndez Fleitas his chance for a comeback. Already, so rumor had it, *epifanista* officers were waiting for the right moment to strike. Still other rumors claimed that nonparty military "professionalists" were demanding that Stroessner ditch the Colorado party altogether and form an all-military government. For a while it was even believed that the professionalists had seized the government and put Stroessner under house arrest.[10]

The uncertainty lasted until the first week of February, when Stroessner—apparently sure now of his military backing—suddenly moved against the remaining pockets of *epifanista* strength. On 4–5 February he ordered the arrest of General Vega Gaona, Admiral Patiño, and General Quintín Parini, the head of the First Military Region. Soon afterwards some twenty officers of the Fourteenth Infantry Cerro Corá Regiment were taken into custody, as well as another forty police officials from Battalion 40. It was a purge of critical importance, for it gave Stroessner a firmer grip on the armed forces than he had ever enjoyed before. Captain Benito Pereira Saguier was given command of the navy, while an old and trusted friend, General Leodegar Cabello, took over the First Military Region forces around Asunción.

Stroessner was now in a position to finish off Méndez Fleitas. He, Colonel Ortega, and Major Candia were sent into exile—although it was euphemistically called a cultural mission. The lower-ranking officers were not so lucky, however. Most of them went to Fort Ingavi, a military camp in the arid part of the Chaco, or to the mosquito-infested island prison colony of Peña Hermosa on the northern Paraguay River.

In the denouement to this struggle, Stroessner called a cabinet meeting on 12 May and asked for the ministers' collective resignation. In the massive reshuffling that followed, six of the old ministers were not reappointed. Morínigo, Sánchez Quell, and da Silva were given ambassadorships, Romero Pereira was brought back later in the year as minister without portfolio, and Velilla and Martínez Miltos were simply dropped.[11] At the same time, Ynsfran was raised to the cabinet as minister of interior, and two other Guionists, Raúl Sapena Pastor and Martín Cuevas, were made ministers of foreign affairs and agriculture, respectively. In this way the delicate balance of forces was maintained vis à vis the *democráticos*, and the stage was set for the next struggle.

Chapter 6. Taming the Colorados

By disposing of Méndez Fleitas, Stroessner had proven to be more durable than the Colorados had originally supposed. Still, he had by no means completely secured his position. The *democráticos* were determined to win back power for the party, and they were still the largest faction in the Junta de Gobierno, the Congress, and the cabinet. In his characteristic fashion, Stroessner had encouraged the revival of the Guionists in order to maintain the balance of power. With his backing the Guionists had acquired the potent weapons of the Interior Ministry and the police, and they had once again penetrated the upper echelons of the party. But this involved a risk, for thus armed, Ynsfran and his followers might turn those weapons on Stroessner himself someday. Thus, all three groups in the struggle had formidable bases of strength. In winning out as he did, Stroessner showed himself to be an unusually skillful politician.

The Purge of the *Democráticos*

The *democráticos* had evened scores with Méndez Fleitas by refusing to oppose his removal from power by Stroessner. They had expected that after he fell they could claim a reunited party, which would make them better able to challenge Stroessner. Instead, they found themselves facing a new threat in Edgar Ynsfran and his Guionists.

Ynsfran claimed that he wanted to forget the past and work for party unity. At the signing of the *Re-encuentro* pact the previous October he had proclaimed:

> The Party needs the help of all those who, inspired by a generous spirit of forgiveness, want to work for its common goals. If

we must remember the past at all, let it be to learn the bitter lessons that our mutual errors and suffering have taught us. But we should never raise old issues that could rekindle rancor in our hearts. The memory of all that strife should prevent any feelings of revenge, because to carry on a chain of old hatreds means that no one can ever be sure that he had added the final link. May our links be, instead, those of Christian fellowship—which is the foundation of Colorado ethics.[1]

But these fine words proved to be merely a smoke screen. Immediately he began to prod Stroessner for more power. Not only did he ask for more jobs for his Guionists, but he also asked that Tomás Romero Pereira and Enrique Zacarias Arza be dropped from the cabinet. Not all Guionists were so greedy, however. A moderate splinter group, headed by Martín Cuevas, wanted to continue in the spirit of the *Re-encuentro*.[2]

Anxious to preserve his leverage against the *democráticos*, Stroessner gave Ynsfran much of what he asked for. Romero Pereira was left out of the new cabinet formed on 1 May 1956, although he retained his position as party president. Zacarias Arza was too dangerous to drop that quickly, but Ynsfran got promoted to interior minister, from which vantage he could direct the police and local government officials—the party's grass-roots patronage. His friend Colonel Duarte Vera succeeded him as police chief. Over the next several years that combination was to prove terrifying for all of Ynsfran's enemies. On the other hand, Sapena Pastor's appointment as minister of foreign affairs was little more than a sop to the Guionists, since he was far more interested in diplomacy than in factional intrigues. As it turned out, he became one of Stroessner's most useful and trustworthy subordinates. Also, the appointment of Martín Cuevas to head the Agriculture Ministry was a masterful stroke of politics, for while it increased the Guionists' nominal strength on the cabinet it also gave representation to a rival of Ynsfran's.

Meanwhile, the *democráticos* were partly compensated for the dismissal of some of their ministers. Besides Zacarias Arza, Raúl Peña was also retained, and the appointment of Ezequiel González Alsina as minister of justice and labor put one of their most promising young figures on the cabinet. A talented writer and speaker who, like Méndez Fleitas, had a real facility with Guaraní, González Alsina was perhaps the party's leading propagandist. Although he began his career as a Guionist, serving briefly as Natalicio González's presidential secretary, he had switched sides and supported the *democrático* cause. It was he who constructed the subtle compromise among the political factions in the 1954 provisional cabinet. Because he had remained loyal to Cháves during the Méndez Fleitas schism, the *democráticos* now put him forward as one of their trusted men. That was a mistake, as events were to show.

Stroessner's friends did well too. Colonel Barrientos moved to the sensitive post of finance minister, while also staying on, ad interim, at the Ministry of Industry and Commerce. General Samaniego became the new defense minister, while General Mario Coscia Tavarossi took his place as head of public works. General Leodegar Cabello replaced Coscia Tavarossi as the army's chief of the General Staff. Gustavo Storm was already presiding at the Central Bank, having taken over when Méndez Fleitas was fired.

Such intricate balancing of factions and subfactions left only the ex-*epifanistas* out in the cold. But Stroessner soon remedied that. Romero Pereira was too tough and wily a veteran not to be of use. He had followed Méndez Fleitas for a while, but in the crisis he had hesitated before abandoning him for Stroessner. His dismissal from the cabinet had been a warning, but now, it was felt, he would be an obedient *stroessnerista*. In June, therefore, Stroessner announced the creation of a new cabinet post, minister without portfolio, whose job would be to link the government with its official party. "In this way," he told the Congress, "our ties have been strengthened with the Party whose ideals and forces stand behind our Government. This ministry will facilitate and apply [the party's] creative initiative, and will call attention to various matters that lie beyond the competence of other high State organs."[3] What he really meant, though, was that creative initiative would run the other way—from Stroessner to the party. Romero Pereira, who still hung on as party president though he had no support from either the *democráticos* or the Guionists, was to be Stroessner's wedge to pry open the Junta de Gobierno. Not only were Barrientos and Samaniego appointed to the junta, but the latter even became the party's treasurer. Thus, Stroessner could exercise some control over the Colorados' financial resources.

All of the major factions shared in the apportioning of ambassadorships too. Expresident Federico Cháves had been named ambassador to France in January, right after his declaration of support for Stroessner. Now his nephew Osvaldo Cháves replaced Guillermo Enciso Velloso—Méndez Fleitas's friend—as ambassador to the United States. The two Guión Rojo founders also received appointments. Victor Morínigo went to Lima, and Natalicio González, who was already residing in Mexico, became the ambassador there.

Stroessner was not long in tapping the obligations he had created by his generosity, for his presidential term was due to run out in 1958.

Accordingly, a Colorado convention was scheduled for November 1957, and Romero Pereira began canvassing support for the president's reelection. Since the Guionists were still riding on Stroessner's coattails and since the *democráticos* still felt too weak to oppose him openly, Romero's job was not difficult. The convention renominated Stroessner unanimously, and he went on to win the February 1958 elections unopposed. The mood of national unanimity was broken only once, when *El Orden*, a Liberal party newspaper that began to circulate in late 1957, made fun of Stroessner's vigorous barnstorming back and forth across the country in a one-party race. Stroessner failed to share *El Orden*'s amusement and had the paper closed down.

Despite his easy electoral victory, Stroessner had reason for concern. Besides the *democráticos* and Guionists who were jockeying quietly behind the scenes, open opposition to his regime was growing more dramatic. On the night of 1 April a small band of Liberals and Febreristas crossed the Paraná to attack a police station in the town of Coronel Bogado. The mayor of the town was wounded and two policemen were killed before the invaders were driven off. It was the first of many guerrilla raids.

Paraguayan exiles had remained adamant opponents of the government. In 1958 they received unexpected support when the military dictatorship in Venezuela was overthrown by Romulo Betancourt, one of Latin America's leading figures of the democratic left. Betancourt vowed to rid the rest of the continent of military regimes, and soon money and moral support were flowing to the Febreristas and Liberals. In the following year an even more dramatic event stirred Latin America: Fidel Castro defeated the Batista regime in Cuba. Thrilled by these examples and armed by the Cubans as well as the Venezuelans, the guerrillas were busy throughout the early months of 1959 harassing the Paraguayan government with sharp attacks over the border and violent manifestos that predicted a horrible fate for those in power.

Both publicly and privately, Stroessner raged against the opposition parties, claiming that he had offered them, time and again, a reconciliation, only to be spurned. He had let the Liberals hold their first public convention in eleven years in July 1958, he pointed out, and they had answered his tolerance by passing resolutions calling him a dictator and demanding an end to the state of siege (which had been in effect, with brief exceptions, since 1947). Now he was through with compromise. He vowed that five rebels would die for every Colorado killed.

This was the sort of language Edgar Ynsfran liked to hear. He and

Duarte Vera were already busy filling the jails. When university students had begun striking and demonstrating in 1956 and 1957, the police had cracked down hard. During one all-out riot some 120 students were reported injured and another 250 were arrested. In 1956, Colonel Franco had made a bizarre attempt to fly back to Paraguay, demanding to discuss "the future of Paraguay" with Stroessner. In that crisis, Ynsfran had ordered the roundup of hundreds of Febreristas, many of whom had joined the hapless *epifanistas* in the jungle concentration camps. There was no real limit to the power of the police, for the use of martial law suspended all constitutional guarantees, and the so-called Law For the Defense Of Democracy, passed by the Congress in 1955, identified any antigovernment activity with communism and made it unlawful.[4] Indeed, the first victims under this law were the leaders of the Liberal party. Some of them were exiled, and others were sent to Fort Ingavi, in the Chaco.

With Stroessner's complete backing, Ynsfran and Duarte Vera now began a campaign of counterterror against the opposition. When a guerrilla group called Vanguardia Febrerista led by Arnaldo Valdovinos tried to provoke an uprising in the Fourteenth Infantry Cerro Corá Regiment in February 1959, Ynsfran retaliated by having Valdovinos's brother assassinated in the Argentine town of Pirané. Captured guerrillas, if not put to death on the spot, were taken to isolated camps in the country, where they were tortured for information and then executed. Friends and relatives of militant oppositionists were jailed and roughed up after every guerrilla raid. Beatings and torture had become common police procedure, and the ululating wail of the red police vans (*camiones colorados*, as they were called) was a deeply dreaded sound.

The cycle of guerrilla terror and police counterterror continued to mount over the months until tensions inside Paraguay became unbearable. The *democráticos* were afraid and for two very different reasons. If the Cuban Revolution were repeated in Paraguay, they could expect little mercy. On the other hand, if Ynsfran were suddenly to turn his brutal police on them, and there was little guarantee that he would not, they could be crushed. Ynsfran was already demanding that the old party urban guard of civil war times be revived and put under his command. As Ynsfran saw it, the urban guard, with proper weapons and a little training, would be able to furnish a militia of twenty thousand men to secure the towns while the regular army tackled the guerrilla invaders. Naturally, the militiamen would have the right to enter any home and arrest any suspect.

The *democráticos* decided to move before it was too late. José Zacarias Arza, Federico Cháves's brilliant strategist in earlier battles against the Guión Rojo, came out of retirement to lead the fight. His brother Enrique (Stroessner's minister of health) kept him in touch with what was going on inside the administration. Another brother, Evaristo, lined up support in Congress. Waldino Lovera, a promising young legislator, had organized the party youth into the Juventud Vertical to use as the shock troops of the *democráticos*. The intellectual leader of the group was Osvaldo Cháves, a former professor of philosophy who held a doctorate from the University of Buenos Aires. A peppery little man with a quick tongue, he had resigned as ambassador to Washington to come back and join the fight. The *democráticos* also gained a prominent recruit in Mario Mallorquín, who had lost his ambassadorship to Mexico when Natalicio González was appointed. Mallorquín, in turn, sought to win over his old friend, Eulógio Estigarribia, the president of the Congress, but Estigarribia refused to commit himself. He had worked hard after his misstep in 1955 to get Stroessner to trust him with this new position. However, he promised to think it over.

The mood of the country favored a *democrático* campaign, for there was growing discontent with the regime. Police brutality had provoked some prominent Catholic bishops and priests to speak out against the continued state of siege. Cases of torture were being publicized. At the same time, the shaky economic situation was causing farmers to complain about inadequate subsidies. In early 1959 protest meetings were being held in the open marketplaces of many country towns. But most dramatic of all was the general strike called by the Paraguayan Workers' Confederation in late August 1958 to force the government to grant a 30 percent wage increase. Nothing like that had ever been tried before in Paraguay. González Alsina, the justice and labor minister, was caught by surprise, but Stroessner reacted quickly. The CPT was the last stronghold of *epifanista* populism, and he came down on it mercilessly. Soldiers occupied the labor unions' headquarters, while the police seized more than two hundred CPT militants. One of those arrested was Vicente Cortesí, the CPT's general secretary, who was also a congressional deputy. As such, he was supposed to have immunity. In any case, Stroessner appointed Enrique Volta Gaona—one of the original and one of the most violent Guionists—as his CPT interventor, a job which Volta Gaona had performed for Morínigo during the civil war. As for González Alsina, Stroessner's firm backing of him during this crisis converted him into an ardent and faithful *stroessnerista*.

Nevertheless, the *democráticos* took the offensive. Led by Evaristo Zacarias Arza and Waldino Lovera, they mobilized their strength in Congress and succeeded in getting it—in one of its rare displays of courage—to protest the arrest of Vicente Cortesí. Surprised, Stroessner retreated, and Cortesí was set free. Next, the *democráticos* demanded the lifting of the CPT's intervention. They succeeded again, for, in March 1959, Volta Gaona stepped aside to let a labor congress select a new CPT executive. The voting was tightly controlled by the government, however, so that the result was the "election" of one of Duarte Vera's police commissioners as the CPT president. Finally, the *democráticos* were able to get González Alsina replaced as justice and labor minister by César Garay, a liberal Colorado whom they trusted more. Stroessner kept González Alsina in the cabinet as agriculture minister, however, and was to find him a useful ally in the coming struggle.

These were unusual concessions for Stroessner, but Ynsfran's talk of an urban guard had frightened the military. The generals were determined to prevent Stroessner from creating any armed force that would lie outside their control. They had already forced him to dismantle police Battalion 40 after Méndez Fleitas's fall; now they were putting pressure on him to give in to the regime's critics and end the police state. Suddenly, Stroessner was on the defensive. Rumors spread that the military was preparing to abandon him and that the regime would soon fall.[5]

The *democráticos* pressed their advantage. On 12 March 1959 they issued a manifesto demanding an end to the state of siege, a general political amnesty, freedom of press and assembly, and the naming of a commission—embracing all Paraguayan parties—that would work toward "institutional normalization."[6] A meeting of the Junta de Gobierno was called on 24 March, at which, surprisingly, the party leaders approved the manifesto by a unanimous vote. Even Ynsfran, Romero Pereira, Barrientos, and Samaniego, all of whom were present, did not dare oppose it.

On 1 April 1959, Stroessner opened the year's first parliamentary session with the momentous announcement that, after twelve years, the state of siege was at an end and that Liberals and Febreristas were free to come home. His speech contained a heavy note of bitterness, however; he reminded the Colorado congressmen of the Liberal party's "legionnaire" origins and its "traitorous" record of "selling out Paraguay to foreign interests." Nonetheless, he said, he would attempt a reconciliation.[7] Despite his sour attitude, Stroessner followed up his message with executive decrees legalizing the exiled parties, ending press censorship, permitting political meetings to be held in public, and freeing all political prisoners. He even talked of calling a constitutional convention to replace the 1940 Constitution, which the Liberals considered a "totalitarian" document.

Despite the turn of events, Ynsfran and Duarte Vera tried to give as little ground as possible. The police chief tried to dampen the ebullience of the opposition by forbidding any public gatherings near government buildings and any meetings without written permission from the police—which required two days' notice and the submission of an agenda of the intended activities. But the tide of public criticism could not be stemmed, as Liberals and Febreristas, returning to the country in droves, began circulating their newspapers on the streets once again.

Indeed, the minister of interior and his police chief were very much on the defensive. Yet Stroessner insisted that his government would stand by its promises. To make sure that everyone understood that, he called a meeting of cabinet ministers, army officers, provincial *delegados*, and police officials to instruct them in the new guidelines. And to make the point clear that literally everyone was expected to conform, he gave Ynsfran the embarrassing task of outlining the government's policy to the gathering. What is more, when the *democráticos* in Congress took up the question of police torture, Stroessner formed a commission to investigate the matter. To the surprise of all the cynics, charges were soon brought against Juan Erasmo Candia, the chief of detectives. Despite Ynsfran's efforts to protect him, Candia was tried, convicted, and sent to jail.

No wonder, then, that Ynsfran was feeling touchy. One night he lost his temper at a private party when he and Osvaldo Cháves suddenly found themselves face to face. The puckish Cháves apparently twitted him about the charges of brutality that were being aimed at the Ministry of Interior. What Ynsfran replied is not recorded, but an angry exchange followed which climaxed when he challenged Cháves to a duel. In true Latin *macho* style, Cháves accepted.[8] The two men went home and began calling up their friends to act as seconds.

It was a ridiculous situation for Cháves. He was short, soft, plump, and bookish. Ynsfran was lean, wiry, and—as a former policeman—knowledgeable about pistols. If Cháves went through with this duel, he would be killed. On the other hand, if he backed out he would be disgraced and the *democráticos* would be laughed at. José Zacarias Arza needed all of his skill to work out a solution. Finally, as Cháves's chief second, he went to Ynsfran with a compromise. His man had not intended any personal insult to the interior minister, but he would apologize anyway. At the same time, he would continue to insist on his right to disagree publicly with Ynsfran's policies. For his part, Ynsfran had decided in the meantime that to kill Cháves might cause himself more complications than his honor was worth. He agreed to the proposal, and the duel was called off.

In any case, Ynsfran's ordeal was nearly over. The heady effervescence of freedom finally culminated on 28 May 1959 in a student riot over the raising of bus fares. The demonstration started peaceably enough in the Plaza Italia, but when the police tried to break it up, a ferocious fight erupted. More than eighty protesters were injured, and many more were arrested, including some *democrático* congressmen who had come out to cheer on the students. Before the crowd was finally dispersed, the students had smashed store windows, broken street lamps, and turned over several automobiles and a trolley car. Seven policemen were hospitalized.

The next day Congress engaged in a heated debate over the three deputies who had been beaten and jailed. Once again congressional immunity had been violated, and the police had returned to their brutal tactics. The *democráticos* demanded a resolution calling for the dismissal of Ynsfran and Duarte Vera. While the Guionists protested angrily, masses of angry students in the hall outside demanded to be allowed into the chamber. Eulógio Estigarribia, the beleaguered presiding officer, was losing control of the situation. At the height of the confusion an aide informed him that a telephone call awaited him. As if to wash his hands of what he knew was about to happen, he excused himself, turned the chair over to Waldino Lovera, and left the room. The call was from President Stroessner, asking him to adjourn the session so as to give both sides a chance to cool off and find some compromise. Estigarribia agreed, but when he returned to the floor Lovera refused to relinquish the chairmanship. Instead, over the noisy protests of the Guionists, he rammed through a resolution repudiating Ynsfran and Duarte Vera and calling for their prosecution. As for Stroessner's request, Lovera refused even to put it before the meeting. Indeed, rather than adjourn, the *democrático* majority declared Congress to be in permanent session.[9]

After a quick meeting with Estigarribia and certain members of his cabinet, including Ynsfran, Stroessner issued two presidential decrees. The first one reimposed the state of siege, "in order to establish order," and the second one dissolved Congress. Police went to the National University to disperse the students who had occupied the buildings, while other units broke up any sign of a street gathering. By the end of the day cavalry reinforcements had arrived from Campo Grande. In the meantime Ynsfran's security police had started a vast roundup of his enemies. The three Zacarias Arza brothers, Osvaldo Cháves, Mario Mallorquín, and Waldino Lovera were only a few of the more than one hundred *democráticos* taken into custody. While this was going on, Romero Pereira was in touch with local party committees, calling for discipline and obedience.

The blow had fallen so swiftly that the *democráticos*, perhaps over-confident of their strength, had been caught off guard. Now their leadership had been lopped off in a single stroke, and their rank and file were disorganized. The efficiency of Ynsfran's operation suggests that it must have been planned long in advance. Only the students were left to carry on the fight. To head off a threatened university and high school strike, Raúl Peña, the minister of education, declared a fifteen-day school holiday. Even so, violent street clashes persisted, and units from the Fourteenth Infantry were called in to support the police and cavalry forces. Driven off the streets, the students reoccupied the *Colegio Nacional* and the law school. Once again the police and army dislodged them with clubs and tear gas. They next occupied the schools of medicine and dentistry, only to be driven off again. At one point it was rumored that the CPT was about to call a general strike in support of the students, but Rodolfo Echeverría, the policeman who controlled the labor confederation, kept a firm grip on his organization. By 4 June the exhausted students were forced to call off any further demonstrations. By then the number of persons under arrest had climbed to over three hundred.

Over the next few days most of the student prisoners were released. Some of the *democrático* politicians, including José Zacarias Arza, were allowed to go into exile. Many others, however, were sent to prison camps. The struggle was over. Now came the rush to be identified with the winning side. On 1 June, Romero Pereira called a meeting of the Junta de Gobierno to declare the party's support for Stroessner. After hearing a report from Edgar Ynsfran about recent events, the junta passed a resolution approving all of the government's acts, including the arrest of seven out of twenty-five of its own members. Only Virgilio Cataldi voted against it, and on the next day the brave Sr. Cataldi was removed as head of the post office, to be replaced by Enrique Volta Gaona. Another late casualty of the downfall of the *democráticos* was César Garay, who also resigned on 1 June. Juan Ramón Cháves, a cousin of Osvaldo's who had sided with Stroessner, took his place as minister of justice and labor.

On 3 June, Romero Pereira held a mass demonstration of the faithful at the Colorado party's sumptuous downtown headquarters and read an official statement released by the junta, which attacked the seventeen signers of the original manifesto of the *democráticos*, calling for liberalization. They were anarchists and Communists, he said, and those sentiments were echoed by Ezequiel González Alsina, who pleased the crowd by addressing them in Guaraní. Finally, on 5 June the remaining loyal congressmen, led by Eulógio Estigarribia, issued a statement of their own, pledging their support for Stroessner and

condemning their excolleagues for provoking a constitutional crisis.
Of the sixty deputies in the Congress at the beginning of the crisis,
only twenty-nine were left to sign the statement. The rest were either
in jail or in exile.[10]

The Fall of Ynsfran

The new Junta de Gobierno comprised three types of men. Some,
like Romero Pereira, Gorostiaga, and Juan Ramón Cháves, having
abandoned their former friends in order to keep their jobs, had lost
their independence and were *stroessneristas* out of necessity. Another
group was *stroessnerista* out of conviction. That included Gustavo
Storm, Barrientos, Samaniego, and, to some extent, González Alsina.
The third group was the Guionists: Ynsfran, Volta Gaona, Domingo
and Sabino Montanaro, Saul González, and J. Augusto Saldivar. Up
to this point they had aided Stroessner in order to subdue their rivals
and to get power. But they were not *stroessneristas*. They intended to
win the government for themselves.

Following Ynsfran's lead, the Guionists used smear tactics to intimidate their opponents. They professed to be militant anti-Communists.
Therefore, anyone they disliked was ipso facto a Communist. According to one report Ynsfran read to the junta, Méndez Fleitas
enjoyed "vigorous foreign support" from "subversive elements." The
ranks of the Liberals, and especially the Febreristas, were riddled with
Communists. Indeed, he said, they had been tools of Moscow ever
since they joined forces with the Communist party during the civil
war. He also charged that the naval revolt of 1947 had been engineered in Moscow, and that such exiled *democráticos* as Osvaldo
Cháves were, at the least, fellow travelers. Nor, he warned, should it
be thought that the Communists had been thoroughly beaten. On the
contrary, they were still at work inside Paraguay, tirelessly gnawing
away at the foundations of the state. In fact, he suggested that they
might even be at work inside the government.[11]

To be fair, however, it must be allowed that Ynsfran's charges
sometimes contained an element of truth. The Communist party
really had been active underground during the civil war, although it
was never dominant in the tripartite Comité de Resistencia. It was
also true that Communist money and advice from Cuba was being
funneled into guerrilla movements such as the United National Liberation Front (FULNA), which attracted for a while many militant
young Liberals and Febreristas. But it was also true that the Liberal
and Febrerista party leaders had repudiated FULNA and had ordered

their members to pull out of it or face expulsion.¹² Nonetheless, Ynsfran's smear tactics were effective in generating enthusiasm among his followers and in putting his opponents on the defensive.

Despite this, Ynsfran was gradually becoming a liability to Stroessner. He had been useful as a ruthlessly efficient organizer of repression when that was needed against the *epifanistas*, the *democráticos*, and the exile guerrillas. Ynsfran was a master of organization who never tired of exhorting the provincial *delegados* (centrally appointed local intendants) under his command to be "representatives of the Executive Power and act in its name . . . so that no corner of the Republic can exist where the thought and action of the National Government does not penetrate." Knowing the value of enlisting the peasants' support in the antiguerrilla campaign, he urged the *delegados* to be "exemplary fathers" to the peasants of their districts. Those instructions paid off, for it was usually the peasants who tipped off the authorities whenever a band of guerrillas crossed the river. But the very efficiency of his operation created the conditions that eventually made him expendable to Stroessner.

By mid-1962 opinion shifted noticeably inside the exile parties. For four years enthusiastic young rebels had been invading the country in hopes of duplicating Fidel Castro's triumph. However, Stroessner had easily smothered every invasion, and his hold on power was as strong as ever. The only result had been hundreds of dead young men, whose horribly mutilated bodies occasionally floated down the Paraná to be washed ashore as warnings to the other exiles. A mood of discouragement had settled over the more militant activists, while more moderate and pragmatic exile leaders were winning people over to the idea of trying to come to an accommodation with Stroessner.

Stroessner was quick to encourage the idea, for he knew that a pacified country would be easier to rule than a convulsed one. Furthermore, by giving his government a more democratic image abroad, he hoped to attract more foreign aid.¹³ In June 1962 he announced that general elections would be held the following year and invited the other parties (but not the exiled Colorados) to participate. One group of Liberals calling itself the Renovationists took him at his word. Although they were drummed out of the Liberal party as renegades, they went back to Paraguay, held a convention, and nominated a slate of candidates for the February 1963 elections. Thus, for the second time in Paraguay's history, more than one man ran for the presidency.¹⁴ Although the Renovationists were swamped at the polls, they were allotted twenty out of the sixty seats in Congress, and their defeated presidential candidate, Ernesto Gavilán, was consoled with the ambassadorship to London.

So began the period of "liberalization." Encouraged by the Renovationists' example, the Febreristas petitioned for legalization and received it in August 1964. That left in exile only the Liberal party— besides the *epifanistas* and *democráticos*, with whom Stroessner absolutely refused to negotiate. It was clear that the process of political decompression would never be complete until the Liberals were back in Paraguay too, but such a concession required compromises by both sides. Since the Liberals were the only party with a mass base sufficient to compete with the Colorados, they would have to prove their willingness to go along with Stroessner. On his side, Stroessner would have to show that he was not just preparing another trap. Finally the Liberals would have to keep their hotheads under control or expel them, and Stroessner would have to sacrifice the more bloody-minded henchmen around him.

As the negotiations proceeded, Romero Pereira and Domingo Montanaro, an old Guionist war-horse, were quietly dropped from the cabinet. But Ynsfran and his brutal understudy, Ramón Duarte Vera, were still in control of the police. Ynsfran, of course, tried to stop the new liberalizing trend by harassing the Renovationists and Febreristas whenever possible. He arrested their leaders every time there was a disturbance at the National University, and hecklers always showed up at their meetings. *El Enano* (The Dwarf), the Renovationists' four-page weekly, often had to shut down its printing presses for lack of electricity, and the police suppressed the Febreristas' *Prensa Campesina* after only one issue. Also, during the 1963 elections there was an ominous spate of terrorist bombings, including one that went off at the Ministry of Interior. Ynsfran charged that the Liberals, Febreristas, *epifanistas*, and, of course, the Communists were responsible. In turn, the opposition accused Ynsfran of setting off the bombs himself in order to create a climate of tension.

But Ynsfran was fighting a losing battle, for he no longer had Stroessner's confidence. Their personal relations had once been friendly, but now they were growing cooler. In 1963, Ynsfran had gone so far as to resign temporarily from the government to manage Stroessner's reelection campaign. By 1966, however, he was growing impatient over Stroessner's apparent determination to be president for life. Plans were already afoot at the Presidential Palace to write a new constitution that would give Stroessner two more legal terms in office. That meant that he would be eligible to serve until 1978—with no guarantee that he would not change the constitution again. For

Ynsfran, who was beginning to harbor presidential ambitions himself, the prospect was intolerable. Stroessner, on the other hand, was aware that Ynsfran was becoming a rallying point for those hard-liners who were critical of the new policy of liberalization. If that policy went awry and Stroessner were made to look foolish, Ynsfran might become dangerous. In any case, he was the last Colorado politician with a personal power base.

When Stroessner opened his attack against Ynsfran, he moved against his power base in the police—not against the minister of interior personally. The job proved easier than expected, for events aided the president. In May 1966 a spectacular scandal was exposed, involving police chief Duarte Vera, two German embezzlers, Interpol, and the West German embassy. By the time the investigation was over, an ugly network of almost unbelievable corruption had been revealed, and twenty top police officials had been placed under arrest. Not only was Duarte Vera out, but so were other Ynsfran proteges such as Alberto Planas, the chief of criminal investigations; Benigno Villasanti, Planas's secretary; Victor Martínez, the chief of the political section; and Washington Anazco, the head of detectives. In one quick sweep Ynsfran's coterie was out of power.

After that the minister of interior's own demise was an anticlimax. The government accepted his resignation on 28 November, and on the following day the local newspapers ran a short column which expressed the president's appreciation for Ynsfran's ten years of service. And that was all. Thereafter, Ynsfran was no longer news.

Nor was he important to the Colorado party. Immediately following his resignation he was dropped from the Junta de Gobierno. Some of Ynsfran's Guionists had made their peace with Stroessner beforehand, while others followed their fallen leader into disfavor. J. Augusto Saldivar, an old veteran of many past battles, survived the purge and saved his seat in Congress. As a reward for his switch in loyalties, he was made president of the lower chamber when a new constitution went into effect the next year, creating a bicameral legislature. Sabino Montanaro and Saúl González stayed in the cabinet, with Montanaro taking over Ynsfran's old job at the Ministry of Interior. Meanwhile, Victor Morínigo, whom Ynsfran recently had gotten appointed to the junta, was dropped, and Enrique Volta Gaona suddenly found himself the target of a government investigation into "irregularities" at the post office. He was later fired in disgrace.

In February 1967, just three months after Ynsfran's fall, the government extended legalization to the Liberal Party,[15] and the country entered a brief period of political peace based on the opposition's tacit acceptance of Stroessner's right to rule. In May 1967, just three months after that, Stroessner called a constitutional convention, which ratified a new document giving him two more five-year terms.

The Personalist Party

By 1967, then, no factions divided the Colorado party. Everyone was a *stroessnerista*. To be sure, some of those in high party and government posts had once identified themselves with some other leader. Romera Pereira had been an *epifanista*; González Alsina had been a *democrático*; and Raúl Sapena Pastor had once called himself a Guionist. Yet all had repudiated their former connections and in doing so had cast their lot irrevocably with Stroessner. Since their safety and prosperity rested on the continuance of the regime, they were forced to support it wholeheartedly. Stroessner also packed the party executive with his old army comrades. Besides controlling key cabinet posts, Samaniego and Barrientos also sat on the Junta de Gobierno. Indeed, as party treasurer, Samaniego controlled the flow of party patronage. Later on Stroessner added another close friend to the junta: Mario Abdo Benítez, who was to do double duty as party secretary and presidential secretary to General Stroessner. Finally, in this era, a new generation of young men rose to prominent positions in the regime. This group had reached political maturity long after the disappearance of notables like Molas López, Natalicio González, and Federico Cháves from political life. Even Méndez Fleitas, who had been out of the country for over ten years, was more or less a shadowy figure to them. Political nobodies before Stroessner elevated them, these new faces also owed everything to the president.

Although Stroessner wanted a pliable party, he did not want a mere paper organization. On the contrary, the party was to have an important function in his regime. He envisioned an efficient, cohesive, and obedient organization—like a military division. Accordingly, shortly after he purged Ynsfran, Stroessner created a new party office—the general secretary of coordination, and he appointed Colonel César Gagliardone, an army surgeon who was then serving as intendant (mayor) of Asunción, to the post. Gagliardone's task was to reorganize the party along the lines Stroessner indicated. All real opposition having been eliminated, he accomplished his task in a short time. By the following year, Gagliardone had created a monolithic machine which could carry out orders with an efficiency and dispatch that were most untypical for Paraguay. The party organization was based on the principle of "verticality," which meant that orders flowed from the top down. The duty of the ordinary member, said Gagliardone in his report, was to obey his leaders—and above all, General Stroessner. Since, in Gagliardone's opinion, *asambleas* (meetings) only opened up possibilities for factionalism and disorganization, the party had few elections or open meetings. Finally, the individual member was to respect the absolute authority of the party's designated leaders at every level.[16]

Gagliardone argued that success in any group enterprise—whether it be a soccer team, a business, an army unit, a surgical team, or a political party—depends on a clear hierarchy of command, with a supreme leader at the top. "Our slogan," he wrote, "is always: One sole authority in the hands of a single Director, surrounded by his collaborators, for all our institutions." Gagliardone insisted that a natural division separates those who have an aptitude for command and those who are fit only to be led. Whenever those roles become confused, the organization begins to break down. This happens whenever certain "negative" people try, out of jealousy, to resist the director's will, but a competent director eliminates such negative elements before anarchy takes over. In short, there must be no opposition to the director's policies. "Discipline, Order, and Work Equal Progress."[17]

Party and state have often been intertwined in Paraguay ever since General Bernardino Caballero created the National Republican Association to be his patronage machine. Stroessner's regime is no different, as table 2 shows. But in 1968 he had a far more disciplined phalanx of apparatchiki at his service. Beyond that, several of Stroessner's friends, such as Abdo Benítez, General Samaniego, Colonel Barrientos, and General Leodegar Cabello were longtime members of the Junta de Gobierno. The first of these controlled its agenda while the second controlled its finances. Thus, the linkage of party and regime are complete.

TABLE 2. *Government Elites in the Party*

Members of the Junta de Gobierno	1959 (N = 25)	1968 (N = 35)
Cabinet ministers	10	9
Congressmen	7	18
Ambassadors	2	0
Other high officials	3	2

The many functions that this renovated party performs for the regime will be examined later, but one that ought to be mentioned here is periodically to renominate and reelect General Stroessner to the presidency. It did so in 1973, and in 1976 its majority in Congress obediently took up the question of revising the nation's constitution to permit Stroessner to remain in office beyond the two terms allowed by the 1967 Basic Law. Accordingly, Congress proposed an amendment to extend the incumbent's eligibility to two more terms and called elections for a constituent assembly to ratify the amendment. Since the opposition boycotted those elections in protest, all of the delegates at the assembly, which met in March 1977, were Colorados. Having cleared Stroessner's path, the Colorados then renominated him for his sixth term. The following February he won handily, rolling up almost 90 percent of the vote. Clearly, Stroessner was to be dictator for life, and at only sixty-five years of age he could expect to serve many more terms.

During earlier regimes such *continuismo* had been sure to provoke resentment from subordinates who were anxious to achieve the presidency for themselves, but Stroessner's subordinates had no power bases of their own. Moreover, the top Colorados reaped substantial rewards from the continuation of the regime, while hundreds of lesser figures also came in for modest portions of the largesse.

Yet exiled Colorados claimed that a great many party members still inside Paraguay felt embittered over the party's loss of independence. Obviously, this could not be verified. But a curious incident which occurred in November 1974 revealed that some pockets of anti-Stroessner feeling still existed among the Colorados.

The minister of interior, Sabino Montanaro, received a tip that a band of guerrillas had set up a hideout in a farmhouse just outside of Asunción with the intention of using it as a base to carry out terrorist attacks. Immediately police went to the site and caught the guerrillas by surprise. A brief battle followed, in which several of the guerrillas, including their leader, were killed. Seven were taken prisoner, however, including four university students who had been attending college in Argentina, where, it was revealed, they had been in touch with leftist terrorist groups. Proud of their success in crushing this operation before it even got started, the police invited reporters to the farmhouse to show them the underground cells, or "people's prisons," that the guerrillas had dug to hold kidnapped government officials.[18]

But a local news blackout abruptly fell over the incident because further investigations led to disturbing discoveries. Under questioning the terrorists revealed a plot to assassinate Stroessner. High explosives were to have been planted along the president's route during a forthcoming procession. The arrested students displayed extremely accurate and detailed knowledge about the preparations for the parade, knowledge that only someone high in the administration could have furnished them.

Up to that time only a few leftist Liberal and Febrerista students had been picked up for questioning. But now Stroessner and Montanaro realized that some disaffected Colorados were conspiring to bring down the regime from within. Immediately they began making arrests. According to Montanaro in an interview he gave to the press, more than a thousand high government officials and party members were brought to police headquarters and interrogated. Among them was Edgar Ynsfran, but authorities held him for only one day before releasing him.[19]

The real suspicion fell on the exiled Colorados. The Paraguayan *peronista* Méndez Fleitas, for example, might well have had contacts with some of the guerrilla movements in Argentina. The only way to identify their accomplices inside Paraguay was to question the exiles themselves. Accordingly, agents went to Brazil and Argentina to kidnap exiled Colorado leaders and spirit them back into Paraguay. They captured ten exiles in Brazil, and Agustín Goiburu, a member of the Colorado executive committee in exile, barely escaped being grabbed in Argentina.

The result of the investigation was a major purge of the government and party. Twenty policemen from the secret Department of Investigations were fired and Pastor Coronel, the head of that section, was sharply reprimanded for failing to uncover the plot earlier. Among the party members disciplined were several presidents of local *seccionales*. Once again, Stroessner's domination of the Colorados was complete. A last flicker of rebellion occurred in late April of 1975 when the Colorado Youth issued a manifesto calling on Stroessner to step down when his presidential term expired in 1978.[20] As with other such futile challenges in the past, this one was snuffed out quickly, and with a touch of irony. After the incumbent student leaders were purged and replaced by more pliant ones, it was precisely the "reorganized" Colorado Youth which, in June 1976, opened up the party's propaganda campaign to amend the constitution so that Stroessner might run again.

PART 3. THE MACHINERY OF DICTATORSHIP

Chapter 7. Maintenance from the Top

Fly into Asunción from abroad and your airplane takes you to the Presidente Stroessner International Airport. Approach Paraguay by the main highway from Brazil and you must pass through the river port of Puerto Presidente Stroessner. Come up from Argentina on the Paraná and Paraguay rivers and you may take passage on one of the Paraguayan river steamers, the *Presidente Stroessner*. As it churns upriver the chances are that music will be blaring from its loud-speakers, for the "amusement" of the passengers, and one of the songs you may hear is the bouncy polka "Don Alfredo." Disembark in Asunción and walk up from the port toward the heart of town: you cannot help but notice the old election posters slapped here and there on the buildings displaying Stroessner's heavy, leonine face. His picture hangs in all the government offices, of course, as well as in most commercial establishments and in quite a few private homes. A new suburb of Asunción bears the name Colonia Presidente Stroessner, and on the Plaza de Independencia, the city's central square, a colored neon sign over the Central Bank building proclaims *"Paz, Trabajo, y Bienestar con Stroessner"* (Peace, Jobs, and Well-being with Stroessner).

All this only emphasizes that Paraguay's dictatorship is a personalistic one, not a dictatorship of party or principle. Stroessner rules in the name of the Colorado party, but it has no more role in decision making than what he cares to allow it. Stroessner also stands at the head of the army. Unlike many other traditionalist dictatorships, it is he who directs it, not vice-versa.

In short, Stroessner is the guiding, cohesive force of the regime. Without him it might dissolve into a welter of incoherent factions. He has overcome Paraguay's seemingly endemic anarchy only by exiling all independently minded politicians and by gathering an overwhelming amount of power into his own hands. He exercises a close, personal supervision over the three bureaucracies that undergird his regime: the military, the party, and the government civil service. Every military assignment and promotion, every party meeting, resolution, or election, every majority member of Congress, every legislative act, every judgeship, every executive post, and every cabinet decision must bear his seal of approval.

Is he popular? It is not possible to measure any dictator's real popularity because the free expression of public opinion is not allowed. Yet, at the same time, the existence of dictatorship is not, ipso facto, a confession of unpopularity either—it may simply be that the contending political groups do not play by the democratic rules of the game. In any case, Stroessner's busy round of duties, which he performs with heavy dignity, makes for good propaganda. His sychophants in the Colorado party pour out an endless stream of praise, lauding him as "El Gran Conductor" or "El Gran Líder," who single-handedly has brought peace and material progress to the country. Beyond that, Stroessner takes credit for every school, road, clinic, sewer, or electric power line that gets built. It is not for nothing that he spends a great deal of his time attending ribbon-cutting ceremonies, digging the first spadeful of dirt, or laying the first brick. Stroessner makes up for his lack of charisma by claiming to have done more to modernize Paraguay than any president since Carlos Antonio López. As the far-seeing leader, he becomes the nation's "indispensable man."

Despite his ponderous style, Stroessner is an active campaigner at election time. Although his reelection is never in doubt, he stumps the country as though he were in a real race. Every *barrio* in Asunción and every town of any size in the interior is sure to receive at least one visit. All of his appearances are surrounded by a great deal of hoopla—fiestas, dances, barbecues, parades—which dazzles and delights the peasants. There are huge Colorado rallies and marches, with red flags and red sashes and red ponchos. There are torchlight parades and stirring polkas praising Stroessner's deeds. And posters with his picture are everywhere.

As a speaker he is something less than electrifying. His speeches are heavily larded with references to the great leaders of the past— Carlos Antonio López, Marshal Solano López, and General Caballero— and to the patriotic spirit of the battles of Cerro Corá and Boqueron. While he identifies these symbols with his administration, he has nothing but scorn for the Liberals and the Communists, and for the foreign press too. Finally, he is given to lengthy enumerations of all the public works projects completed since he came to power.

But if Stroessner is usually stiff and formal, he can also unbend at times. At his second inauguration, in 1958, he was in the reviewing stand watching a huge victory parade that the Colorados had assembled by bringing in people from all over the country. There was an enormous mass of people, all swathed in red, while long red banners hung down from the buildings along the jampacked street. Suddenly, as the police band struck up the Colorado polka, Stroessner came down to the crowd, took hold of the president of the Colorado Women's Association, and danced to the music while the delighted onlookers whooped and cheered.[1]

One crucial characteristic of Stroessner's political style is that he knows how to keep open important channels of information. That is vital in a dictatorship because in the absence of a free press the ruler may become isolated from reality. Surrounded by flatterers who tell him only what they want him to hear—or what they think he wants to hear—he may fail to adjust his policies when they are no longer effective. Stroessner tries to avoid this by staying on the move. During the course of a year he visits every region in Paraguay, from the Chaco to Misiones and from the hill towns of the central highlands to the boom towns along the Brazilian border. An avid amateur pilot, Stroessner may even fly himself to some town in the backlands for an unannounced visit. On these tours he keeps a busy schedule, visiting military posts, checking on government projects, and meeting with local party chiefs.

All of this keeps him in touch with local problems and allows him to size up his army and party officials throughout the country. That, in turn, helps him to assess the information he gets through police and military intelligence or through the party's network of spies. In short, his personal knowledge of the people who serve under him is one of the important elements of his ability to survive.

The Ceremonial Leader

High political office tends to confer a kind of majesty on its possessor. Amid the grandeur of the Presidential Palace the shadiest opportunist may look like a statesman. One reason for this is that the president, whoever he may be, is the nation's ceremonial leader, just as ancient kings and tribal chiefs used to be. The office itself is a symbol of national unity and sovereignty, and the man who occupies it performs certain rituals that deeply touch the emotions of many citizens. Thus, a Paraguayan president, like his American counterpart, wears many hats. Besides being the head of the executive branch of government, the leader of the party, and the commander in chief of the army, he is the officer in charge of the nation's most solemn secular rites. A successful leader can use those rites to build up his own prestige.

The ceremonial function is especially important in Paraguay, for it is still a traditional society in which rituals and symbols are taken seriously. What is more, as citizens of a small, poor country Paraguayans are touchy about their national dignity. Since one major aspect of the ceremonial function is to represent Paraguay before other states, the president's standing rises among his countrymen if he can show that important international personages court his goodwill and that he is able to obtain concessions from them. As head of state he receives ambassadors and other foreign dignitaries, such as representatives of international banks, military missions, parliamentary delegations, and big businessmen. The glittering ceremonies that surround such functions are amply recorded in the press, lending an added aura of glamour to the occupant of the palace. Beyond that, Stroessner also tries to improve his image abroad by making himself available to touring student groups or the foreign press.

Stroessner must also affect the "common touch." Paraguay is fundamentally a peasant society where homey, country manners prevail. So, on the first day of the soccer season, Stroessner is in the stands. On graduation day he is in great demand to make commencement speeches or to hand out diplomas, and he usually accepts two or three such invitations. Naturally, he also attends the final exercises of the military cadets. In addition, Stroessner is usually present when a street is paved, a new school is opened, a wing is added to a public clinic, or some newly purchased military equipment is unloaded to cut the tape, break the champagne bottle, or make a short speech. On Independence Day (14 May) or Asunción Founders' Day (15 August) he is in the reviewing stand; sometimes he even marches at the head of the parade. On more solemn holidays, such as the birthday of one of the country's heroes or the memorial day for soldiers killed in the Chaco War, he goes with his attendants to the Pantheon of Heroes to lay a wreath.

Personalismo—the inclination to attach one's loyalties to a particular political leader—is a strong force in Paraguay as it is in the rest of Latin America. To take advantage of it, a leader must make himself accessible to the public. Thus, Stroessner sets aside large blocks of time for meeting with petitioners and well-wishers of all kinds, from the representatives of important pressure groups to humble individuals who, in accordance with Paraguay's shirt-sleeve populism, have decided to carry their personal troubles all the way to the president. Moreover, the presidential calendar is filled with appointments to appear before business and farm groups, veterans' associations, the medical society, labor union meetings, women's clubs, the Boy Scouts, and various functions sponsored by the Colorado party.[2]

Because Paraguay is a military regime, Stroessner must keep in close personal contact with his officers. Unlike his civilian predecessors, he is his own commander in chief, a role which he carries out conscientiously. This involves him, of course, in many other ceremonies having to do with the various service branches—recruitment, promotions, and special training courses.

Since Paraguay is a Roman Catholic country, the president is also expected to take part in ceremonies celebrating important religious holidays such as the Corpus Christi procession or the pilgrimage every 8 December (the feast of the Immaculate Conception) to Caacupé, to pay homage to the Virgin Patroness of Paraguay. On national holidays he attends Mass at the National Cathedral.

The President's Formal Powers

Closely related to the mystique of the ceremonial function is the Latin American tradition of the strong president, which Jacques Lambert calls the tradition of presidential dominance.[3] This preeminence of executive power is based in Hispanic customs of personalism and paternalism, both of which are contrary to the democratic ideal of equality. They are predicated on the assumption that inequality is inevitable and that the weak must subordinate themselves to some sympathetic superior. In postindependence Latin America, these same customs were expressed in *caudillismo* and the need for forceful leadership to prevent the disintegration of the fledgling republics.

In line with this tradition, Paraguay's constitution provides for a strong president. The chief executive's formal powers are so great by themselves that, without ever violating the strict letter of the law, he could govern practically as a dictator. Moreover, he can always secure approval from the acquiescent Congress for a grant of emergency powers that suspends constitutional procedures. Paraguayan presidents since 1947 have removed the few restrictions on their powers by getting the legislature to renew periodically the state of siege.

Up to 1968, Stroessner governed under Estigarribia's constitution of 1940, which set out the qualifications for being president, limited the term of office, and defined the range of executive power. The president had to be at least forty years old, native born, and a Roman Catholic. Elected by direct, popular vote, he served a five-year term and could be reelected once. Showing his contempt for legal forms,

Stroessner ran for a third term in 1963 without even bothering to get the constitution amended. But in 1967, during his "liberalization" program, he avoided repeating that unlawful act by ordering a new constitution to be written. That made him eligible for another two terms beginning in 1968. Then, in 1977, he had the new constitution amended to permit him to run again.

The 1967 constitution was much like that of 1940. Most important, the broad scope of executive power was retained. The majority of the changes concerned Congress. In place of the unicameral congress (officially called the Chamber of Representatives) two houses were created: an upper house called the Senate, and a lower house called the Chamber of Deputies. Also, provision was made for the representation of opposition parties.

In addition to normal powers granted by the constitution the president has access to two types of extraordinary power. First, the state of siege power allows the president to suspend all constitutional guarantees, including habeas corpus, in times of serious political crisis.[4] Although this grant of power is hedged about with formal restrictions, in practice these are easy to sidestep because Congress has granted Stroessner complete discretion through such supplemental legislation as the Law for the Defense of Democracy. In fairness to Stroessner, though, it should be pointed out that all of his predecessors since Morínigo justified their arbitrary authority by having their hand-picked congresses extend the state of siege. As a result, Paraguay has been under martial law almost constantly since January 1947. Second, the president has the right to intervene in local government whenever serious disturbances or evidence of malfeasance seems to warrant it. Paraguay has a centralized administrative system under which local officials serve as subordinates of the Ministry of Interior. Thus, they may be removed practically at will. But the right of intervention does not stop at local government. Private associations that have a political character, such as political parties and pressure groups, are also regulated by law. To function publicly they must obtain juridical standing. If this is rescinded, their executive committees may be taken over and their assets seized by the government.

Although there is a formal separation of powers between the executive, judicial, and legislative branches, in reality the president completely overshadows the other two branches. For example, even though the Supreme Court can declare laws and presidential acts invalid, it has never done so under Stroessner. After all, judges have only five-year appointments, and the renewal of their terms depends on presidential favor. While in office, they earn salaries which are not fixed, and they are at the mercy of Stroessner's solid majority in Congress, which could easily impeach them. Finally, given Stroessner's hold on the party and the party's dominance of Congress, only safe men are likely to be nominated and approved in the first place.

Congress is no more free than the courts, although in theory it is the lawmaking body. Significantly, the constitution includes no provision for the impeachment by Congress of either the president or his ministers. As with the courts, Stroessner's control of the Colorado party gives him the whip hand over Congress. Both the Senate and the Chamber of Deputies are directly elected, with two-thirds of the seats going to the party gaining the most votes (that is, the Colorados) and the remaining one-third distributed proportionally among the remaining parties. Since Stroessner personally supervises the party's nominations for Congress, a two-thirds majority is solidly behind anything he wishes.

The Senate and the Chamber differ in the following ways: (1) senators must be forty years old, whereas deputies need be only twenty-five, (2) the Senate has the exclusive right to ratify treaties, to participate in the naming of Supreme Court justices, to initiate laws dealing with the national defense, and to approve laws expropriating or regulating property, (3) the Chamber has the right of initiative on taxing and spending bills. Again, however, since Stroessner sets the legislative agenda, Congress has little to do except approve the bills sent to it. In addition, it serves as a forum for opposition opinion; it is one of the few places where the other parties are permitted to voice their dissent and even to try to make changes in the government's policies. But with only a minority of the seats, the opposition can do little except protest. The outcome of every debate is certain.

Only on rare occasions has the legislative branch dared to challenge Stroessner. In May 1959 the *democráticos* briefly took control of the Congress and pushed through their resolution condemning the interior minister and the chief of police. Stroessner's response was to dissolve the legislature, purge the party, and arrest the mavericks. In 1969, as representatives of well-to-do business and farming groups, Colorado congressmen protested the government's proposed income tax bill. In this case their delaying tactics and quiet pressure persuaded Stroessner to relent and accept certain modifications. Beyond these few examples of independent action, however, Congress has done little. Even the often bitter attacks on government policy by the opposition probably have had little impact, since ministers have not been required to appear before investigative committees to answer questions.

Even if faced with a difficult Congress, the president has an overwhelming arsenal of weapons. Ultimately, of course, he can dissolve

Congress, claiming a constitutional crisis. In Stroessner's case this power is buttressed by his control of the army. Although the president must call for new elections within three months after dissolving Congress, in the interim he rules by executive decree. Despite Stroessner's use of that device in 1959, however, it is seldom necessary to go that far. The president has easier means to get his way. First, if he has pressing legislation to be considered, he may extend the legislative session, which ordinarily runs from 1 April to 20 December. Also, he may call an extraordinary session. Second, article 158 of the constitution prevents Congress from ignoring or pigeonholing the president's bills. Unless they are disposed of in the same legislative session in which they are introduced, they become law anyway. Third, the president's annual budget has priority over all other legislation. Each house has only one month to debate it, and they can reject it only by an absolute majority of both houses. Since that is extremely unlikely, it means that the president alone really decides how government funds are to be allocated. That by itself would make him the central political figure.

The president, not Congress, has the initiative in the lawmaking process. Every 1 April, Stroessner opens the legislative session with a presidential message, reviewing the state of the nation and the government's record over the past year and proposing the government's agenda for future action. During the session the executive branch sends over most of the bills considered by Congress. Those originating in the legislature are generally private bills for the relief of some individual. When Congress passes one of the president's bills, it does so in very general terms as a broad grant of power, leaving it up to the executive to "issue rules and instructions" for the law's application. By such executive decrees the president and his ministers really determine the content of legislation.

Finally, the president continues to govern by decree during those months when Congress is not in session. Although the legislature has the right to review any of his actions taken during that time, there is no record of its ever having overruled him.

The President's Informal Powers

Patronage greases the wheels of a political machine. Used wisely, it aids the dictator to keep his ruling coalition together and to recruit new support. A patronage job represents to the recipient an opportunity to raise his income, to gain valuable experience, and perhaps even to begin his own career as a political influential. A franchise, a government contract, or a tax exemption offers a privileged source of gain, which, in turn, creates an obligation of loyalty to the giver. Stroessner has a great amount of patronage to dispense. The constitution grants him a wide latitude in making executive appointments. Moreover, his control of the Colorado party makes him the ultimate arbiter of who shall hold office in all branches of the government, as well as in many nongovernmental associations. This is an important source of power in a country like Paraguay, where good jobs are scarce. Public or semipublic employment is one of the few avenues of enrichment.

The constitution places very few limits on the president's right to name executive personnel. He needs the Senate's approval to appoint ambassadors and other official representatives abroad, Supreme Court justices, and military officers above the rank of lieutenant colonel. Also, he consults the Supreme Court before naming inferior court judges. Finally, the constitution dictates the makeup of the Council of State, an advisory body made up of cabinet ministers, retired generals and admirals, and representatives of powerful pressure groups. Beyond those limitations, however, the president has a free hand. He alone appoints his cabinet and presidential staff and delineates the functions of his ministers; he has the last word on the promotions and assignments of all junior military officers; he appoints all sub-cabinet personnel, as well as the rector of the National University, the heads of the Central Bank and the Development Bank, and the members of the Agrarian Reform Institute, the Institute of Rural Welfare, and the National Economic Council; and he appoints and removes the police chief and all subordinate police department heads.

Local government also provides many patronage opportunities. Paraguay is divided into sixteen departments, plus a federal district (Asunción). Each department is headed by a presidentially-appointed *delegado* (delegate), who reports to the minister of interior. The capital has an elected junta, or council, and an intendant who is also a presidential appointee. Below the departmental level are the municipalities and, in rural areas, the *partidos*, or counties. The municipalities elect their own councils, which in turn select one of their number to serve as the local *alcalde* (mayor). The *alcalde*, however, is responsible to the departmental *delegado*, who may intervene the municipality in the event of a disagreement and remove its officials from their posts. Thus, indirectly, the president controls even this last corner of nominally independent power—all the more so since the local Colorado organization is sure to see that no troublemakers get elected in the first place. The rural *partido* is under the authority of the local *comisario* (police chief), who has a deputy chief and a number of conscript policemen serving under him. He, too, is answerable to the *delegado*, although as a police officer he also falls under the direct authority of the minister of interior.[5]

One final constitutionally recognized area of appointment power is the president's right of ecclesiastical patronage, which he exercises under a concordat with the Vatican. Under its provisions the state is required to maintain the church's property and its clergy, in return for which the president nominates men for all clerical offices down to the parish priests. While his nominations are not binding on the Holy See, it would be a serious matter to overrule him.

The constitutional scope of presidential authority and his control of patronage constitute an enormous reservoir of power. Yet, this would not suffice without Stroessner's firm control over the Colorado party. For it is the party's subservience that allows him to influence the composition of the other two branches of government, as well as the leadership of many nongovernmental associations. Since elections are always rigged to insure a Colorado majority in Congress and since all of the party's candidates must be approved by Stroessner, the principle of separation of powers has no real meaning. Moreover, the Colorado party embraces a large number of ancillary institutions such as professional associations, veterans' groups, student clubs, women's organizations, peasant groups, cultural societies, and the party press. Such groups offer another source of jobs, and they often exercise great influence in their respective areas. For instance, hospital appointments or judgeships are likely to be cleared through the Colorado medical and law associations. The same is true of appointments to the National University. Similarly, the party exercises a close supervision over the country's labor unions and makes certain that the executive committee of the Paraguayan Workers' Confederation is acceptable to the government. And at the university, where student politics is frequently the first stepping-stone to a political career, the party is usually successful in electing its handpicked candidates to leadership positions. In sum, the spoils system extends beyond the government to include key political positions in other walks of life. All lines of power eventually converge on Stroessner.

The Men around the President

Stroessner's personal control over the political system is helped by Paraguay's very backwardness. Here is a rural nation with no really large city, no complex industrial economy, and no highly organized system of interest groups. The vast majority of the population is illiterate, ignorant, passive, and obedient. Public opinion, insofar as that is politically relevant, is limited to a small segment of the population. In order to rule an ambitious person has only to win over a core of loyal followers in that small segment, uproot those who are determined to oppose him, and buy off the remainder.

Nevertheless, a dictator cannot be everywhere at once, no matter how active he is. He may have the power to make final judgments, but in the everyday administration of the state he must delegate some of his authority. As a result, a governing elite stratum forms just below him. That constitutes a problem, for it is often within such inner circles that coups d'etat begin. Thus the dilemma: how can subordinates be given responsibility, yet kept under control?

When delegating power, a dictator has a choice between two strategies. On the one hand, he can constantly shift elite personnel so that no subleader ever gets a chance to build up his own institutional power base. Although this device is often effective in keeping the dictator independent of his subordinates and potential rivals, it has the disadvantage of lowering the administrative efficiency of the regime. Morale in the army, police, or civil service may suffer from frequent shakeups, so that they may suddenly disintegrate in the face of a serious challenge by the opposition. On the other hand, a dictator may try to put together a team of trusted men to whom authority may be delegated. Such an approach requires good character judgment, and that is an area in which many men overestimate their ability. If the dictator succeeds in building his team, however, the regime will have greater coherence. The danger of this approach is that the team ages and its members may become elderly, inflexible, and unable to meet new challenges.

Stroessner has tended toward the second approach, which is more in keeping with his cautious, conservative temperament. Still, circumstances have forced him from time to time to overhaul his top administrative structure. Table 3 shows the major changes and general trends in the composition of Stroessner's cabinets from 1954 to 1978.

The table charts a more or less orderly turnover of cabinet personnel. However, a core of ministers has stayed in office since the early days of the regime, and another group of long-tenured men were dropped from the cabinet at one time, only to be brought back later. The stable core group plus those who have been brought back constitute the real political ballast of the government. Unfortunately for Stroessner, after almost a quarter of a century in power those trusted subordinates are beginning to show their age. When Stroessner was preparing to celebrate his sixth presidential inauguration, in 1978, Romero Pereira was eighty-nine years old, General Samaniego was

TABLE 3. *Stroessner's Cabinets*

Cabinet Post	1955[a]	1956[b]	1957[b]	1958[c]	1959[c]	1960[a]	1961[a]	1962[a]	1963[a]	19
Agriculture	Fabio da Silva	Martin Cuevas ——→			González Alsina ——					
Defense	Gen. Herminio Morinigo	*Gen. Marcial Samaniego* ———————————————→							Gen. Leódegar Cabello ——	
Education	Raúl Peña ———————————————→				J. Bernardino Gorostiaga	*da Silva* ——→			*Gorostiaga* ——	
Finance	Carlos R. Velilla	*Col. César Barrientos* ————————————————————————————								
Foreign Affairs	Hipólito Sánchez Quell	Raúl Sapena Pastor ————————————————————————————								
Health	Enrique Zacarias Arza ———————————————→				*Peña* ——→	Dionosio González Torres ——				
Industry and Commerce	Col. César Barrientos ——→ [d]			*Coscia*[d]	*da Silva* ——→ [d]		Domingo Montanaro →	José Antonio Moreno Gonzále		
Interior	Tomás Romero Pereira	Edgar Ynsfran ————————————————————————————								
Justice and Labor	Luís Martínez Miltos	Ezequiel González Alsina ——→			Juan R. Cháves[b] ———————————————→				*J. R. Cháves*[d] M	Sa
Public Works	Gen. Marcial Samaniego	General Mario Coscia T. ———————————————→				Romero Pereira ——→			*Samaniego* ——	
Without Portfolio		*Tomás Romero Pereira* ———————————————→				*Gorostiaga* ——→			J. R. Cháves ——	

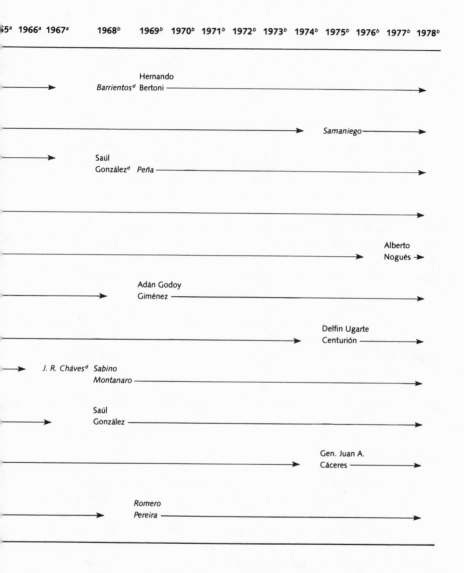

Note: Names in italics served in previous cabinets.
a. As of January.
b. As of May.
c. As of August.
d. Interim appointment.
e. Cesar Garay served as minister of justice and labor from September
  1958 to June 1959.

sixty-seven, and Colonel Barrientos was over sixty. Sapena Pastor had retired the year before at sixty-nine, and Stroessner himself was approaching sixty-five. Thus, the inner circle was becoming a gerontocracy.

There have been five major renovations in the cabinet's personnel: in 1956, between 1959 and 1960, in 1963, between 1967 and 1969, and in 1974. The first came after the showdown between Stroessner and Méndez Fleitas. Méndez Fleitas's ouster was followed by a purge of his friends. In 1959, after Stroessner surmounted the challenge from the *democráticos*, there was a large turnover and shuffling of cabinet ministers. Between then and 1964 seven new men were brought into the government, and some of them were shifted around until Stroessner had another stable team. Then, after Edgar Ynsfran's fall from power in late 1966, the cabinet went through another extended period of renovation. Four new men were recruited, while older ministers were moved around. After came another stable period, which lasted until 1974. Age forced more changes. General Cabello and Moreno González stepped down because of old age and poor health. Raúl Sapena Pastor followed soon after. In the process, a new generation was coming to power.

Stroessner's inner circle around which he built most of his cabinets, including the latest one, consists of a handful of loyal aides: Generals Barrientos and Samaniego, who are old military comrades; Romero Pereira, an aging party hatchet man; Raúl Peña; and Alberto Nogués, who is new to the cabinet but who served for many years as Stroessner's presidential secretary. A second group of ministers came to the cabinet during the middle period of the regime but seem to have kept Stroessner's confidence: Sabino Montanaro, the interior minister and former Guionist; Saúl González, the justice and labor minister, who was Edgar Ynsfran's protege; Hernando Bertoni, an agricultural engineer, the regime's "technocrat," whose appointment to the Agriculture Ministry in 1968 shocked Colorados because he was a nonparty man; and Adán Godoy Giménez, the young health minister. To some extent this latter group balances out the agedness of the inner circle. Finally, four exministers were once considered very close to the president: General Leodegar Cabello, who acted as Stroessner's stand-in with the army; José A. Moreno González, an old party hack who ran the Industry and Commerce Ministry; Raúl Sapena Pastor, who served Stroessner very ably for twenty years as foreign minister; and Edgar Ynsfran, the former interior minister, who was once considered to be the second most powerful man in Paraguay until Stroessner suddenly dropped him from the cabinet in 1966. Leaving aside the commanders of key military installations—who will be discussed later—these men constitute, or constituted, the elite within the elite.

In general cabinet renovation has come slowly and grudgingly. Compared with other long-established Latin dictators, Stroessner keeps his ministers in office a long time. Their average tenure, nine and a half years, is extraordinary when compared to, say, Franco of Spain or Salazar of Portugal. In those cases, ministerial tenure averaged only about two and a half years.[6]

Stroessner's ministers have varied backgrounds. Half of the twenty-eight ministers were lawyers. The next largest group (six) were military officers. Medical doctors (four) constituted the only other significantly large group. There were two journalists—Ezequiel González Alsina, though the holder of a law degree, was put in this category—one architect, and one agricultural engineer. Of the first three groups it is interesting to note that the military men stayed in the cabinet for the longest time—on the average, slightly over eleven years, to seven and a half years for the doctors, and six and a half years for the lawyers.

Thirteen of Stroessner's ministers had served in some important political post during previous regimes. Five (Domingo Montanaro, Sabino Montanaro, Ynsfran, González Alsina, and Sapena Pastor) had participated in the Guionist governments of Morínigo, Natalicio González, or Molas López. Nine (Juan Ramón Cháves, da Silva, Gorostiaga, Moreno González, Raúl Peña, Romero Pereira, Sánchez Quell, Zacarias Arza, and González Alsina again) had served under Cháves. Many of them had held only minor posts, but some had been cabinet ministers. Others had been on the Colorado party executive committee, in Congress, or in the corps of ambassadors. Sánchez Quell and González Alsina had edited the Colorado newspaper, *Patria*; the latter, along with Sabino Montanaro, had also served on the party's Youth Affairs Committee. Moreno González, besides being Federico Cháves's foreign minister, had once been president of the Central Bank. Sapena Pastor's long career in public service included service on the Supreme Court, in the Central Bank, in the deanship of the law school, and in many subcabinet posts.

To sum up, at least half of Stroessner's ministers were recruited from the already established political elite, and all of them were drawn from the upper class or respectable middle class.[7] This points to the essentially conservative nature of his regime, as well as to its continuity with the past. In part, this is because the Colorado party itself provides the basis for such continuity. But even so, the old warhorses have been kept in office for a much longer time than might have been expected. Another sort of dictator might have purged them and brought in his own men. Instead, Stroessner preferred to keep them and to use old factional quarrels to play them off against one another.

In Paraguay defeated factions are seldom completely purged, although their leaders are eliminated at the first opportune moment. Stroessner seems to prefer to co-opt useful people into his personal following rather than eliminate them for the sake of principle. Consequently, his cabinet ministers display an assortment of political antecedents. Romero Pereira was once a close ally of Méndez Fleitas. Raúl Peña, González Alsina, Fabio da Silva, and Moreno González were once close to Federico Cháves. Sapena Pastor, Sabino Montanaro, and Saúl González have Guionist backgrounds. Yet, Stroessner has succeeded in blending them all into a cohesive, loyal government.

Other ministers, of course, were brought to the government because of close personal friendship with Stroessner. Generals Morínigo and Cáceres collaborated with him in coup plots back in the late 1940s. Indeed, Cáceres went into exile with Stroessner after the botched attempt against Natalicio González. Samaniego and Barrientos are other old military comrades. Nogués, as Stroessner's secretary, has probably worked more closely with him than has any other cabinet minister.

Political criteria were the most important in choosing ministers for the early cabinets. Factions had to be carefully balanced against each other: *epifanistas* versus *democráticos*, and *democráticos* versus Guionists. More recently, however, the new recruits have had to show some special skill or to prove their usefulness by previous service in the government or party. Some were ambassadors, some served in Congress, some sat on the party executive, and some acquired a standing in their profession. Even "repeaters" such as Romero Pereira and Raúl Peña had to serve in the Senate and on the Junta de Gobierno before being brought back into the cabinet. Peña also went to Brazil as ambassador for a brief time. Ambassadorships were the means of ascent as well for Juan Ramón Cháves and Moreno González. After being replaced by Abdo Benítez as Stroessner's secretary, Nogués served as ambassador to Uruguay before succeeding Sapena Pastor as foreign minister. Gorostiaga, González Alsina, and Fabio da Silva (before his second appointment to the cabinet) had to prove their loyalty by following Stroessner's lead unswervingly on the Junta de Gobierno.

Sabino Montanaro and Saúl González had long apprenticeships before coming to the cabinet. Montanaro was elected *suplente* (alternate) to the Junta de Gobierno in 1959, after the purge of the *democráticos*. At the same time, he was elected to Congress. Later, in 1962, he became a full-fledged member of the junta. Then, in the following year he succeeded Juan Ramón Cháves as minister of justice and labor when the latter became party president. González had a similar career. His first really important job was as chief of investigations in Ynsfran's police force. Later he was elected *suplente* to the Colorado party executive and then, in 1966, became a full member. He also served as the junta's secretary. After getting elected to Congress, he moved over to the executive branch as director of penal institutions and, briefly, as interim minister of education. When Montanaro took Edgar Ynsfran's place as interior minister in 1966, González entered the cabinet permanently as the new minister of justice and labor.

The directorship of penal institutions was also the stepping stone for Domingo Montanaro, Sabino's elder brother, who came to the cabinet in 1960 as the minister for industry. In his case, though, he had already proven his competence as a cabinet minister under Natalicio González and as ambassador to Mexico under Federico Cháves. By contrast, Adán Godoy Giménez had practically no political experience other than a term in Congress before being picked as health minister. Similarly, Raúl Sapena Pastor, Dionosio González Torres, and Hernando Bertoni seem to have been chosen by Stroessner largely on the basis of their professional backgrounds in the fields of law, diplomacy, medicine, and agronomy.

In democratic systems exministers usually retire to private life; totalitarian dictatorships, however, usually liquidate fallen chiefs or at least punish them with expulsion from the party and with obloquy. But not all dictatorships are as severe as that. According to Juan Linz, merely authoritarian dictatorships are more pluralistic and less ideological; thus shifts in power occur in a more humane fashion. "Turnover in . . . elites can take place without purges, by retiring people to secondary or honorary positions, if not to private life." Linz goes on to explain that "venomous hatred of defeated elite members is not always absent, but the lack of ideological clarity, of self-righteousness, contribute to making this infrequent. On the other hand, the more pluralistic, open structure of society may help make the loss of power less painful."[8]

Stroessner's government fits more comfortably into the "authoritarian," rather than the "totalitarian," category in this respect. Of the twenty-eight men who served under him, twenty resigned or were dismissed at one time or another. Only five of those were dropped unceremoniously, and only one was exiled (Zacarias Arza). None of them were imprisoned, executed, or publicly humiliated. Ynsfran, it is true, went into immediate obscurity after being removed from office. After eleven years as Stroessner's right-hand man he is no longer mentioned in the press at all, and if he still has political opinions they are not circulated in the media. But even he is still at liberty to enter or leave the country, or to travel around inside it. Ten of the other ministers were transferred to Congress: eight to the Senate and two to the Chamber of Deputies. Five of the exministers eventually obtained ambassadorships. Two were appointed to the Supreme Court, one was made president of the Colorado party, and one was made rector of the National University.

In fact, ambassadorships, congressional seats, and other prestigious political posts have been used frequently to reward people other than former cabinet ministers. One of the lagniappes of the new bicameral congress under the 1967 constitution was to create more honorific positions for Stroessner to fill, and he has taken advantage of this privilege. For instance, in order to secure the support of Eulógio Estigarribia and his faction, Stroessner gave him a seat in the old Chamber of Representatives. Later, Estigarribia became president of the Chamber, and today, having behaved himself, he has a seat in the Senate. So too has one of Estigarribia's followers, Ramón Méndez Paiva. And so has General Raimundo Rolón, the expresident, whom Stroessner helped to overthrow. Crispín Insaurralde, a former Guionist and another of Eulógio Estigarribia's backers, was given the rectorship of the National University, where he served until 1969 when the former health minister, González Torres, replaced him. Rigoberto Caballero, one of Federico Cháves's old friends and cabinet ministers, was recently rehabilitated and given a seat in the Chamber of Deputies.

Ambassadorships can be compensatory and honorable appointments for services rendered—or they can be one way of getting a troublesome person out of the country, as a face-saving alternative to exile. General Herminio Morínigo's appointment to West Germany in 1955 mollified the Argentine government, which was putting pressure on Stroessner to remove all pro-Peronist elements from his regime. Rather than drop an old military chum completely, Stroessner sent him to Europe to live under comfortable circumstances until conditions improved. Today Morínigo has a seat in the Chamber of Deputies. Hipolito Sánchez Quell, a powerful *democrático* politician, was dropped from the cabinet at the same time as Morínigo, but he was amply compensated with the responsible post of ambassador to Brazil. After that he was rewarded with the most sought-after diplomatic appointment of all for a Paraguayan: ambassador to France.

Other ambassadorial appointments are made for very different motives. Sometimes they are a way of making a peaceful gesture to members of a defeated faction, who are to go abroad temporarily while the situation stabilizes. This must have been at least part of the reason for the appointments of Federico Cháves as ambassador to France in 1956 and of Guillermo Enciso Velloso, a longtime friend and patron of Méndez Fleitas, as ambassador to Spain and the Vatican. Sometimes, however, the expatriation is intended to be permanent. It is said that Natalicio González was promised the ambassadorship to Mexico on the understanding that he was to stay out of Paraguay. Similarly, Osvaldo Cháves, the hotheaded nephew of the former president, was sent to Washington as Paraguay's ambassador to the United States and the Organization of American States in order to keep him out of the way.

Of course if the bribe fails, exile is possibly the only alternative. In 1958, Osvaldo Cháves resigned his posts and returned to Paraguay to lead the *democrático* challenge to Stroessner. Thus, when Stroessner purged the party the following year, Cháves received no second chance; he was cast into exile. After being ousted from the Central Bank, Méndez Fleitas was offered the prestigious ambassadorship in London. When his *caudillo* pride prevented his accepting the post, he was exiled. Of course, Méndez Fleitas had another good reason to turn down the offer. He had no reason to trust Stroessner, who had tricked him once already. The president could easily countermand the appointment once his opponent was safely out of the country. Only this time, Méndez Fleitas would be in England, across the ocean, instead of just across the border.

During the process of purging and taming the Colorado party, Stroessner has succeeded in putting together a ministerial team that facilitates the extension of his presidential powers. They come from a variety of backgrounds. Some are close personal friends, others have been won over from rival factions, others have been recruited because of their skills. In most cases they came to the cabinet after a period of apprenticeship during which they proved their trustworthiness. Once in office their tenure is usually secure, for Stroessner likes to deal with men he knows well. All of the ministers are well above the average Paraguayan in education and experience. Drawn from the higher strata of the population, they, like Stroessner, tend to be conservative in outlook. Although they may not have the professional backgrounds to merit being called a technocracy, they constitute an elite corps whose competency is quite adequate for Stroessner's purposes. Through them he controls the rest of the machinery of the regime.

Chapter 8. Guarding the Guardians

Every government needs its security forces. It is not enough to organize an administration; there must be sufficient power to coerce
those who would deny the government's claim to rule. Besides protecting the country's borders, the army must put down any large-
scale violence against the authorities, and the police must try to prevent conspiracies from forming in the first place. Such concerns are
common to all regimes, but they are central to dictatorships, which
come to power in divided polities, lack public consensus on their legitimacy, and so must maintain themselves in power by force. For dictators like Stroessner, however, the very instruments of coercion they
depend on may be turned against them. In Paraguay the army has
been the means for every change of regime since 1936. In the eighteen years between the February Revolution and Stroessner's rise to
power it put nine presidents into the palace and removed seven of
them (Estigarribia died in office). Only Stroessner was able to break
that pattern.

To accomplish that, he has been able to take advantage of several
circumstances. First, he is a soldier himself, and he has an expert
knowledge of the institution. The officer corps is small, so that each
man's character and connections are well understood. That is an aid
in handling such things as promotions, assignments, and retirements.
In addition, Stroessner has made certain that the military receives a
large portion of government spending and favors. Military appropriations in Paraguay are, in proportion to the population, among the
highest in Latin America. Moreover, senior officers participate heavily
in patronage and graft.

Nevertheless, such methods by themselves do not guarantee that
the military will stay under control. Other Paraguayan presidents tried

to buy military support and surrounded themselves with trusted officers. In the end, however, they failed to keep the greedier or more ambitious soldiers in line. Stroessner has achieved a real advantage over his predecessors in the fashioning of a dominant single-party regime, based on a purified and obedient mass organization. This instrument, in conjunction with the lavish distribution of rewards, makes it risky and unprofitable for the officer corps to conspire against him.

How Internal Security Is Organized

Paraguay's armed forces are divided into an army, a navy, and an air force. The total fighting strength is slightly over 20,000 officers and men. The army is by far the largest branch, with about 17,500 troops, of whom about half are draftees. The navy has about 2,000 men, including a marine infantry and a small air detachment. The air force's strength is estimated at somewhere between 800 and 1,000 men.[1]

The army is further divided into cavalry, infantry, artillery, engineers, signal corps, transport, and supply services. No official figures are available, but very rough estimates suggest a breakdown like this: (1) one cavalry brigade (Campo Grande) of motorized troops, 2,000 men; (2) three infantry regiments, 2,700 men; (3) three artillery regiments, 1,800 men; (4) one presidential escort battalion, 1,500 men; (5) six engineering battalions, 9,000 men; (6) a signal corps, a transport command, and repair crews, 500 men; for a total of 17,500 men.[2]

Of the three infantry regiments, the Fourteenth Cerro Corá Regiment is the largest by far, with about half of total number of foot soldiers; of the three artillery regiments, the General Brúgez Regiment in Paraguarí is the dominant one. Along with the Campo Grande cavalry and the Presidential Escort Battalion they constitute the most important military units in the country, politically speaking. Yet it is also worth noting that more than half of the soldiers are in branches that do not relate directly to fighting. Specifically, the six engineering battalions point up the army's sizable role in carrying out the government's development projects.

The Marshal Francisco Solano López Military College trains the officer corps for all three branches of the armed services. The course of study lasts five years, at the end of which the cadets are commissioned as second lieutenants or naval ensigns. Later, those who show unusual promise may be sent to the Superior War School, where a two-year program prepares them for the command of large units. That is a crucial step in an officer's career, for it is a good sign that he is on the way to the top of the military hierarchy.

In Paraguay, as in many other countries, the constitution makes the president the commander in chief of the armed forces. As a rule, though, Paraguayan presidents—especially if they were civilians—found it advisable to delegate the real power of command to some high-ranking officer. That is because the military in Latin America has a tradition of resistance to any interference from civilian authorities in its internal affairs, a tradition that goes all the way back to the *fueros* (special privileges) that the Spanish crown granted to its officers. Thus, military men are sensitive about their "rights" and their "honor," and it is risky to appoint commanders over them without their consent. It is from that same tradition of *fueros*, too, that disobedience to civilian presidents originates.

Stroessner, however, rose to power as head of the armed forces and has never relinquished that authority. He is his own commander in chief, and he intervenes directly in promotions and assignments. Every Thursday he goes to General Staff headquarters and puts in a full day's work, meeting with unit commanders, discussing their tasks, and reviewing all equipment orders.[3] As a result, he has a very detailed understanding of his military personnel—including the junior officers—which he supplements by frequent personal visits to bases all around the country. More than that, he has assumed the direct command of Campo Grande on at least two occasions and once made himself interim head of the air force.

Immediately below the president are the minister of defense and the chief of the General Staff. The minister of defense is not concerned with the command of troops. Rather, his duties involve drawing up the military budget, disbursing money for pay and pensions, and supervising the system of military tribunals. Since he is in charge of supplies, however, he wields a lot of power. The chief of the General Staff commands all of the armed forces in the name of the president, and when the latter is a civilian, the chief of the General Staff is the de facto commander in chief. Under Stroessner he has been relegated more to the position of a liaison officer. However, since Stroessner's time is inevitably divided among several concerns, it is necessary that the chief of the General Staff be a man of unquestioned loyalty and capability, for he is required to keep a close watch on the three services.

The General Staff's main duties are to coordinate the activities of the army, navy, and air force. Since the army is the predominant branch, the chief of the General Staff is usually its ranking officer.

Below the General Staff the army, navy, and air force each have their own general staffs, divided into sections dealing with personnel, intelligence, operations, supply, finance, and public relations. Finally, Paraguay is divided into six military regions, whose commands cut across the vertical hierarchies of the three branches. The First Military Region includes Asunción and the surrounding area. It comprises the Campo Grande cavalry, the Fourteenth Cerro Corá Infantry Regiment, the General Brúgez Artillery Regiment, and the main naval and air force units. Consequently, the command of this region is of crucial importance. Other territorial divisions are the Second Military Region, with headquarters at Villarica, controlling the center of eastern Paraguay; the Third Military Region, headquartered at San Juan Bautista de Misiones, guarding the southern frontier with Argentina; the Fourth Military Region, with headquarters in Concepción, protecting the north; the Fifth Military Region, with headquarters in Puerto Presidente Stroessner, defending the main eastern route to Brazil; and the Military Territory of the Chaco, which is responsible for both defending and administering the western zone.

The police may also be considered practically an adjunct to the armed forces. Ever since the May 1956 purge, when Battalion 40 was downgraded and the police lost their role as a countervailing power to the military, more and more key police positions have been held by army officers. Except for Edgar Ynsfran, all of the police chiefs to serve under Stroessner have been army men: Mario Ortega (1954–56), Ramón Duarte Vera (1956–66), and Francisco Brítez (1966 to the present). Under General Brítez army men have controlled such sensitive posts as head of the Department of Instruction and Operations (the planning office), commander of the Security Guard Battalion, director of Communications, and director of the Center for Military Police Instruction.

Despite this militarization of the police, however, they fall under the authority of the Ministry of Interior, not Defense. It should be noted, too, that even with the cutback of Battalion 40 the police maintain an impressive level of manpower: about 8,000 men in all, of whom 4,500 are assigned to the capital and the remainder spotted throughout the interior. A scaled-down version of Battalion 40 still exists in the Police Security Guard, a tough, well-trained unit whose job is to provide special protection for the president. It numbers some 400 men, who are divided into two rifle companies, a support company, and a headquarters company.

Besides the Security Guard, other chief divisions within the police are the Department of Public Order and the Department of Investigations. The former is in charge of the regular police and handles ordinary breaches of the peace. It is further divided into traffic, mounted, and motorized police. The Department of Investigations deals with political affairs. It is the secret police. A long line of ruthless directors, which includes Edgar Ynsfran, Ramón Duarte Vera, Saúl González, and Pastor Coronel, has given it a sinister reputation. Its grim influence is everywhere: tapping telephones, opening mail, and listening to the reports of spies and informers. It is generally believed to use torture as a common method for extracting information and confessions.

This by no means exhausts the repertoire of police activities. Some police units are assigned to keep order in the interior. In rural counties they are under the authority of the local police commissioner, while in the towns they report to the *alcalde*. In either case they are still under the Ministry of Interior, which pays their salaries and provides funds for their services. The rank-and-file policeman is a conscript serving a two-year stint. As a rule, these draftees are not sent to serve in the areas from which they came.

Another branch of the police that deserves mention is the Police of the Presidency. This is the Paraguayan secret service: a corps of about one hundred specially trained plainclothesmen who guard high government officials and their families. Also, there is the Police Academy, which gives promising career policemen a five-year course in modern police techniques. It graduates about fifty officers a year, who then rise to the middle and upper levels of the police hierarchy.

The Cost of Internal Security

Paraguay is a praetorian state. The ratio of both military and police personnel to the whole population is one of the highest in the world. In Latin America only Cuba and post-Allende Chile have higher percentages of men in the armed forces. Indeed, Paraguay has a larger percentage of its people under arms than many of the world's middle-level powers, like Great Britain, France, West and East Germany, China, India, and Pakistan.[4] The size of the police in relation to the population places Paraguay ahead of such notorious regimes as Bulgaria, East Germany, and South Africa. Only Albania, Liberia, Libya, Viet Nam, and Singapore have larger police forces compared to size of the country.[5]

Estimates of the cost to maintain such an enormous security apparatus vary and are hard to compare because different researchers use different yardsticks to measure the relative amount of expendi-

ture. For example, Henry D. Ceuppens put the 1970 costs at 2.25 percent of the gross national product. Furthermore, he argued, some of
that went to essentially nonmilitary projects, such as road building,
construction, and the maintenance of Paraguay's airlines and river
fleet. Purely military expenditures amounted to only 1.6 percent of the
GNP. In Ceuppens's view that contrasted well with other Latin American countries such as Peru, Argentina, or Brazil, where the costs ran
to 3 percent of the GNP, or with the United States, where they reached
12 percent. Indeed, he concluded that the current military budget was
a bargain because "chiefly due to the austerity of the Armed Forces . . .
Paraguay does not misspend money in superfluous arms, or in big
exhibitions, or in displays of military power. If we take into account
that 1.6 percent of the GNP is able to maintain the country's internal
peace, no one will disagree that the cost is very low. Any revolution
or coup d'etat costs more than the equivalent of ten years of military
spending."[6]

The *Area Handbook for Paraguay* arrives at an estimated cost that
is very similar to the one given by Ceuppens: 2.7 percent of the GNP.
It also agrees that about one-fourth of the defense budget goes to
finance a variety of works that are not strictly military in nature. The
armed forces provide, for instance, a broad range of engineering
services for road, school, and church construction, as well as for the
extension of telephone and telegraph lines. They also run several
commercial enterprises, including passenger and cargo airlines,
ranches, farms, and a ship repair service for the merchant fleet. As
part of its civic action program the military has developed medical
assistance facilities for rural areas, a radio communication service,
and local air and river transport. It also runs the weather bureau.[7]

Nevertheless, there is other evidence to suggest that the military
receives an inordinately large slice of the national budget. Lewis Taylor and Michael C. Hudson arrive at an estimated 2.9 percent of the
GNP as the military's share, not much different from those of Ceuppens and the *Area Handbook*. However, they conclude that this is one
of the highest levels of military spending in Latin America, with only
Cuba (7.1 percent) and the Dominican Republic (3.6 percent) ranking higher. In fact, they contradict Ceuppens directly, for they show
Paraguay tied with Brazil and Peru in military spending as a percentage of the GNP.[8]

The cost of internal security bulks even greater when the police
forces are added. T. N. Dupuy and Wendell Blanchard put the combined cost of the military and police at 4 percent of the GNP in 1970,
which was the second highest level (after Cuba's 6.4 percent) in

Latin America. Robert Sellers's estimates were even higher (5 percent of GNP), although he still had Paraguay second to Cuba (6.1 percent).[9] It should be kept in mind, too, that these estimates have been expressing Paraguay's military expenditures as a percentage of the total value of goods and services produced during the year. A different impression is gained by relating the Ministry of Defense allocations to the total government budget. According to Edwin Lieuwin, a veteran student of Latin America's civil-military relations, the military's share of the national budget shot up to 50 percent after Stroessner's takeover in 1954. In 1959 the *New York Times* reported that out of a total budget of around $21 million some 40 percent went to the armed forces. This seems to have declined since then, for in 1966, Willard Barber and C. Neale Ronning claimed that the military's share of the budget was 27.5 percent—which was still the highest percentage for military spending in Latin America.[10]

But in fairness to Stroessner it should be noted that official statistics show a somewhat different picture, and these cannot be simply brushed aside as being hopelessly distorted. Up to 1961 they were gathered with the aid of American technical advisors in the Servício Técnico Interamericano de Cooperación Agricola (STICA), and thereafter by the Central Bank. What they show is a steady decline in the portion of the budget going to the military and the police. Table 4 takes the percentage of the total allocations received by the ministries of Defense and Interior and contrasts them to those received by Education and Health. By doing this for three-year intervals, beginning in 1949, Stroessner's government can be contrasted with that of his predecessor, Federico Cháves.

According to the figures in table 4, the military's share of the budget went down after Stroessner came to power—not up, as Lieuwin claimed—and the cost of internal security never reached 50 percent of total government expenditures, even including the entire budget for the Interior Ministry.[11] If those figures are taken as accurate, it would seem that Stroessner has brought internal security costs under control. However, this was not done by cutting the military and police budgets, because the actual amount of money spent on the military has gone up steadily. In 1953, Cháves allotted 180.5 million *guaranis* to the Defense Ministry; that amount was raised to 258.8 million by Stroessner in 1955, to 616.6 million in 1960, 1.04 billion in 1965, and 1.68 billion in 1970. Those raises do not simply reflect inflation, for the *guaraní* has been, since 1956, one of the most stable currencies in Latin America. It is just that the total government budget has expanded faster than the military's share of it. Also,

Stroessner has had help from the United States in keeping the generals satisfied. In 1970 Paraguay received about $800,000 in American military aid, making a total of some $8.7 million received over the past twenty years.[12]

As table 4 also shows, however, the percentage of the budget allocated to much-needed educational and health services has changed very little since Cháves's time. Indeed, with only 1.6 percent of the GNP going to education, Paraguay in 1972 ranked near the bottom in this category for all Latin American countries—tied with Nicaragua and ahead of only Guatemala, Haiti, and Uruguay. In this instance poverty cannot be offered as an excuse, because equally poor countries, like Bolivia, the Dominican Republic, Ecuador, and Honduras, spent proportionally much more.[13] Clearly, then, internal security still figures uppermost in the regime's list of priorities.

The Rewards of Loyalty

Direct military allocations are only the apparent cost of military security to Paraguay. Other costs are hidden. Much of the patronage Stroessner distributes goes to military men. As a result, they hold some of the more lucrative positions in the state. One important area of patronage jobs is the state enterprises, or "autonomous agencies." Because of the lack of private capital or because some economic activities are considered too essential to the public welfare to be trusted to private firms, the Paraguayan government has established certain state monopolies. Thus, the public utilities, the ports, the merchant fleet, the railroad, and the three airline companies (two domestic and one international) all fall under Stroessner's patronage authority. Many of those enterprises are managed by military officers. The transportation companies in particular are considered to be desirable posts, for they offer great opportunities for smuggling—probably Paraguay's leading industry. Two other very profitable enterprises are the Paraguayan Alcohol Administration, which controls the wholesale market for alcoholic beverages, and the Paraguayan Meat Corporation, which provides meat for Asunción. Both are headed by military men. The government-owned businesses in ship repair, furniture making, quarrying, lumber, and cattle raising also offer economic opportunities for favored military officers and Colorado party politicians. In addition, the National Development Bank, which is ostensibly set up to promote economic development by extending loans to businessmen and farmers, favors applications from those who stand well with

TABLE 4. Percentage of the Government's Budget
Allocated to Selected Ministries, 1949–1978

Ministry	1949	1952	1955	1958	1961
Defense	32.5	33.9	31.6	21.2	21.3
Interior	12.1	13.4	13.6	8.0	9.6
Total	44.6	47.3	45.2	29.2	30.9
Education	12.8	13.3	15.0	11.8	15.4
Health	5.7	3.7	4.6	4.4	4.7
Total	18.5	17.0	19.6	16.2	20.1

Source: Servício Técnico Interamericano de Cooperación Agrícola, *Manual estadística del Paraguay, 1941–1961*, pp. 87–88; Banco Central del Paraguay, Departamento de Estudios Económicos, *Boletín estadístico mensual*, 1962–78.

the regime. Top military men are seldom turned down for a loan.

Moreover, the senior officers live far better than the rest of the population. From the $1.5 million Defense Ministry, to the officers' club and casino, to the various new barracks and parade grounds, they move in the most modern, comfortable environment the government can provide. They are an elite group and know it. They get handsome salaries, which are quite comparable to those of top managers in civilian life, family allowances, ration allowances, free medical care, and a good pension system. Officers have easy access to loans for building a house or starting a business, and they run some of the most important enterprises in the country. After retirement most have the prospect of high-paying managerial opportunities. As Leo Lott puts it: "The Paraguayan armed forces have little reason to complain. They do not have to pay license fees for their cars; they have a good deal of influence in getting friends and relations on the public payroll; and they may—and do—augment their income through various concessions to import goods duty free."[14]

The police are treated almost as well. Recently an $800,000 police complex was built, with officers' quarters, a casino, a bar, and shops selling imported duty-free food, clothes, hardware, pharmaceuticals, toys, and sporting goods.[15] Such items are not available to the general public at such bargain prices. Party and government officials who go abroad may also obtain special permits to bring luxury goods such as cars and electric appliances into the country without paying import duties.

Top officials can also extend their earnings through influence peddling. It is no accident that retired military officers and Colorado

1964	1967	1970	1972	1975	1978
23.1	22.4	20.3	19.7	20.3	18.6
11.9	9.4	9.4	9.3	9.4	8.5
35.0	31.8	29.7	29.0	29.7	27.1
19.0	16.6	14.9	14.8	14.6	15.7
5.0	3.8	3.6	3.2	2.7	3.4
24.0	20.4	18.5	18.0	17.3	19.1

party chiefs often appear on the directorates of private companies, especially in the fields of construction, tourism, or exports, where the obtaining of a government franchise or license can be facilitated by someone with *entrada* (contacts) in the regime.

For those who have no *entrada* or who have somehow incurred the displeasure of a government official, life can be hazardous. Not only are they passed over for favors but they may find it hard to get a job at all or their business prospects may be blocked in favor of someone else with better connections—say, a military officer who has decided to enter the same field. Corrupt police officials, feeling no legal restraint, may subject them to extortion.

One notorious example of this involved Colonel Ramón Duarte Vera, who was then chief of police. Two West German embezzlers, Dieter During and Wolf Eckhard Kocubek, disappeared one day in March 1966 with about $400,000 worth of various European currencies from the Metropole Bank of Frankfurt. With the help of Interpol the West German authorities traced the two men to Rio de Janeiro, but just as the Brazilian police were about to pick them up, they disappeared again. When they resurfaced a short while later they were in Asunción, staying at the Gran Hotel del Paraguay, a large old establishment in a quiet, residential section of the city.

Having located their men once more, Interpol agents went to the Asunción police and asked to have them arrested. But when Duarte Vera heard about the money he began to formulate his own plans. Instead of arresting the embezzlers he went to the hotel and made them an offer. In return for handing over the loot to him he would let them escape. A light plane would fly them to Paraguay's eastern border and leave them off in a small jungle village. There they would be met by a guide who would take them by a little-known path into Brazilian territory. After that they would be on their own.[16]

Since Duarte Vera's men were all over the hotel, watching their every move, During and Kocubek had no choice but to accept the terms. The next morning the two embezzlers took off before dawn, and Duarte Vera and Alberto Planas, his chief of investigations, went to the hotel to collect the money from the safe. Instead of turning it over, however, the woman behind the desk went to her German-born employers. They, in turn, called the German embassy. Soon afterwards, Stroessner got a personal call from the German ambassador. Immediately, special agents went to the hotel and arrested Duarte Vera and a score of his top aides.

The political repercussions were tremendous. Not only were Duarte Vera and his clique removed from their jobs but the minister of interior, Edgar Ynsfran, who had been Duarte Vera's protector, was eventually purged, thus ending the long era during which those two men had commanded the nation's police power. As for the two embezzlers, they were never heard from again.

An even more shocking example of police blackmail was the kidnapping of Ian Duncan Martin in September 1973.[17] Martin was an executive of Liebig's Meatpacking Company, a British firm and one of the largest factories in Paraguay. This happened at a time when left-wing guerrillas were very active in neighboring Argentina. It was common for such groups to kidnap foreign executives and hold them for large ransoms, so the Paraguayan police first speculated that Martin's disappearance was the work of guerrillas who had extended their activities into Paraguay. The nature of the ransom demand, however, caused Police Chief Francisco Brítez to revise that theory; he concluded that a gang of common criminals was holding Martin. Rather than pay the ransom, Liebig's offered a $300,000 reward for the gang's arrest.

Soon after the reward was posted, the police "discovered" the kidnappers' hideout. Most of the gang were "shot trying to escape," but the few who were taken into custody told a curious story. Although the details were never published, it is certain that at least eight police officers were behind the plot to seize Martin and split the ransom money. The officers implicated were arrested, and an indignant Junta de Gobierno read them out of the party. Even so, some ugly rumors would not die down—that Pastor Coronel, the chief of investigations, had been the real brains behind the scheme, and that higher-ups in the Ministry of Interior were also involved.

Top military and police leaders also have access to the enormous rewards of smuggling in Paraguay. Situated in the heart of the continent, with extensive and sparsely settled frontiers, the country is a smuggler's paradise. This sort of illegal activity is encouraged even more because Brazil and Argentina tax luxury imports heavily, thereby creating an even greater market for contraband goods. Some of these circulate in Paraguay too. In downtown Asunción dozens of women and children peddle American cigarettes, sun glasses, nylons, underwear, sweaters, and scarves at prices far below those in the neighboring countries. The best imported Scotch whiskey is a bargain compared to what people in Buenos Aires or São Paulo have to pay. That is why Paraguay has become such an entrepôt for clandestine trade in those items. The volume of illegal merchandise is impossible to fix exactly, of course, but it is said to amount to around two billion dollars annually.[18] Consequently, one of the main sources of income for high army and police officials is the so-called in-transit tax, which is simply a rake-off on all contraband going in or out of the country.

Each area of the contraband trade is parceled out, like a fiefdom, to highly placed officers. The more important the man, the more lucrative is the racket apportioned to him. Like other patronage systems, the smuggling operations are organized into networks of patron-client relationships and provide jobs and incomes for a large number of people.

Since economic opportunity has always been limited in Paraguay, smuggling might be defended as an unfortunate but unavoidable alternative to poverty—perhaps even as a laudable response to restrictions on free trade. In fact, so long as Paraguay's smuggling was confined to whiskey, cigarettes, and fancy underwear, it aroused little international concern other than an occasional crackdown by foreign border patrols. Around 1970, however, Paraguayan smugglers began branching out into gunrunning and drugs. As a result, the country's relations with Argentina and the United States have deteriorated somewhat, often leading to embarrassing incidents.

For example, Stroessner was forced to replace Admiral Hugo González as head of the navy in April 1976 because it was revealed that he had been smuggling guns to Argentina. All of this came out after a fierce battle between Paraguayan marines and Argentine border guards on 19 February, during which several people were killed. Stroessner resisted pressure from Buenos Aires at first, but he finally made González step down when he was presented with evidence that the weapons were being sold to left-wing, as well as right-wing, terrorist groups.[19]

Evidence that top officers in Paraguay were at the center of a drug network covering the whole Western Hemisphere began to crop up between 1970 and 1972. As American narcotics agents became more successful at intercepting shipments from Europe, a new route was opened up. Heroin was sent from Marseilles to Asunción, where it was transshipped to Miami and New York. According to one calculation, as much as 582 kilograms of pure heroin with a value of around $145 million arrived in the United States every year by this route. The mastermind of the operation was an expatriate Frenchman named Auguste Ricord, who went under the name of André and used a night club he owned outside of Asunción as his cover.[20]

Obviously, Ricord needed the connivance and protection of powerful men inside Paraguay in order to operate on such a scale. According to published accounts based on the testimony of American narcotics agents, Ricord's chief backer was none other than General Andrés Rodríguez, the chief of Campo Grande. Another influential *patrón* was General Patrício Colmán, one of Stroessner's oldest and closest friends, who headed the Fourteenth Infantry Cerro Corá Regiment. Both Rodríguez and Colmán had made their fortunes from the whiskey and cigarette concessions in the early 1960s, but now they were making bigger profits by turning their extensive ranches near Asunción into airstrips where private planes came and went by night, hauling their cargoes of narcotics. Indeed, it was said that Rodríguez, as a major stockholder in an air taxi service, even furnished some of the planes. A third key official was Pastor Coronel, who headed the secret police. His job was to keep an eye out for American or Interpol agents. Police undercover men took photographs of suspected agents and turned them over to Ricord. Coronel also supplied the smugglers with false passports and any other needed documents.[21]

Not all of Paraguay's top officials were involved in this arrangement, however. Stroessner has never been linked to it, although it is inconceivable that he didn't know about it. Nor were General Brítez, the police chief, and his boss, Sabino Montanaro, the interior minister, ever tied to the drug traffic. Therefore, when American narcotics agents finally penetrated the smuggling operation in April 1971 and asked for Ricord's arrest and extradition, something of a power struggle ensued. Montanaro wanted to turn him over, but Rodríguez and Colmán were determined to protect him. Although Ricord was taken into custody by the police, the extradition proceedings dragged on for eight months. Finally the Paraguayan court handed down its decision: the extradition request was refused on the grounds that Ricord had committed no crime in the United States. Since he had violated Paraguay's laws, he would remain confined there.

That was unacceptable to the Americans, who were convinced that

Ricord's protectors would eventually arrange his escape. So, Stroessner received a personal note from President Nixon reminding him that under the 1971 Foreign Aid Act the United States could cut off economic aid to any country that refused to take action against the international drug traffic. Paraguay stood to lose about $11 million in direct aid, plus considerably more if Congress went ahead with its threat to cancel Paraguay's sugar quota. Nevertheless, Stroessner refused to budge, pleading that he could not overturn a court's decision. Perhaps he was being loyal to his old friend Colmán. Or maybe he feared the consequences if Colmán and Rodríguez ganged up on him. Whatever his reasons, he took a trip to Japan at that time to explore the possibility of securing financial aid there should the Americans cut him off.[22]

A sudden turn of events rescued Stroessner, however. In August 1972, General Colmán became seriously ill from the effects of an old bullet wound. Two years before he had been involved in tracking down a guerrilla leader named Arturo López Areco and had finally discovered him hiding in the trunk of a car. Colmán, whose often-flaunted bravery made him a hero to his men, insisted on being the one to pry open the door to the trunk. But when it sprung open López Areco came out shooting. Although the guerrilla was immediately shot down by the soldiers surrounding the car, Colmán was hit twice in the abdomen. He was rushed to the hospital and operated on immediately. A long convalescence followed, but finally he seemed recovered. Now, however, serious complications suddenly flared up. Stroessner had Colmán flown to the United States, where he was admitted to Walter Reed Hospital, but a few days later he was dead. On the very next day an appeals court in Paraguay reversed the decision about Ricord's extradition. Soon afterwards the gangster was on his way to New York and twenty years in prison.[23]

Internal Controls

For officers who cannot be bought, Stroessner has developed a system of checks and balances inside the military. In addition to promoting his friends to the top ranks and placing them in the most important commands, Stroessner takes time to cultivate the junior officers. After all, senior officers are powerful only so long as they are backed by their subordinates. As a rule, captains, majors, and lieutenant colonels, not full colonels or generals, are in direct command of troops in Paraguay. Although the latter may run the General Staff Head-quarters, without the allegiance of the junior officers the units do not move. In the past, in fact, unhappy junior officers have led troops against the government despite the protests of their superiors.

Stroessner's good relations with junior officers have served him well on crucial occasions. They were the key to his triumph over Méndez Fleitas in 1955. Méndez Fleitas depended heavily on the support of the Campo Grande cavalry, which was under the command of his friend Major Virgilio Candia. But Major Candia lost control of his garrison at the critical moment because of the defection of three out of four of his regimental commanders: Major Sixto Duré Franco, Captain Roberto Cuba Barbossa, and Captain Andrés Rodríguez. In the maneuverings to subvert them, Stroessner was not able to deal with those junior officers directly, lest he raise suspicions, but he had an able go-between in Captain Luís Maria Argaña, the head of his palace military staff.

Two days before Stroessner launched his preventive coup, Argaña met with Cuba Barbossa, Rodríguez, and a first lieutenant from Campo Grande named Diáz Delmas. What they talked about can only be guessed at, but when Argaña arrived at Campo Grande two nights later, bearing a presidential order deposing Candia as commander of the cavalry, all four regiments declared their loyalty to Stroessner. When rewards were passed around afterwards, Major Duré Franco became the new Campo Grande chief and was promoted to lieutenant colonel. Rodríguez succeeded Duré Franco in 1961 as head of Campo Grande and still holds that command. Many people consider him the second most powerful man in Paraguay.

The 1955 coup provided Stroessner with a golden opportunity to purge the military's ranks. He retired dozens of officers suspected of *epifanista* sympathies and even sent a few to prison camps like Peña Hermosa. Stroessner's hold on the military was considerably strengthened, but the process was not completed until the *democrático* purge of June 1959. The most outstanding casualty that time was Colonel Epifanio Ovando, the air force chief, who had led the reformers' demand for a lifting of the state of siege. At the same time, Stroessner was able to edge out some former collaborators who were showing signs of acquiring presidential ambitions. Though his opposition had never been out in the open, Colonel Duré Franco had quietly supported Ovando in the hope of undermining Stroessner. Once Stroessner was sure of his support in the army and the party, he sent Duré Franco to Uruguay as military attaché and Colonel Cuba Barbossa, who should have been next in line as Campo Grande chief, to another overseas assignment. As a result of those shifts Stroessner's inner circle of military chiefs consisted of Major Andrés Rodríguez (the new cavalry head), Colonel Patrício Colmán (head of the Fourteenth

Infantry), General Leodegar Cabello (chief of the General Staff),
Colonel Juan Antonio Cáceres (the new air force head), and Captain
Luís Maria Argaña (who continued to head the presidential military
staff). All of them were close friends or proteges.

Two other innovations have been crucial for keeping the generals
in line. First, the command of troops and the supplying of materiel
have been divided between two parallel army chains of command, the
first extending from the General Staff and the second from the
Ministry of Defense. Thus, the senior officers are dependent on
Stroessner's decisions for their equipment. Second, Stroessner has
built up his own, personal, heavily armed Presidential Escort Battalion, an elite unit of 1,500 men, each of whom was carefully
screened by the secret police before being allowed to join. Considering
its size, firepower, and esprit de corps, this force raises the ante considerably for any military officer thinking of attacking the Presidential Palace. Stroessner also has a well-armed Police Security
Battalion of 400 men, personally loyal to him. Thus, it is extremely
unlikely that any officer could hope to supplant Stroessner by a coup,
unless he had the backing of the rest of the country's key military
units—and that is unlikely.

The Colorado Party as a Counterweight

In some ways the Colorado party in Paraguay performs functions
similar to those of official parties in more advanced totalitarian dictatorships. It provides popular support for Stroessner, even to the
point of building a personality cult. It also disseminates propaganda
and serves as an organizational network to control various inter-
mediate groups: labor, students, professional associations, and
veterans. Furthermore, it engages in surveillance, for the militant
Colorado is expected to watch his non-Colorado neighbors and report
their suspicious doings. All of these functions, taken together, constitute still another check on the military, for Stroessner's dictatorship
rests upon a stronger and broader organizational base than most.
Many officers are involved in the party, and others have friends and
relatives who are Colorados. Those who might be indifferent or even
disaffected must take into account the party's mass following, which,
presumably, would be behind Stroessner in a revolt. The example of
the armed *py nandi* in 1947 is worth keeping in mind.

To understand how the Colorado party is able to assume such a
pivotal role as a counterweight to the military it is necessary, first, to
understand its structure and organization, and then to explore the

sources of its popularity. The Colorado party's present basic structure was laid down by its 1947 convention. In theory, its highest organ is the National Convention, which convenes every three years. Delegates to it are elected by local committees on the basis of one for every 1,500 members. Since official membership figures are put at around 700,000, there should be some 450 delegates at the convention.[24] Extraordinary conventions may also be convened whenever some crisis arises. To do business a convention must have a quorum, and that requires the presence of an absolute majority of all the delegates elected.

The National Convention has certain specific duties. First, it hears reports from the Junta de Gobierno, or national executive committee, and either approves or disapproves them. Since Gagliardone's reforms, of course, approval is a foregone conclusion. Second, it hears complaints from local committees, ancillary organizations, or individual members. As an appeals court it has the power, in theory, even to discipline the junta. Third, it nominates the party's slate of presidential and congressional candidates—although in practice its deliberations in this are only pro forma. Fourth, it proclaims the party's official platform. Fifth, it may choose to modify the party statutes. Sixth, it elects the Junta de Gobierno for the next three-year term.

In reality the National Convention has little power. It meets too infrequently, its size is unwieldy, and it is composed largely of obscure people. Obviously the Junta de Gobierno runs the party, and it manipulates the convention as it likes. The junta consists of thirty-five members and sixteen *suplentes* (alternates), who are elected by the convention by a simple majority vote. Once constituted, the junta proceeds to elect its own officers: a president, three vice-presidents, three secretaries, one treasurer, and one protreasurer. Actually, though, since the convention votes for an entire slate of candidates to the junta it is already known who will occupy these posts. The vote taken at the junta's first meeting is merely a formality.

The junta's duties are wide-ranging. It administers the party's property and finances, keeps membership records, fixes dues, and exercises discipline over the local committees. In its public role it represents the party's views to the government and keeps in touch with its congressional bloc to make sure they know which way to vote. In this connection, Colorado cabinet ministers and congressmen, as well as heads of local committees, have a right to attend the junta's meetings, although unless they were also elected to the junta they do not vote. Finally, other vague grants of power give the junta the right to "dictate rules which it believes convenient for the carrying out of the Statutes, and for the progress of the Party." Thus, it combines "all the necessary powers for the fulfillment of Party interests, being able . . . to take whatever legitimate measures may be necessary to insure the success of those proposals which constitute the Party's goals."[25]

The most influential member of the junta is the party's president. He chairs the meetings, fixes the agenda, and votes on all proposals (indeed, he may cast a double vote if that is necessary to break a tie). He may also call the junta into emergency session on his own initiative or at the request of three of its members. In conjunction with his secretaries the president is responsible for all party documents and correspondence. With the advice of his treasurer and pro-treasurer he carries on all financial transactions. Beyond that he is the party's official representative before the government and in dealings with any other party or political group.

So varied are the junta's duties that its work must be divided among several committees and subcommittees. The most important of these is the Political Committee, which maps out party strategy and is the first to discuss crucial issues facing the organization; it is the inner circle within the junta. The party president is always a member. Also, General Marcial Samaniego—the party treasurer and Stroessner's personal representative to the junta—has been on the Political Committee since the regime's earliest days. When the party must make a critical decision, the Political Committee meets first in secret, thrashes out its position, and presents its recommendation to the rest of the junta. If it passes there but is still considered controversial enough to warrant a full party discussion, an extraordinary convention may be called.[26]

Committees dealing with labor (Comisión Obrera), peasants (Comisión para la Campaña), women (Comisión Central de Damas Coloradas, and its subordinate committee for girls, Niñas Coloradas), and youth (Comisión Central de la Juventud Colorado) are next in importance. Party youth affairs are, in turn, divided into committees specializing in the National University and in the high schools. The junta also includes a committee for legal matters (Comisión Jurídica) and one for publicity (Comisión para Propaganda). The latter is in charge of issuing party pamphlets, as well as series such as *Cuadernos Republicanos* and *Reflexiones Republicanas*, which publish articles on party history and doctrine. It also overseas the publication of *Patria*, the Colorados' official daily newspaper, and *El Colorado*, a weekly.

The junta also keeps in touch with key segments of the public through its ancillary organizations, such as the Colorado Medical Association, the Colorado Law Society, and the Retired Colorado Military Officers' Association. It also sends *asesores* (advisers) to the

Paraguayan Workers' Confederation and the National War Veterans' Association. Probably the most active groups of all, however, are those connected with university and high school students, for the party is well aware of the importance of recruiting new generations to its ranks. Thus, the secretary for university affairs runs a very busy social and cultural organization called the Ignacio A. Pane Center For University Students, as well as a political club called the Colorado University Federation, whose job is to win elections for student representation on the various university governing committees. The secretary for high school students has a similar social club in the Blás Garay Cultural Center. He also administers a party leadership training program for young boys and girls, as well as a very popular preuniversity training course—a night school curriculum which prepares Colorado teenagers for taking the university entrance examinations. In all these committees the party activists are constantly busy, drumming up enthusiasm by their propaganda and seeing to it that members of their ancillary organizations receive preferential treatment from the government.

One last important junta committee, the Committee on Party Organization (Comisión de Organización Partidaria), deals with the party apparatus. Given its many different functions it too is divided into subcommittees which specialize in various facets of mobilization and control. Policy originates in the Political Committee, but its application begins in the Committee on Party Organization. Its members make frequent trips into the interior, visiting local committees to explain the junta's directives and to keep themselves informed about local problems. The committee is particularly active during election campaigns in order to get out a big vote, and it periodically launches special recruitment drives. Probably its most sensitive work comes during those periods when local committees are preparing to elect delegates to a national convention, for that is when factionalism is most likely to crop up. When it does, it is the task of the Committee on Party Organization to keep it localized and within bounds, if possible. If that is not possible, then it must intervene diplomatically in the local committee *asambleas* (assemblies) to make sure they select delegates who are congenial to the national leadership.

The local committees are called *seccionales*. There are twenty-five such committees in Asunción, representing the neighborhood or ward organizations, and more than a hundred and sixty scattered throughout the rest of the country. In turn, the *seccionales* may be divided into *subseccionales*. Each local group has an executive committee of nine members and six *suplentes*, all of whom serve for three years. The executive is broken down into a president, a vice-president, a treasurer, and a secretary, plus the other five members. Party regulations require local committees to meet at least once a week. Among their duties are: (1) to look after the welfare of their members and provide assistance when needed, (2) to maintain discipline, (3) to keep a registry of members, (4) to encourage the formation of worker and peasant clubs, (5) to organize local conferences to publicize the party's work, (6) to arrange for the orderly election of local party officials and delegates to the National Convention, and (7) to carry out faithfully the orders of the national leaders. The *subseccionales* do not choose their own leaders. They are creations of the executive committee of the local *seccional* which appoints and removes them at will.[27]

The Junta de Gobierno keeps a close watch over the *seccionales*. Part of Gagliardone's reforms in the late 1960s was to assign permanent delegates from the junta to each local committee to act as advisors. Besides making sure that the *seccionales* conform to the national party line, the permanent delegates help local leaders to hold membership drives or to sponsor activities that help the party's public relations. Above all, their job is to keep peace in the local organization, to resolve disputes among members, and to insure that local officers are loyal to the junta.

In theory, the *seccionales* are free to elect their own officers and delegates to the National Convention. Also, when more than one slate is contesting the election, the resulting local executive committee or convention delegation is supposed to represent the various factions in proportion to the vote they got. Electing is done at an *asamblea*, which is partly a local convention and partly a fiesta, replete with dancing and a barbecue. In practice, the permanent delegates and the Committee on Party Organization usually work behind the scenes to make sure that factional fights are avoided and that a single slate (*lista única*) is presented for the members to vote on. The junta representatives have many ways of bringing pressure on local leaders to accomplish this. For example, they control the parceling out of favors and promotions, and in extreme situations can impose sanctions, such as removal from office. They can also control the machinery of the elections. In April 1973 the Committee on Party Organization issued firm instructions to the *seccionales* concerning the upcoming *asambleas*, which were to elect National Convention delegates. The committee put strict limits on the use of propaganda by rival candidates: no graffiti to be painted on walls, no provoking jingles or slogans, and no defamatory allusions. Moreover, the use of microphones and sound trucks was prohibited.[28]

Yet the junta's permanent delegates must be careful about how they apply pressure in the local situation. Clumsily applied pressure can backfire, intensifying factional differences and generating antagonism toward the national leaders. As Frederick Hicks points out, the delegates prefer to persuade.

> The chief of the delegation is usually a nationally prominent politician whose name has appeared frequently in the newspapers and is familiar to the people, except for this occasion they would probably never be privileged to actually meet him. But as the alcohol and the general festive mood breaks down reserve, ordinary peasants engage him in conversation and present to him their problems, he dances with the local girls and the feeling is fostered that the leaders of the Colorado government, however exalted, maintain a close personal interest in the well-being of their fellow party members, however poor, in all parts of the country.
>
> The occasion also provides an opportunity for young men seeking political advancement to bring themselves to the attention of the delegates (offering toasts and making impromptu speeches is one way of doing this) and to make contacts which may later be useful. At the same time, the delegates representing the national party leadership come to know and evaluate the principal party leaders in the community.[29]

The *seccionales* also have their special committees for labor, peasants, women, and youth. All of these work to disseminate party propaganda and to administer programs like the youth leadership courses. The local executive committee maintains its hold over these ancillary organizations, in the last analysis, by its power to suspend any member for up to three months. Such a disciplinary measure requires a two-thirds vote. When that happens, an account must be rendered to the junta, justifying the action. Any harsher penalties can be imposed only by the junta itself.

Finally, the party's rank and file expect certain services from their leaders. Looking after the welfare of local members is one of the principal functions of the *seccionales*. This may mean using influence to get people jobs on the public payroll, or it may involve helping some unfortunate family that has lost a Colorado breadwinner. The latter sort of aid is financed by allocations from the junta, which gets its funds from a 5 percent "donation" from all government employees, sometimes supplemented by local collections.[30] Such paternalism is an important ingredient in Paraguayan politics, where the patron-client relationship is the basis of organizational cohesion.

How the Masses Are Mobilized

Party identification is practically universal in Paraguay, and member-ship in one of them is almost always a lifetime commitment. An American researcher who distributed a questionnaire to some 269 Paraguayans living in the capital asked: "Have you ever thought of changing parties?" Three-fourths of his respondents answered no. Another 15 percent refused to reply, and only 10 percent admitted that they had ever considered it. The same study found that Para-guayans usually selected their friends, and even their marriage partners, from the same party affiliation.[31] Parties in Paraguay tend to seal people in total party environments, somewhat like the Social-ist, Communist, Fascist, and Christian parties of pre–World War II Europe.

Therefore, it is a serious matter to switch party allegiances. In his study, Byron Nichols tapped a deep-seated taboo which is summed up in the Guaraní word *yeré*. *Yeré* means to turn, to change one's mind about a pledge. It connotes treason. Paraguayans often use an-other term when referring to fellow party members: *co-religionario*. Even a member of another faction within the same party is a *co-religionario*, but those who do not belong to the party cannot be *co-religionarios*, whatever else they may have in common. When a crisis occurs, *co-religionarios* of different factions are expected to lay aside their quarrels and close ranks against outsiders. To change parties would be to betray one's *co-religionarios*, and that would con-stitute a serious example of *yeré*. Such a person would be unprincipled and treacherous. He would risk being made a pariah, cut off from friends and family.

Thus the Paraguayan wears his party colors proudly: a red, blue, or green poncho or necktie, depending on whether he is a Colorado, a Liberal, or a Febrerista. Some observers, in fact, believe that party membership is little more than family loyalty and tradition. Hicks, for example, concludes that the Colorado party is essentially an in-tricate web of personal ties with no real set of principles separating it from the other parties. In Paraguay politics involves almost everyone, Hicks argues, because in such a poor country, controlling the govern-ment is the best way for someone to escape poverty, and to do so one must either be the leader of a political band or else be a follower in it. Family membership in a party is passed down from generation to generation, reflecting family feuds that have been carried over since the past century.[32]

In the opinion poll conducted by Nichols, however, the respondents were asked why they had joined a particular party. Over 60 percent of them answered: "Because of its ideals and program." When asked What is the best way for a party to increase its membership? more than 75 percent answered that the best way is for the party to develop an ideology that explains all aspects of social life.[33] In fact, Paraguayans do believe that ideologies are important in their political lives, although they also recognize the influence of inherited party preferences. Consider, for example, the following statement by Epifanio Méndez Fleitas.

> When I came into the world, you were born in Paraguay as either a "Liberal" or a "Colorado." Just as in the United States, with its blacks and whites, partisan prejudice was absolute and it was almost impossible to imagine someone of Liberal origins turning into a Colorado or vice-versa. As you know, this could not have been possible without the existence of an Ideology conditioning the sentiments of each group. That is to say, there had to be a system of ideas and experiences specifying what was "Liberal" or "Colorado" behavior; in sum, a powerful factor of autochthonous alienation that defined the mentality of the thinking class of the two traditional parties. In this sense I was "born" a Colorado. Temperamentally, I fell in love with its symbols, its forebears, and its cultural creations. This outlook is so complete in a person that one is tempted to speak of a Colorado "civilization," and identify it to some extent with Paraguayan civilization. Perhaps Marxism, as an international ideology, possesses the same *elan vital* as Coloradism, but it could never compete with it in Paraguay. Nevertheless, as my father was a farmer and liked men to be free to think without interference, he told us children to consider things carefully before making a decision. Because of that—and principally because of the lack of political opportunities, for the country was going through a long period of institutional abnormality—I became an active member of the Colorado Party relatively late, in 1939. Today, thanks to the potent ideology on which I was nursed since childhood, I have never experienced any ups or downs in my convictions, nor have I ceased to believe in the manifest destiny of Coloradism.[34]

The reader will perceive that this quote makes no reference to the actual content of Colorado ideology. That is characteristic of Colorado leaders—indeed, of Paraguayan party leaders in general. They prefer to talk of their party's history, its symbols, and its great leaders of the past. When asked to explain his party's beliefs, a Paraguayan politician is almost certain to begin a long lecture on the nation's history from independence to the present, with a heavy emphasis on the earlier period. Such discussions seem futile unless one remembers that Paraguay's political conflicts of today grew out of the unresolved questions of the past, such as should Paraguay federate with Argentina, or be an independent nation? Should the property rights of the upper classes be protected, or eliminàted? Should the new state be a liberal democracy, or a populist dictatorship? At first the left won out, resulting in the socialistic tyranny of Francia and the Lópezes. But the losers returned with the allied armies in 1869 and imposed a different type of government. It was as if the Tories had come back a half century later to overthrow the American Revolution—or better yet, as if the Russian emigres had returned during World War II and restored the czar. In Paraguay the restoration was cut short when General Caballero came to power in 1877, but the Liberals returned in triumph in 1904.

Thus, Paraguay was saddled with two sets of founding fathers, each set representing a vastly different concept of legitimate government. The country had no George Washingtons or Benjamin Franklins to act as unifying symbols. One either accepted the tradition of Francia and the Lópezes or rejected it in favor of the more moderate tradition of democratic, free enterprise liberalism. Either Francia was a patriot or he was a villain; either the Paraguayan Legion rescued the country from tyranny or it did the dirty work of foreigners. There was no middle ground. The modern Liberal party looks back to the democratic "Plan of Government" drawn up by the original junta of 1813, to the public proclamation of the Legionnaire Triumvirate on their entry into Asunción in 1869, to the Legionnaires' constitution of 1870, to the founding of the Centro Democrático, forerunner of the Liberal party, in 1887, and to Captain Benigno Ferreira's revolution of 1904 as milestones in Paraguay's struggle toward freedom.[35] Colorado writers trace a chain of patriotic endeavor running from Francia, through the two Lópezes and General Caballero, right down to Stroessner.[36] In a typical campaign speech, given on 14 December 1962 in Asunción's soccer stadium before an enormous partisan crowd, Stroessner mentioned Francia twice, Carlos Antonio López seven times, Marshal Solano López six times, the War of the Triple Alliance twice (including a reference to Cerro Corá, López's last battle), and General Caballero three times.[37] His other speeches, particularly his state of the union addresses, are much the same. In his speeches before Congress for the years 1957, 1959, 1962, and 1973, the only Liberal figure mentioned was Captain Benigno Ferreira, whom Stroessner described as "that Legionnaire sergeant who destroyed our country."

Translating historical experience into general principles, the Liberal party ideology fears a strong state. It is for limited government and individualism. "Liberals are individualists," says the *Manual del ciudadano liberal*, "inasmuch as they recognize that the individual . . . is the end for which everything exists."[38] On the other hand, Colorado ideology favors a much greater degree of state control over people and property. The party still propounds the principle articulated by Natalicio González at the National Convention in 1947: "The state, servant of the free man, should intervene in the social and economic life of the nation in order to prevent abuses by private interests and to promote the general welfare, but without prejudice to anyone." In other words, national interests take precedence over individual liberties. While most Colorados do not carry this argument all the way to statism or collectivism, their outlook still contains a strong element of populism. Such populism is reminiscent of the rural radicalism found in the American South in the 1930s. Its main ingredients are the sentimentalizing of poor farmers, an appeal to the lower classes' prejudices against the rich and educated, and a contempt for formal procedures.[39] That sort of barefoot radicalism constitutes the "ideals" that give spirit to the Colorados' *co-religionario* mentality.

The *co-religionario* mentality places at Stroessner's service a large mass of fanatical supporters, which represents an important check against the military. The effect of this can be seen in the great "spontaneous" demonstration on 14 August 1973 when more than fifty thousand Colorados—an enormous number of demonstrators by Paraguayan standards—paraded in support of the president. During this period, Stroessner was encountering strong criticism over a proposed hydroelectric treaty with Brazil. According to his opponents, Stroessner and his foreign minister, Sapena Pastor, had agreed to terms that endangered Paraguay's sovereignty over her territory and resources along the border. What made the criticism particularly ominous was that the commander of Campo Grande and the commander of the General Brúgez Artillery Regiment also ventured to speak out publicly against the treaty. With two such influential generals taking a critical stand, even the normally timid daily papers *La Tribuna* and *ABC Color* dared to write editorials attacking the government. Rebellion was in the air, and Stroessner had to react quickly.

Thus the Colorado party began a massive campaign to demonstrate support for the president. Party organs such as *Patria* and *El Colorado* appeared on the streets with banner headlines heralding a new era of prosperity for Paraguay as a result of the proposed treaty. A new journal, *La Opinión Republicana con Stroessner*, was created, and its entire contents were given over to applauding the president for negotiating the Brazilian treaty and to outlining the great benefits to the country that were to flow from it. At the same time, letters and testimonials supporting Stroessner began pouring in to *La Tribuna* and *ABC Color.* The pages of those two papers were practically covered with bold-print advertisements by cabinet ministers and high party officials condemning the critics as shortsighted and unpatriotic. Above all, the advertisements said, the people were with Stroessner and would show it on August 14.

The publicity campaign for the demonstration was saturating. Posters, handbills, full-page newspaper advertisements, and sound trucks barraged the public with the message: all loyal Colorados would parade through Asunción on the appointed day. In every *seccional* and *subseccional* across the country party activists signed people up for the spectacular "March on Asunción." All of the ancillary organizations—the lawyers, doctors, students, women, and veterans—announced that they would participate to show their support for Stroessner.

The logistical problems of moving such a great number of people into and out of the city and of feeding them while they were there challenged the party's organizational ability. First, some fourteen hundred cars and trucks were assembled all around the country, in every town and in every suburb of the capital, to transport the demonstrators. Before dawn on 14 August thousands of peasants clambered aboard those vehicles and began heading for Asunción. When they got to town, they were taken to the party's magnificent headquarters near the Plaza Independencia. Everyone was given a red scarf to wear. In the meantime, dozens of cooks fried sausages, cut rolls, and opened wine for the free lunch that was to follow the march.

All public servants and their families were also required to show up, from cabinet ministers down to grade school teachers and humble clerks. All of them had been contacted and reminded of the importance of showing their loyalty at such a time. Thus, by midmorning there were more than fifty thousand red-bedecked party members milling around the headquarters and the street out front, listening to warm-up speeches and polka music, smelling the cooking food, and getting into a fiesta spirit.

When the time came to march, the participants were tolled off into small groups, each with its own leader. Besides a red scarf everyone got a large portrait of General Stroessner to wave and a button with his picture on it to pin on his shirt. Some people also carried Paraguayan flags, while others simply got red pennants. Everyone was to stick with his leader and cheer when he gave the signal. The streets were all decorated with red flags. As Stroessner stood in the reviewing stand, Tomás Romero Pereira, dressed as a gaucho and riding on horseback, led the cheering marchers past. Other high party officials came galloping along too, waving their cowboy hats.[40]

Fifty thousand people in a quiet, colonial town like Asunción make for an impressive show. At least the military were impressed, for they immediately dropped their criticism of the government. The "popular majority" had spoken, and, no doubt, lurking in the background were memories of the fighting spirit of the *py nandi* during the civil war. Above all, the Colorado party had shown what it could do—or rather, Stroessner had shown what he could accomplish through it—to mobilize mass power in support of his rule.

But popular demonstrations are not the only way in which the Colorado party's masses can be mobilized against the military. Another function of an authoritarian mass party is to provide a network of unpaid spies and informers to keep all potential enemies under surveillance. Loyal Colorados are encouraged to watch their neighbors and to report any suspicious doings to the police or their party leaders. Military officers come under these *vigilantes*' scrutiny as well.

The party has over 180 *seccionales* scattered over every *barrio* of Asunción and every town and hamlet of the interior, and many of those units are further divided into *subseccionales* on a block by block basis. Moreover, many of the officers, their servants, and the enlisted men serving under them are Colorado *co-religionarios*. Thus the power of surveillance of the party is pervasive and formidable and the risks of plotting against the regime are very great. It would be hard for army officers to escape the vigilance of the party's spies, and the loyalty of their troops would be doubtful if the Colorado leadership called for the soldiers to rally behind Stroessner. Although this falls short of complete penetration and control of the military— as practiced, for instance, by the Russian Communist party through its political commissars—Stroessner's use of the Colorado Party's mass organization constitutes a far more formidable weapon against the officers than Paraguay has seen since the time of Solano López. It reduces practically to zero the likelihood of a successful coup against him.

Chapter 9. The Political Role
of Economic Development

On the first day of April, President Stroessner, in accordance with the constitution, appears before Congress to give his state of the union address. A reading of those speeches finds that they follow a predictable pattern in presentation and theme. The opening remarks are broad and general, referring to the government's patriotic spirit and to the inspiration provided by the country's great traditions—above all by the Colorado party. The main body of the speech begins with a long listing of the accomplishments of the past year. The maintenance of law and order and of a stable currency usually head the list. After that the president quotes facts and statistics concerning such things as how many schools were built, how many kilometers of road were paved, how many bridges were finished, how many towns are now receiving electricity, how many clinics were established, how many rural cooperatives were started, how many families received how much land under the agrarian reform program, how much new foreign investment was attracted, how many new sewer lines were built, and what improvements were recorded in agricultural and industrial production—a review which sometimes involves a product by product summary.

Such seemingly dull accomplishments form an important part of the foundation for Stroessner's regime. He has presided over an era of unprecedented economic expansion in Paraguay. Whether achieved through his efforts or not, this expansion has become a major theme in the propaganda to justify his rule. That is why the neon sign over the Central Bank flashes its message to evening strollers: "Peace, Jobs, and Well-being with Stroessner," and Colorado apologists place their greatest emphasis on the material progress recorded since 1954.[1] To understand even better why this is so, it is useful to recall the conditions in Paraguay before Stroessner took over. The 1947 civil war had left the society and the economy in shambles. Production had collapsed, trade was practically at a standstill, almost a third of the population had emigrated, and the victors—instead of restoring order—had turned to squabbling over the spoils.

The various post–civil war Colorado governments had made some half-hearted attempts to check the deterioration, but their ill-conceived plans only made matters worse. When they tried to restore the trade balance by laying heavy duties on luxury imports, smuggling and black marketeering spread. When they decreed price controls to hold down the cost of living, even more goods were diverted to the black market.

A primary cause of inflation was the dizzying growth of the money supply in the form of easy loans to businessmen. According to a study by the International Monetary Fund, in 1955 alone the Central Bank increased the availability of credit by almost 100 percent. Those loans did not go to farmers or industrialists, who might have raised production and boosted the country's exports. Instead, the large bulk of them went to contractors who were building apartment houses on speculation. Without saying so explicitly, the IMF report supported charges that the Central Bank president—who was none other than Epifanio Méndez Fleitas—was using the government's money to build a personal following.[2]

The Central Bank was also involved in other operations that, though legal, discouraged commerce. All foreign currency earned from exports had to be exchanged at the bank for highly overvalued *guaranis*. The bank then sold that currency at much higher black market rates. In 1955 the bank realized a profit of 366 million *guaranis* from just this sort of manipulation. But this practice cheated exporters, and as exports dropped, exchange reserves were used to cover balance of payments deficits. When those ran out in 1955, Paraguay was unable to continue importing the machinery, fuels, and industrial parts needed to keep the economy running—to say nothing of certain foodstuffs like wheat, which the country was in the habit of purchasing abroad.

In sum, the state of the economy could not have been worse. Paraguay was on the brink of complete economic collapse. Severe measures were necessary, but Méndez Fleitas opposed any belt-tightening, which he said was "antipopular." With Méndez Fleitas's fall in December 1955, however, the administration made sweeping changes in the Central Bank's policies and personnel. Gustavo Storm, the new Central Bank president, appealed to the IMF for an emergency loan to help Paraguay meet its immediate financial crisis. The agency not only granted the loan but sent a commission to Paraguay to work out a plan for reforming the country's finances. The result was the Stabilization Plan of 1956, which became a blueprint for Stroessner's subsequent development strategy.

The Stabilization Plan

Stabilization was to proceed in certain stages. First, credit was to be restricted and the money supply kept stable. Second, the system of currency exchange at the Central Bank was to be changed in order to encourage exporters. Third, the government was to undertake a program of internal improvements, to include new roads, schools, port facilities, sanitary works, electrification, and so forth, which would stimulate industry and commerce and upgrade the labor force. Fourth, the tax system was to be reformed in order to raise the revenue for financing those improvements. One tax reform was to be implemented immediately: the high duties on exports were to be abolished.[3]

Controlling credit and the money supply was a politically sensitive task, for businessmen who were loyal Colorados had grown used to easy loans. Similarly, labor unions looked to a paternalistic government to decree higher wages every time the cost of living rose. Moreover, a large proportion of organized labor worked in the public sector—that is, they were loyal Colorados who expected to be taken care of. Any politician who refused to reward these groups as they expected was running the risk of mass defections. Sticking to the stabilization plan was a high-risk strategy for Stroessner.

Nevertheless, loans to private firms dropped by two-thirds during the first year. Labor received an initial wage boost of 20 percent to offset the effects of a projected currency devaluation, but after that their wages were to rise less than 5 percent annually. These policies lowered the rate of monetary expansion dramatically over the next four years, from 700 million *guaranis* in 1955 to only 25 million in 1959.

The next step was to eliminate the old artificial currency exchange rates and price controls. The *guaraní* was left to float to its free market rate—in effect, to be devalued. Currency devaluation and the lifting of price controls combined to spur production in both industry and agriculture. Not only did the total volume of exports rise, but more goods were available for the domestic market. In fact, the increase was so great that even with the abolition of price controls inflation actually decreased by 18 percent by the end of 1956. Although there was still a long way to go, it was clear that an economic turnaround had been achieved.

The government now had the beginnings of a coherent economic plan and needed only the necessary institutions to put it into effect. Fortunately, two top-level advisory bodies were already in existence: the Council of State, a corporative chamber in which cabinet officials in charge of economic ministries met with representatives of the country's key pressure groups, and the National Council on Economic Coordination. Created in 1948, the latter organization was chaired by the president and was composed of the ministers of Treasury, Agriculture, and Industry and Commerce, plus the president of the Central Bank. After 1961 the president of the National Development Bank became a member as well. A third organization, the Central Bank, had up until that time determined credit and currency policies.

More specialized institutions were needed, however, to focus on certain economic bottlenecks. In banking, for instance, the IMF had warned against giving the powers to expand the money supply and to make loans to the same agency. Therefore, the government chartered the National Development Bank in 1961, which handled all loans. Decisions about monetary expansion and foreign exchange were reserved to the Central Bank. Central Bank authorities were to make only a limited, specified amount of money available to the National Development Bank, thus limiting the volume of loans. This system both insulated the Central Bank from political pressures and gave it a mechanism to stimulate or cool off the rate of business expansion—an important factor for keeping inflation under control.[4]

New public bodies were also created to manage budgetary reform, education, sanitation, housing, agrarian reform, foreign trade, planning and investment, transportation, and public utilities. Indeed, the vast majority of public policy institutions in Paraguay today were created after 1960.[5] Together with such older public institutions such as the railroad company, the maritime fleet, the telecommunications company (ANTELCO), the meat corporation, the sugar and alcohol monopoly, the Port of Asunción Authority, the Social Security Institute, and the Central Bank, they furnish the government with considerable leverage to direct economic development.

They also represent an enormous increase in the number of government jobs, for the bureaucracy today employs well in excess of 40,000 people. Yet, political and family connections are still the most important criteria for securing a public post. In this aspect of the economy, efficiency and potential economic payoff have been sacrificed to the considerations of politics and patronage.

Financing Development: The Role of
Private Domestic Capital

Investment capital comes from three primary sources: the state, local
entrepreneurs, and foreign investment or loans. The political ideology
of a regime determines how much .weight each of these receives.
Stroessner has taken advantage of all three sources, but he favors
using private capital whenever possible.

The entrepreneurial community in Paraguay may be divided into
two broad groups. The first group, which is heavily dominated by
foreign firms, produces mainly for the export market. Its establishments are well financed, efficient, modern in outlook, and corporate
in structure. The second group, which serves mainly the domestic
market, is owned by Paraguayans. Its businesses are family owned
and poorly capitalized. Although domestic private capital is the preferred route to economic growth, local businessmen have played a
very secondary role in the development effort in Paraguay. Attitudinal
studies show that local Paraguayan businessmen see themselves as
innovators rather than traditionalists, but there are few real go-
getters among them. Lack of capital, limited opportunities in the local
market, and long periods of political insecurity have produced conservative business habits.[6]

Nevertheless, evidence suggests that the Paraguayan business
community may be ready to assert more leadership in the future. For
example, two pressure groups, the Federation of Production, Industry,
and Commerce (FEPRINCO) and the Paraguayan Industrial Union
(UIP) have begun to actively represent private enterprise. Founded in
1952, FEPRINCO tries to coordinate the political activities of farming,
ranching, industrial, and mercantile associations, thereby allowing
the private sector to present the government with a common front on
economic policy.[7] Because of its importance it has representation on
such high-level government policy bodies as the Council of State, the
Council on Foreign Trade, and the National Electricity Administration. From the government's point of view, FEPRINCO is also a handy
device for marshaling the business community behind its policies.
For instance, in 1963 Stroessner called on the private sector for help
in combating inflation. Having already persuaded the labor unions to
accept a wage freeze, he was able to pressure FEPRINCO to accept a
schedule of officially set prices. Influence and cooperation work both
ways.

The private sector does not always speak with a single voice, however. In 1973 the UIP, which embraces 22 different industrial federa-

tions and 180 individual firms, pulled out of FEPRINCO in a dispute over tariff policy. Most of FEPRINCO's members support free trade, whereas the industrialists favor protectionism. Because of its size and importance the UIP also has representation on the Council of State, the Council of Foreign Trade, the Industrial Board of the Ministry of Industry and Commerce, and the administrative board of the Central Bank.[8]

Whatever their disputes over certain policies, Paraguayan businessmen share many basic attitudes. They are generally favorable to the Stroessner regime, but are critical of certain aspects of it. Like businessmen elsewhere, they feel that the government is not providing enough tax incentives and credit to encourage the private sector, and they view with concern the expansion of the public bureaucracy and the growing tendency toward government economic planning. They are also severely critical of the "political discrimination" and "personal pull" involved in getting a license, a loan, or a government contract. Above all, they complain about the officially tolerated smuggling, which undercuts the profits of law-abiding merchants and manufacturers.[9]

Nevertheless, Paraguayan businessmen admit that they have gained from the government's economic program. They make no secret of their admiration for the authoritarian-capitalist approach to development as exemplified in the Brazilian model—which is Stroessner's approach too. In their view, Brazil's recent progress began when the generals overthrew the radicals and demagogues, restored labor discipline, and encouraged the private sector.[10] Stroessner has taken a similar tack. In Paraguay the labor unions have been under government control since 1958. Economic and political stability has encouraged savings and investment. Trade and industry have been stimulated by improvements in transportation and electric power.

Tourism is another area in which the government has encouraged the growth of private enterprise. Enjoying their country's new prosperity, Brazilian tourists have flocked to Paraguay in increasing numbers to take advantage of the cheap prices. Their number has grown from some thirty thousand in 1966 to nearly two hundred thousand visitors a year by 1978, which brings in around $250 million annually. The National Development Bank has been eager to extend loans to local entrepreneurs who will expand the country's tourist facilities, causing a large increase in the number of hotels, restaurants, gift shops, tourist agencies, exchange houses, and similar services. In turn, this generates many new jobs in the service sector.

To reform the agricultural sector, Stroessner has enlisted the support of the economically influential. The government paid lip service to agrarian reform and set up an Institute for Rural Welfare, but very little private property has been redistributed. The agrarian reform law exempts all holdings of ten thousand square hectares or less from expropriation, and affects only that portion of the estate in excess of ten thousand hectares. Agrarian reform, which in Paraguay means setting up peasant colonies on state-owned lands, is poorly financed and administered. Often the land to be colonized is not cleared, and the new settlers are furnished only a few hand tools for the job. Beyond that they receive little technical assistance or credit to help them through the first years. In brief, not much has been done to change the lopsided land tenure system in which a few giant *latifundios* dominate rural life. Stroessner has preferred not to antagonize the powerful Paraguayan Rural Association (the ranchers' pressure group) or the big farmers' National Society of Agriculture.[11]

This does not imply a lack of interest in modernizing agriculture, however. Stroessner's economic program depends for its success on his ability to induce landowners to raise agricultural production— especially for export—in order to earn capital for investment. The large farmers, who already have the money and experience, can contribute the most if they agree to modernize. Therefore, the regime is doubly concerned not to antagonize this key group by policies aimed at land redistribution. Moreover, giving land to the peasants might actually lower output in the short run. More production, not social justice, is the paramount value for Stroessner.

But to modernize production the traditional elite must cooperate. So far the government has been successful in using fiscal incentives to encourage farmers to diversify production by introducing new cash crops, such as soybeans and coffee. One interesting experiment of this sort was the national wheat plan introduced by Humberto Bertoni, who took over the Ministry of Agriculture in 1968. His aim was to get more farmers to raise wheat, so that domestic production might rise from seven thousand to twenty thousand tons yearly. Since Paraguay consumes about one hundred thousand tons of wheat a year, this bit of import substitution was expected to save the country around $8 million annually.

To get the program started the Central Bank authorized the National Development Bank to extend up to 20 million *guaranis* in loans to farmers who would increase the acreage sown to wheat. The farmers' response was highly favorable: between 1968 and 1969 the amount of wheat acreage rose from twenty-one thousand to sixty thousand acres. What is more, fifty thousand tons of wheat were produced—two and a half times Bertoni's goal and about half of Paraguay's needs.

More credits were soon forthcoming for land clearance, seeds, fertilizer, and machinery. Moreover, the government provided other incentives such as high fixed prices and bonuses for exceptional yields. As a result, by the end of 1973 Paraguay was not only supplying all of its own domestic needs, but even exported some $40 million worth of wheat. Moreover, the wheat plan had important side effects. First, the encouragement of mechanization resulted in bigger yields for crops other than wheat, such as corn, rice, beans, and sorghum. Consequently, the growth rates registered for agriculture have risen dramatically, from a yearly average of only 1.7 percent from 1965 to 1970, to 5.8 percent from 1970 to 1974, and to about 11.5 percent from 1974 to 1978.[12] Second, because intensive wheat cultivation will exhaust the land, the government has encouraged rotating it with soybeans or garden crops such as tomatoes, onions, potatoes, or fruit. As a result, these products have become more abundant in the domestic market and have even begun to take their place alongside such traditional products as meat, timber, cotton, and tobacco in the export market.

The Role of Foreign Capital

In August 1959, Stroessner went before a FEPRINCO assembly to answer the businessmen's criticism of his tight money policies. A stable currency, he told them, was absolutely necessary to gain foreign investors' confidence. And attracting capital from abroad was essential to development, for neither the domestic private sector nor the state had sufficient resources for the job. He told his audience, "I feel proud in proclaiming that the general prosperity of this nation is based directly on the factors of firmness and tranquility which my government has managed to establish. . . . Economic development . . . is unobtainable except through the incorporation of new capital and new techniques, which will never be obtained from abroad . . . save through measures that facilitate our access to international investors. To do that the government must guarantee its ability to preserve the Nation's peace."[13] In short, a sound *guaraní* and a strong government capable of preserving order were necessary to create a favorable investment climate.

The attraction of foreign capital has been a favorite theme of Stroessner's almost from the beginning. In early 1955 new investors were offered a variety of incentives ranging from exemptions from customs duties to easy access to the Central Bank's exchange reserves for the purpose of remitting profits. More comprehensive still was the law of November 1970, which provided for substantial tax reductions and easy remittances of profits, interest, and royalties for new industries. Particularly favored were those investments that contributed to Paraguay's exports or found new means to process local raw materials. Other beneficiaries of the law were industries that promoted import substitution by producing goods that previously had been purchased abroad, that increased employment, or that made for a more efficient use of local resources.[14]

Because of the political uncertainty of Stroessner's first years in power, direct foreign investment continued the exodus that had begun after the civil war. By 1967, however, the situation had stabilized. Moreover, Stroessner's program of internal improvements had opened up new opportunities for trade and investment. Since the mid-1960s, therefore, foreign investment has been on the upswing; currently Paraguay receives between $20 million and $30 million a year in private capital from abroad.

In addition to tax inducements and political stability, another large factor in attracting foreign capital to Paraguay has been the building of hydroelectric dams on the Argentine and Brazilian borders, for in the past a chronic shortage of electric power was a major obstacle to industrialization. Now investments by Argentine, Brazilian, American, and Italian firms are flowing into the areas of lumber processing, sugar refining, textiles, cellulose and paper, food processing, and construction. A Brazilian firm may even set up a steel mill. Such stepped-up investment is reflected in the high industrial growth rates that have characterized Paraguay's economy in the 1970s: about 8 percent annually in manufacturing, 9 percent in transportation, and over 11 percent in construction. However, such increases are relative to a very small base; industry still contributes only about 15 percent to Paraguay's total gross domestic product.[15]

Most foreign capital comes in the form of loans rather than direct investments. The bulk of it is from foreign governments and international lending institutions. Almost all these loans go toward underwriting the government's infrastructural projects. Consequently, even though Stroessner favors private enterprise, and even though the rates of foreign private investment and domestic private investment have been rising, the state has assumed a leading role in the development process. Partly because basic internal improvements are so costly and often unprofitable and partly because they are so central to the society, the government's responsibilities have grown enormously.

The Role of the State

In the IMF's original stabilization plan the state's main function was to stimulate private enterprise by creating the conditions necessary for it to flourish. Besides stabilizing the currency and encouraging exports, that meant building roads to facilitate commerce, constructing dams to provide the power to run factories, and improving education and health to develop a more skilled and productive labor force. Government investment in all those areas has increased under Stroessner, and especially since 1965 the rate of spending has accelerated.

More than half of all public funds have gone into improving transportation and communications. In line with the stabilization plan's assumption that economic growth depends on increasing exports, the river fleet has been expanded and modernized, so that today Paraguay's new cargo, passenger, and freezer ships are the most up-to-date on the Paraná River. Other large sums have been spent on building the President Stroessner International Airport and in outfitting the passenger and cargo planes in the state's three airline companies.

But the centerpiece of Stroessner's transportation policy is the system of improved highways and farm-to-market roads that has opened up the interior as well as linked Paraguay to Brazilian markets. Between 1955 and 1975 the road network was expanded from 1,166 to 7,477 kilometers, and the asphalted part of that from 95 to over 900 kilometers. The most important of these roads is the Paraguay-Brazil highway, which gives Paraguay an alternative to its traditional dependence on Argentina for an outlet to the sea. Soon after Juscelino Kubitschek took office in 1955 as president of Brazil, he extended a friendly hand to Stroessner, who at that time was fencing with the military government in Buenos Aires over the Perón question. Substantial loans were made, which permitted Paraguay to extend a paved highway to the Brazilian border and to build a bridge over the Paraná River, thus connecting the cities of Asunción and São Paulo. In addition, Brazil granted Paraguay free-port privileges at the Atlantic ports of Santos and Paranaguá.

Stroessner was quick to seize this new counterweight to Argentina. Shortly before the new president had come to office, the Cháves government had signed an agreement to form an economic union with Argentina that would have turned much of Paraguay's economy over to her stronger neighbor. Stroessner now put this aside, and a pro-Brazilian emphasis became increasingly apparent in his speeches. In his message to the opening session of Congress in 1957, when tension with Argentina was at its height, he told the congressmen triumphantly: "It is no longer just the river which carries us south. A road is about to open us a door to the Atlantic, toward the east, through the territory of Brazil." Two years later, when the highway was completed and paved, Stroessner spoke to Congress in terms that showed more clearly the new diplomatic reality. He noted that Argentina was willing at last to send her foreign minister to Asunción to discuss free navigation on the Paraná—"which makes us glad to be united in overcoming problems that might have divided us." But that was faint praise in contrast with his assertion that Brazil was pursuing a "grand policy of spiritual and material friendship," which offered Paraguay "valiant and generous cooperation." Brazilian goodwill deserved the "affectionate feelings of all Paraguayans," whom President Kubitschek had called "the golden people." As for Kubitschek himself, Stroessner considered him "illustrious"—a "great president" and "brilliant proponent of the Good Neighbor Policy."[16]

Thus, Paraguay's development became intertwined with its foreign relations. As Argentina's economy went from crisis to crisis in the 1960s, its influence over Paraguay declined. By contrast, Brazil's growing prosperity made that country an increasingly important source of development capital. This shift in the regional balance of power, and its relation to Paraguay's internal growth, was highlighted most dramatically by the issue of harnessing the Paraná River's hydroelectric potential.

The Upper Paraná, which flows along the borders of Paraguay, Argentina, and Brazil, is interrupted in several places by huge waterfalls whose electric energy potential is tremendous. As industrialized countries, Argentina and Brazil are eager to build dams along this river, especially since the oil crisis of the 1970s sent their energy costs skyrocketing. To do so, however, they need Paraguay's cooperation, for Paraguayan sovereignty extends to the middle of the river (that is, to the channel). As a result, Paraguay—without having to put up any substantial financing itself—has been able to demand joint control over all such projects, as well as half of the energy produced.

The first joint project, with Argentina, was the Acaray Falls Dam, which opened in 1969 with an output of 90,000 kilowatts. Since Paraguay's share was far more than it needed, it sold the surplus back to Argentina, becoming an exporter of electric energy. The Acaray project was soon dwarfed by an even more ambitious scheme wherein Paraguay and Brazil would collaborate to build a dam at Itaipú, further upstream. When completed in 1988 it would be the world's largest hydroelectric project, generating some 10.7 million kilowatts. Again, since Paraguay could not hope to absorb more than a fraction of its share of the output, it would sell the surplus to Brazil, at an estimated profit of about $200 million a year. Although Stroessner's opponents criticized certain clauses in the treaty that, it was said, failed to protect Paraguay's rights over the project, this criticism could not mar the fact that the projected revenues would just about equal Paraguay's current gross national product.[17]

Argentina, however, was alarmed that its influence over Paraguay was being challenged so directly by Brazil. At first the government in Buenos Aires tried to browbeat the Paraguayans, as it had in the past. It claimed that the Itaipú project might lower the water level on the Paraná to such an extent that Argentine ships could not get up to Asunción. But to Argentina's surprise Paraguay rejected the note and informed its southern neighbor that it was going ahead with the dam. Trying the soft approach, a second Argentine note pointed out that, after all, Itaipú was only a few miles from the Argentine border. Surely some site on the Argentine side would do as well. In fact, the note suggested two possible sites. That note was rejected as well. Raúl Sapena Pastor, the Paraguayan foreign minister, was reported to have told the Argentines that "Paraguay will not involve itself in any project with any other country without the prior agreement of Brazil."[18]

After that Argentina could do nothing but sulk. When the Itaipú treaty was signed in 1973, it temporarily withdrew its ambassador from Brasilia to show its displeasure. For Stroessner's fifth presidential inauguration a few weeks later Argentina canceled its plans to send a big delegation and instead sent only an anti-Brazilian historian. Perhaps in reply, Stroessner ordered the border closed for a few days, alleging guerrilla activity on the Argentine side.

Subsequently, however, Paraguay and Argentina realized that they, too, had a common interest in exploiting the Upper Paraná's hydroelectric potential, and Argentina recovered some of the diplomatic ground it had lost. Two of the important new projects planned were the Yaciretá and Corpus dams. Although Brazil insisted that Corpus was incompatible with the Itaipú project, Paraguay informed the Brazilians that Corpus was an exclusively bilateral affair between Paraguay and Argentina. To underline the Paraguayans' independence, Stroessner announced that his country would not change its electric grid, which was compatible with Argentina's, to make it conform to Brazil's. The diplomatic negotiations concerning the La Plata Basin and the coordination of the several hydroelectric projects planned along the Paraná are complicated. But through it all, Stroessner has managed to play a clever neutralist game, playing off the two giant rivals and reaping advantages from both sides.[19]

After transportation and energy most the government's spending on infrastructure goes to education, health, and housing. The amounts allocated to them are far from adequate, however. Stroessner's boast that an average of one new school building has gone up for every week that he has been in power may or may not be true. But at least an effort is being made to bring primary schooling to every village and hamlet in the nation, and official figures indicate that illiteracy has declined from one out of three to only one out of five Paraguayans. However, qualified teachers are still in short supply—especially in the rural schools—and both textbooks and other school equipment are sadly lacking.[20]

In the area of health and sanitation, one of Stroessner's showcase projects is Asunción's system of fresh running water. Until 1958 the houses of the capital had had to obtain fresh water from peddlers who brought it into town in jugs or cans that were carried in carts or tied to the backs of donkeys—a picturesque survival of the pre-industrial world, but also a spreader of disease. More recently, storm drains were installed along the downtown streets, which in years past were often flooded by sudden tropical downpours. Yet another much-vaunted program is the new system of rural clinics, which, though rudely equipped by modern standards, offer medical assistance where none was available before. Today Paraguay has almost 1,300 hospitals and clinics, compared to only 68 when Stroessner first took office.

So little capital has been provided for new home construction (as opposed to commercial buildings, whose market is booming) that it is estimated that there is a shortage of more than a quarter of a million units. Moreover, much of the existing housing, especially in the interior, is quite rudimentary. According to a 1972 census the average Paraguayan house had only two rooms, mud floors, no running water or electricity, no inside toilet, and no system of sewage disposal. To be sure, things were much better in the capital, but even there conditions were still poor when compared with many other Latin American cities.

The Balance Sheet

In order to assess Stroessner's record in fostering economic development, it is necessary to consider first what material benefits have been achieved for the country as a whole, and second what groups have gained most from his policies.[21] Considering the broad accomplishments of the regime, Stroessner can claim with justifiable pride that Paraguay has one of the highest economic growth rates in Latin America—an average annual rise of 8 percent in the gross domestic product since 1974. Moreover, that figure is not bloated by inflation, for Stroessner has remained committed to a hard currency. Between 1964 and 1974 the cost of living rose by a yearly average of only 9 percent, which is very conservative by Latin American standards. The oil crisis of the mid-1970s threatened that policy, however: in 1975 the cost of living jumped over 25 percent. The regime responded with a tough program of fiscal and wage controls, with the result that in 1976 the rise in the cost of living was only 6.7 percent. However, this policy of tight money also threatened to bring on a recession: in 1976 the growth rate, which had been 8 percent the year before, dropped to only 6.5 percent. A looser monetary policy in 1977 allowed inflation to move back up to 9 percent—although the gross domestic product also rose an impressive 11.8 percent. Thus, the regime has been able to keep inflation under control without sacrificing growth.

The economic progress of the 1970s is changing the character of Paraguayan society. Trade figures show a considerable growth in the economy. Between 1953 and 1977 the value of exports went from $30.7 million to $278.9 million, while imports increased from only $56.2 million to $255.3 million. In other words, many more goods are being produced, traded, and consumed. Although Paraguay's exports are still predominantly agricultural, new products such as tung oil, vegetable oils, coffee, and soybeans are helping to diversify the country's approach to world markets. Wheat, which once led the list of imports, is now produced in sufficient quantity at home. Much the same is true of textiles. On the other hand, the purchase of fuels, lubricants, vehicles, machinery, and tools has sharply increased. All of this reflects the steady growth of industry in Paraguay, as well as the mechanization of agriculture.

Economic growth has been accompanied by an increase in population, which just about doubled between 1950 and 1975—from 1.3 to 2.5 million. Asunción has become a burgeoning city of around a half million people, with modern hotels and stores jutting up above the older colonial-style buildings downtown. Cars, trucks, and jeeps have crowded out the donkey and horsecart, so that the once sleepy atmosphere has given way to a boom-town spirit.

Another bustling region is the area lying along the Brazilian border, where new roads have opened up opportunities for trade and colonization. Puerto Presidente Stroessner, along the Paraguay-Brazil highway, has grown in a few years from a rude village into an important commercial center, and the land around the Itaipú dam site has attracted a horde of settlers, speculators, and construction workers. The 1972 census shows that the provinces bordering Brazil are the fastest growing in the country.

That points to a serious problem for Stroessner, however. Part of Paraguay's population growth is the result, of course, of natural increase—especially since the infant mortality rate has been reduced by almost two-thirds in the last twenty years. Another cause is the partial political amnesty granted by Stroessner as part of the liberalization program of the mid-1960s, which encouraged many exiles to return. Yet another cause of growth is that many Paraguayans who lived abroad because economic opportunities were better in Argentina or Brazil have now returned to take advantage of the expanding opportunities at home. Nevertheless, when all these factors have been taken into account, it is still true that a major cause of population growth is the large and steady influx of Brazilian immigrants into the easternmost provinces. Although the Colorado party press lauds these settlers as loyal and diligent contributors to the national economy, many Paraguayans are concerned that in large parts of their country Portuguese has replaced Spanish and Guaraní as the dominant language. The opposition parties have been quick to take up this issue, alleging that Brazilian economic, cultural, and political influence now poses as great a threat to Paraguay's independence as Argentine influence once did. It has become one of their most popular themes.

Nevertheless, economic progress has so far sheltered Stroessner's regime from adverse public opinion, for the benefits of that progress are being shared by a great many people. Between 1953 and 1974 the per capita GNP inched up from $200 to $282. That is certainly no startling jump; most Paraguayans are still living as subsistence farmers. Yet if the population grows by 3.5 percent and the economy grows by 8 percent, as they have in the 1970s, then the country as a whole is getting wealthier.

However, considering Stroessner's conservative bias, it is no surprise that the upper classes have been the biggest gainers from economic development and that the lower classes have gained the least. During the decade from 1960 to 1970 the portion of the total national income received by the bottom one-fifth of the working population dropped from 4 percent to only 3 percent; meanwhile, the portion received by the top 5 percent rose from 30 to 50 percent. Moreover, compensation paid to employees dropped as a percentage of the national income from 37.5 to 35.4 percent between 1962 and 1973.[22] These statistics indicate that the rich in Paraguay are certainly getting richer.

Obviously, in relative terms, this means that the poor are worse off than before. In absolute terms, however, the evidence is less clear. Research gathered by the Organization of American States shows that while wages rose by slightly more than one-third between 1970 and 1975, living costs went up by nearly 73 percent. Considering that labor unions are under firm government control and knowing Stroessner's eagerness to attract foreign capital, it is hard to escape the conclusion that workers' living standards are being sacrificed to promote capitalist economic development.[23] Yet this dreary situation is mitigated to some extent by the fact that the country now has practically full employment. It was estimated that in 1977–78 only about 4 percent of the adult population was without work. More than four thousand Paraguayan laborers had jobs at Itaipú, and the related expansion of the construction and service sectors absorbed thousands more. Furthermore, wages are only one indicator of general living standards. Better health care is also important, and the dramatic decline in infant mortality rates and the rise of life expectancy to sixty-two years, at present, which is one of the longest in Latin America today, indicate modest but real improvements in that area.

But the conclusion is unavoidable that Stroessner's programs have been aimed at securing for him the support of the wealthy and powerful. The traditional landowning class has been left undisturbed by any serious agrarian reform. It has benefited from government incentives and subsidies to mechanize and diversify production. Businessmen have been given relief from labor troubles, and their profits are protected by a stable currency. Foreign investors, especially, have benefited from tax exemptions. Meanwhile, the wide range of government economic activities has given the regime a large number of new patronage jobs to distribute among the military officers and Colorado *políticos*.

Finally, not the least among the regime's beneficiaries are its foreign creditors. Since many of the state's development projects are financed by borrowing abroad, the external debt has climbed rapidly— from about $11 million in 1956, to almost $23 million in 1960, to $115 million in 1973, and to $455.5 million at the end of 1976. That is a large sum for a small, poor nation, and the servicing of that debt—which the Central Bank estimates is equivalent to about one-fourth of Paraguay's export earnings—has now become the largest single item in the government's annual budget. That causes many

Paraguayans to worry about foreign creditors' acquiring too much influence over domestic policy.

However, Paraguay's finances seem essentially sound, and a default seems unlikely so long as current trends continue. Foreign capital, chiefly connected with the building of Itaipú, is flowing into the country at record levels. The Central Bank's foreign reserve holdings have never been higher. Moreover, much of the foreign debt is in the form of low-interest loans from international agencies and could presumably be easily renegotiated in an emergency. Above all, the large anticipated earnings from Itaipú and other similar projects ought to make it possible for Paraguay to repay its creditors with ease. Even at current levels Paraguay's annual debt service payments, in relation to its export earnings, are among the lowest in Latin America. Thus, with all these factors taken into consideration, Paraguay enjoys such a solid reputation in international financial circles that the IMF decided in 1976 to include the *guaraní* among the currencies acceptable for use in IMF transactions.[24]

Stroessner based his economic expansion on heavy borrowing from abroad, and he seems to have won his gamble. Even so, it might have been better to have raised more of that money at home. But Stroessner was afraid to anger his influential supporters by raising taxes, even though the original stabilization plan called for tax reform. Indeed, an income tax bill was introduced in Congress in 1970, but the congressmen, in a rare show of independence, pigeonholed it. Surprised by such resistance, Stroessner preferred to back down. A new bill sent to Congress the following year reduced the tax rates and provided for so many loopholes that it finally won acceptance. Therefore, although Paraguay now has an income tax, the revenues generated from it are insufficient, and that is why the regime still must engage in heavy foreign borrowing.

In sum, economic development has generated additional support for Stroessner. His government has acquired a high reputation with foreign bankers; it has earned the backing of big farmers and businessmen in Paraguay; and it has expanded the patronage opportunities for political loyalists. For members of the poorer classes the benefits of the system are far more modest, yet some do manage to obtain jobs in the government or the private sector, especially those who have a *patrón* in the Colorado party or the army. To the extent that this system provides Stroessner with mass support, it may be said that he is its chief beneficiary.

PART 4. THE OPPOSITION

Chapter 10. The Dilemmas of Opposition

General Stroessner's regime has long been considered one of the most repressive in all of Latin America. For example, in a recent study of the status of political oppositions in Latin America, Robert Dix put Paraguay at the very bottom of the scale in amount of freedom allowed.[1] However, although no one denies that Stroessner is a dictator, it may be questioned whether his regime is more cruel than that of his contemporaries in Brazil, Chile, or Cuba.

The status of the opposition in Paraguay is difficult to summarize neatly. Repression exists, but repression is hard to measure precisely. As W. Howard Wriggins observes:

> There are difficulties in exploring the matter of intimidation. Few cases are documented. Gossip is rife but reliable evidence is scarce. Scholars find it far from the ideal of politics and avoid it. Critics see it where it may in fact not exist. Moreover, since effective intimidation is largely in the mind of the person intimidated, it is extremely difficult to find unambiguous examples of it. A few cases of exemplary sanctions may render men timid who were not intended objects of government intimidation. Does intimidation then apply only when government intends it? If sanctions are threatened but never actually applied, can one say that intimidation was used? In some regimes the level of anxiety is high and intimidation seems ubiquitous. Even without identifiable instances of intimidation men may tiptoe carefully to avoid the sleeping giant of the sovereign's wrath. In others it is easier to associate intimidation with specific political acts.[2]

In Paraguay gossip is indeed rife—but documented cases of repression do exist. In 1966, and again in 1971, Amnesty International published reports on the treatment of political prisoners and concluded that conditions in Paraguay were "medieval." "As regards technique and organization," the latter report said, "the system of torture and repression is far less sophisticated than that of neighboring Brazil; yet it is extremely effective in a country like Paraguay with its history of dictatorship, low educational levels, and small-town atmosphere."[3]

Aid from the United States helped to build up Stroessner's coercive machinery. Until recently, when human rights considerations led to a sharp reduction in American support, the armed forces and the police received about $750,000 a year in various kinds of equipment, under the inter-American defense system set up in 1947 and under the 1964 bilateral military treaty. The aid to Paraguay was tailored to its jungle terrain: armored personnel carriers (instead of big tanks), light artillery, armored helicopters, transport planes, amphibians, patrol boats, landing craft, and light arms.[4] That is not heavy equipment that could stand up to a serious invasion by a large foreign power, nor was it intended for that purpose. American military aid was not aimed at preparing Paraguay for war but rather at controlling internal subversion. For that task the Paraguayan armed forces have the proper weaponry to maneuver rapidly in the country's swamps and forests. To train them in the use of this equipment, Paraguay sends men to the United States Army's School of the Americas at Fort Gulick, in the Canal Zone. Every year this school instructs dozens of Latin American military officers in the latest techniques of jungle warfare and military intelligence. The school also teaches the importance of enlisting popular support against guerrillas through community development programs. Until recently, Paraguay also sent a number of police officers to the International Police Academy in Washington, where they learned modern counterintelligence methods.[5]

The Paraguayan army has gained a savage reputation in its dealing with guerrillas. Its methods are simple and ruthless: they take no prisoners; invaders are shot without benefit of trial. For example, in December 1959 Argentine authorities in the river town of Clorinda reported that some twenty-five captured guerrillas were hauled aboard the Paraguayan gunboat *Humaitá*, anchored on the opposite shore, and were summarily executed in front of the astonished onlookers. In August 1960, seventeen mutilated bodies were fished out of the river near the Argentine town of Posadas. The Argentine government called for an investigation by the Organization of American States, charging that the Paraguayan army was torturing and executing captured guerrillas and dumping their bodies into the river. In reply Stroessner suggested that the rebels may have drowned trying to cross the river and that alligators must have attacked the corpses.

But it is also said that, years later, General Patrício Colmán used to enjoy displaying the preserved genitals of captured guerrillas to horrified members of visiting military missions.[6]

Police procedures have been equally brutal and arbitrary. Suspects are commonly picked up without a warrant and held incommunicado without formal charges. Often such prisoners receive no trial and may remain in jail for years. According to the constitution an individual has the right to legal counsel and to be arraigned before a judge within twenty-four hours of his arrest. In practice, though, the police often ignore writs of habeas corpus. A judge who issues such an order may be informed that the prisoner is being held by order of the president—under his state of siege powers the chief executive may suspend anybody's constitutional rights. Thus, the rule of law does not exist in Paraguay.[7]

Cases of arbitrary arrest and confinement are common. Captain Juan Speratti, a former navy officer who was the Febrerista party general secretary, was arrested in 1963, apparently as the result of a personal feud with a prominent Colorado. He remained in Asunción's Tacumbú Prison for two years without trial. One courageous judge issued a writ of habeas corpus, but the police rejected it. Months had elapsed without even the laying of formal charges against him when two men, Eustacio Arsenio Romero and Bernardo Benítez, were picked up by the police as suspects in a bomb plot. After rough questioning by the police the pair broke down, "confessed," and named a large number of people, including Speratti, as accomplices. Although Speratti had been in jail for the past eleven months and could not have been in contact with the plotters, that made no difference; the police finally had something to pin on him. That was important because the American embassy was pressuring the regime to liberalize and was particularly concerned about the Speratti case. The phoniness of the process against Speratti was soon made obvious, however, when Romero and Benítez were released under a Christmas amnesty. That was hardly the sort of treatment one would have expected for real terrorists. Speratti was also freed a few months later as part of the deal by which the Febrerista party received legal recognition. Later he even represented the Febreristas in Congress, without any objection from the government. That too was curious, for if Speratti had really been guilty of trying to assassinate Stroessner, it is hardly likely that he would have been tolerated inside the country, much less allowed to run for office.

Estimates of the number of political prisoners are always unreliable, but *Latin America*, a British weekly, placed the number in late 1978 at less than 20. That is largely the result of pressure by the

American embassy, which has been demanding that Stroessner improve his government's record on human rights. Previously, the estimates ranged much higher. In 1973, Señora Carmen Lara de Castro, a Radical Liberal party congresswoman who heads the unofficial Paraguayan Human Rights Commission, placed the number of political prisoners at 250. In 1966 Amnesty International put the number at around 150.[8] In any case, such estimates do not cover only prisoners of conscience, as both Señora Lara de Castro and Amnesty International will admit. Some of the people being held actually engaged in illegal acts against the regime, so they cannot really claim to be innocent victims. Other prisoners were jailed not for political reasons, but simply because—as in Speratti's case—they got on the wrong side of some official in the regime. For example, one of Señora Lara de Castro's cases was a taxi driver from the town of Areguá who was sent to jail because he was involved in a traffic accident in which an army officer was killed. In other cases people are held as hostages to discourage exiles who are suspected of plotting. Or the police may arrest someone to extort money from him. Although such prisoners are not, strictly speaking, political, the Human Rights Commission and Amnesty International take an interest in them—and properly so, for such cases are clear indications of the government's contempt for human rights and legal procedures.

The beating and torture of political prisoners by the police appears to be common. Although the regime denies this, the many stories with names, dates, and witnesses make the accusations impossible to ignore. In 1959 Catholic Action fought a case against the government all the way to the Supreme Court, claiming that three of its members had been subjected to police torture. Although the group finally lost the case, the government's action aroused the auxiliary bishop of Asunción, Monseñor Anibal Marícevich, to call on Ramón Duarte Vera, the police chief. At first Duarte Vera dismissed the charges as false, but he quickly backed down when the bishop presented him with a list of former prisoners he had interviewed, together with a description of the scars they had shown him. The police chief admitted that his subordinates had perhaps committed excesses and promised that it wouldn't happen again.[9]

Soon after that pressure from the army and the *democrático* Colorados forced the lifting of the state of siege. In the accompanying reform at police headquarters, Juan Erasmo Candia, the brutal head of the detective squad, was fired from his job and brought to trial on charges of having tortured prisoners. The government's backlash against the reforms at the end of May 1959 brought a new wave of cruelty. On 29 June, Victor Marcial Miranda, an eighteen-year-old student who had been arrested during the protest riots earlier in the month, died in the Asunción jail. According to other student prisoners he had been beaten with a whip and shocked with an electric cattle prod. And that is not the only death that has occurred at the hands of the Paraguayan police. In 1969, Juan José Farias, a member of the Radical Liberal party, died after a week of questioning at police head-quarters. The opposition weekly, *El Radical*, claimed that he had been tortured. All of the opposition parties boycotted the opening session of Congress in protest.[10]

According to several sources a favorite method of torture used by Duarte Vera's police was the "electric bath"—a practice that was invented in Argentina under Perón and was imported into Paraguay when that dictator and his entourage took refuge there in 1955. Here is one description of how prisoners who refused to sign prepared confessions were subjected to torture in a special little room at police headquarters:

> Electric cables hang down from a large box in the ceiling. Some are thick, some are thin, and there is also a tub filled with water in the room. There is also a rubber truncheon and an electric cattle prod. The prisoner is stripped and then beaten with the truncheon to "soften him up." After that they tie his arms and attach the slender electric cables to his fingers. Those cables, in turn, are connected to the thicker ones, through which the current flows.
>
> When everything is ready they turn on the electric mechanism. The victim cannot move, for he is bound tightly by leather straps. If it is necessary to "soften him up" still more he is then thrown into the tub by four or five men who push him under the water one, two, three, and more times, until he is almost suffocated. In the meantime, one of the torturers climbs on top of the tub and kicks him in the guts. Finally, they plunge one of the cables into the water.[11]

The author of that account is E. René Speratti, a brother of the naval officer whose case was discussed above. E. René Speratti is a retired army officer and a highly decorated veteran of the Chaco War, having been awarded the Defender's Cross and the Chaco Cross for his bravery. He and several other Febreristas were arrested in 1956 after an attempt by Colonel Franco to enter the country. He was first held at Tacumbú Prison and later was sent to Peña Hermosa, from which he escaped the following year. He claims that while at Tacumbú he was interrogated in the very room he describes.

Nor were these vicious practices abandoned with Duarte Vera's fall and the switch to liberalization. Amnesty International's investigations in 1971 of police brutality in Paraguay led it to the conclusion that "torture usually takes place immediately after arrest, during the interrogation stages. Both the Ministry of Interior and the Department of Crimes and Vigilance in Asunción carry out torture in their respective centres. Techniques seem to concentrate on physical brutality, although sexual abuse of women prisoners takes place within the comisarias [police stations], and families are also threatened. Torture is frequently witnessed by Army generals and by a prominent political figure, and is carried out by teams whose members include the mentally deficient and sexually disturbed."[12]

No doubt Stroessner would argue that if torture is repulsive so are the terrorists who resort to bombing, kidnapping, and assassination in the name of revolution. To terrorize the terrorists may require calling in brutes and sadists to deal with them. The inability of guerrilla armies or underground cells of revolutionaries to destabilize Stroessner's regime as they have other Latin American governments may be proof of the efficacy of his strategy. On the other hand, the opposition would argue that such internal peace is only a delusion, that it is only silence imposed by fear, and that some day a terrible price will have to be paid for it.

The Velvet Glove

Yet political opposition continues to exist in Paraguay. More than that, it exists openly—in contrast, say, to Cuba. This is one of the many curious features of Paraguayan politics that make it so difficult for an outsider to grasp. In totalitarian systems unbending persecution extends to all critics. In Paraguay, however, the treatment of opponents varies greatly with the individual, for there even enemies know each other on a first-name basis. That is because the political class—which means the university-educated class—is very small. Even among the 3 percent of the male population who form the leadership pool, many prefer to follow their business, professional, or intellectual careers, and others are temperamentally disinclined towards politics. What remains is a tiny group of political activists who are involved in the struggle for power. Often they grew up in the same neighborhoods, knew each other in school, and may even be related.

As a result, the political contest in Paraguay often includes a vicious element precisely because personal hatreds may be involved. But at the same time, because people know each other so well, there are informal pressures to limit repression. After all, the man next door may belong to another party, but he is also a lifelong acquaintance, a fellow professional, a classmate, or a cousin. On the whole, he is not a bad type. Certainly, he cannot be treated as less than human, and at the very least, his wife and children deserve compassion.

Out of this highly personal environment come certain unwritten rules of political conduct, a kind of chivalry which softens the struggle except in periods of extreme tension. Rather than execute their enemies, for instance, the victors in a power struggle exile them, for the positions may be reversed someday. If the requirements of the spoils system are that jobs in the government are reserved for *co-religionarios*, still a few posts may be scattered to opponents who do not cause trouble and who have good connections. This sort of code is similar to that which Juan Linz found operating in Franco's Spain: "In the tolerant stages of authoritarian regimes, even high officials maintain good private relations with persons known as opponents, do favors for them, and unconsciously perhaps, elicit information in return. . . . They are civilized men who can separate politics from friendship or colleagueship in the professions. Politics is not the only and highest value, even when, in moments of difficulty or danger, politics wins out, and contacts are broken off."[13]

Obviously this code cannot apply to the real revolutionary, who is intransigent and violent in his opposition to the regime. When many such radicals are active against the regime and pose a real threat to it, the range of tolerated activity narrows for the rest of the opposition as well. When the regime feels safe, however, the machinery of repression tends to relax.

Even in the worst periods, however, known members of the opposition parties are allowed to live and work in Paraguay. In earlier years they had to tread carefully and stay inconspicuous, but since the mid-1960s they have been permitted to organize their parties legally, to hold meetings, to publish newspapers, to contest elections, and to voice their opinions in Congress. To be sure, there are still limits. They must refrain from public attacks on the president or members of the armed forces, and they cannot organize public demonstrations. Of course they know that they will not be permitted to go beyond their present minority status in Congress.

Censorship of the press still exists, although it is applied somewhat unevenly. Surprisingly enough, severe criticism of the regime does get published, especially in the small opposition newspapers. However, editors run risks if they goad a prominent official too far. The two big

daily papers, *La Tribuna* and *ABC Color*, hew rather closely to government guidelines. They are businesses, and their owners would lose
financially if they were to be closed down or if the regime were to use
its influence to get businessmen to withdraw their advertising. Therefore, they carry little local political news other than government
handouts.

On one occasion *ABC Color* did carry some editorials critical of the
Itaipú Treaty and on another occasion it printed an account of the
arrest of certain prominent suspects, including Edgar Ynsfran, during
the investigation of the November 1974 assassination plot. For the
latter story *ABC*'s editor, Roberto Thompson, was put in *confino* for
three months. That is, the police sent him to a small hamlet in the
interior, where he was kept under close surveillance.[14] Germán
Ballasch Benítez, the editor of a monthly news magazine called
Diálogo, received a similar punishment when he printed a story poking fun at the pressure tactics used by Colorado leaders to get a mass
turnout for one of their public demonstrations of support for Stroessner. The regime was not amused, and Ballasch was "rusticated." Even
so, *Diálogo* continued to appear and held to its line of responsible
criticism.

The journals that belong to the opposition parties are more pugna-
cious. *Comunidad* operated for years as the weekly voice of radical
Catholic protest until the government finally closed it down in 1969.
But that step had been preceded by several warnings including official protests, the seizure of certain issues, and two temporary closures.
During its tenure *Comunidad* promoted a radical anti-Stroessner
campaign, calling for revolution. Not only was it put out of business
but its editor was chased into exile. *El Radical* and *El Pueblo*, the
Radical Liberal and Febrerista weeklies, continue to publish, although
not without harassment. *El Pueblo*'s existence is precarious because
the Febrerista party is so small. *El Radical* is more important. From
time to time the government shuts it down, but it always reappears.
In 1977 the Radical Liberal party split into right-wing collaboration-
ists and left-wing intransigents. At first *El Radical* belonged to the
latter, but when they lost legal recognition, the newspaper was inter-
vened and turned over to the officially recognized collaborationist
wing as a reward for its cooperation.[15]

Stroessner's relations with his opponents have gone through at least
three discernible phases. The first phase, which lasted until 1963, was
the most repressive. Stroessner was struggling to wrest the Colorado
party from the *epifanistas* and the *democráticos*, while fighting off
guerrilla invasions by the Liberal and Febrerista exiles. He was

merciless toward his enemies: the jails were filled, and protesters were clubbed in the streets; the bound and broken bodies that occasionally floated to the Argentine shores were a warning that the general meant business.

During the second phase a partial amnesty allowed many Liberals and Febreristas to return to Paraguay and even to participate in politics, subject to the limitations mentioned above. Political tensions were lessened, and more attention was paid to economic development. It seemed as though a new era of political reconciliation had begun, which might become a first step toward democracy.

However, in the third phase, which began toward the end of the 1960s, political tensions began to build again. A younger generation of Liberals, Febreristas, and Christian Democrats was becoming restive under the restrictions placed on their parties. Also, prompted by the social encyclicals of Pope John XXIII, the Catholic church was becoming an outspoken critic of the regime. Considering that Catholicism is the religion of a vast majority of the Paraguayan people, that was one of the most dangerous challenges Stroessner had faced. Once again he turned to strong-arm methods without, however, canceling all of the concessions made during the liberalization phase. Opposition parties were still allowed to exist and were guaranteed representation in Congress, but radical individuals in the parties and the clergy were beaten and jailed.

A closer look at these three periods will help illuminate the dilemmas that Stroessner posed to the opposition.

Violence and Counterviolence

Shortly after assuming office, Stroessner moved to strengthen his hand in dealing with his opponents. Like other right-wing dictators, he justified his extraconstitutional methods by citing the threat of communism. In October 1955 the Chamber of Representatives passed the Law for the Defense of Democracy, which legalized searches and arrests without warrants, as well as suspending other constitutional guarantees, to enable the president to proceed with his war against communism. Since communism was never defined by the law, the executive was able to interpret his powers broadly enough to justify the persecution of any critic of the regime. The first victims were the Colorados' old nemesis, the Liberal party. A few weeks after the law's passage Justo Prieto, the Liberal party chief, and six other members of his executive committee were seized in Asunción and escorted

across the border. The Febreristas suffered the same fate the following year.

Nevertheless, during brief periods, Stroessner eased the pressure.
In 1958 he told the Liberals that they could return, and he even allowed them to hold their first public convention since the civil war.
When the Liberals met that July, however, one of their first acts was
to pass a resolution condemning the dictatorship. The government
reacted strongly. Duarte Vera's police arrested thirty-two prominent
Liberals, and the party went back into exile. The following year,
Stroessner, under pressure from the army and the *democráticos*, lifted
the state of siege. Back came the Liberals and the Febreristas—only
to be sent scampering for the border two months later when the
government unleashed another brutal crackdown.

During this same period guerrilla warfare was becoming a popular
idea among the younger exiles. The "insurrectionist thesis" of direct,
violent action seemed to hold more promise than the more cautious
approach of the Liberal and Febrerista party elders. Armed groups
began to form outside the regular party organizations.[16] One of these
was the 14th of May Movement, led by Benjamín Vargas Peña, a
Liberal dissident. It launched the first of several invasions on 1 April
1958, when a band of its followers crossed the Upper Paraná and attacked the police garrison of Coronel Bogado, a small town in the
south. Although reinforcements finally drove them off, the attackers
managed to escape with a large quantity of arms and munitions.

A second guerrilla group was the Vanguardia Febrerista, formed
by Arnaldo Valdovinos. It merged with the 14th of May Movement,
and Valdovinos, using his contacts with Latin America's democratic-
left parties, is said to have secured financial support from Rómulo
Betancourt's government in Venezuela. However, Valdovinos and
Vargas Peña soon quarreled over who was to be the top leader and the
Vanguardia left the coalition.

Not long after that the 14th of May Movement split again. This
time Vargas Peña was challenged by a young hothead named Juan
José Rotela. Fired by Fidel Castro's example in Cuba, Rotela had no
time for Vargas Peña's careful organizing tactics. He gathered about
him a splinter group of guerrillas, and on the night of 12 December
1959 he made a two-pronged invasion of Paraguay. The main force
of about 1,000 men, which he headed himself, aimed at the city of
Encarnación. Meanwhile, a smaller diversionary group crossed the
Paraná further upstream. Both units met disaster. Government troops
encircled the diversionary group as soon as it reached the Paraguayan
shore and wiped it out to a man. Troops also drove Rotela's band

from Encarnación, inflicting heavy losses, and blocked its escape route to the river. In panic, the guerrillas broke into small groups and scattered. Only a few of them ever made it back to safety, for Stroessner's soldiers, aided by Colorado peasants, hunted them down relentlessly. Rotela himself was killed.

His fate did not discourage other young revolutionaries, though. It was considered a glorious fate to die fighting tyranny. Besides, for them, Castro's triumph showed that the insurrectionist thesis *had* to work, given the proper implementation. Moreover the Cubans were sending money and advisors to the Paraguayans. A new, Communist-dominated front, called the United National Liberation Front (FULNA), appeared. It soon had the entire field of guerrilla operations to itself, for the 14th of May group never recovered from a second disastrous invasion in April 1960, and the Vanguardia Febrerista lost most of its members when Colonel Franco expelled Valdovinos from the party for insubordination.

On 3 May 1960 FULNA infiltrated a small squad of seventeen men into Paraguay from Brazil and attacked the village of Capitan Bado. The local police repulsed them, however, and a few days later army troops cut them to pieces as they tried to get back across the border. Next, a much larger force, estimated at about two hundred, entered to establish a base in the jungle along the Upper Paraná, but the army quickly discovered them. The government troops wiped out the guerrillas in a pitched battle and threw their bodies into the river. Finally, FULNA launched an invasion on 20 December which aimed almost directly at Asunción. Once again the guerrillas were met almost as soon as they landed. After a short, fierce clash they fled under the cover of night. The next day some twenty-five forlorn survivors were picked up by an Argentine ship as they huddled on an island in the middle of the Paraguay River.

Several factors made the failure of the insurrectionist thesis in Paraguay inevitable. First, the guerrillas had not, like the Cubans, established any base in the peasantry. The vast majority of Paraguayan peasants were Colorado *py nandí*, who simply informed the authorities whenever strangers appeared. Second, Stroessner's army, unlike Batista's, was well trained and spirited. Third, the exile community was riddled with Stroessner's spies, so that the government always knew when and where an invasion was to take place. And fourth, such invasions placed relatives and friends inside Paraguay in danger, for the police would often retaliate by arresting and interrogating them. Thus this radical strategy quickly lost its appeal for the Liberals and Febreristas.

Liberalization

Although the insurrectionist thesis was discarded, Liberal and Febrerista party leaders still felt a responsibility to act. Many of their followers' families had been separated since the civil war. They were
growing more homesick, and they were concerned about their children
growing up in foreign lands, without memories of the homeland or a
sense of patriotism toward it. Moreover, the lives of most exiles were
ones of economic hardship. Unless the party leaders could find a way
to return, they stood a good chance of losing their supporters. In any
case, it was in these leaders' own interest to get back to Paraguay, for
a new generation might grow up unfamiliar with their names.

Some of the more intransigent exiles vowed never to compromise
with Stroessner. As for Stroessner, he refused to have anything to do
with either the Communists or those left-wing Colorados in exile who
had recently formed the Popular Colorado Movement (MOPOCO). But
the majority of exiles, those with moderate or conservative views, began to accept the "accommodationist thesis," justifying it as the highest sort of statesmanship. It was argued that Paraguay had to return
to "institutional normality," which meant that the government and
the opposition had to learn to get along without violence.

Stroessner could also gain by reaching an accommodation with the
opposition. In the first place, the guerrilla invasions had raised tensions inside Paraguay to an uncomfortable level. The government
preferred peace too. After all, as F. G. Bailey observes, political feuding "has to be paid for in the time spent on it, in comforts, and even
necessities foregone, even in lives lost. In this sense political competition is parasitic on other forms of social interaction."[17] In Paraguay
the continued violence and the oppressive atmosphere of an ubiqui-
tous police state frightened off trade and investment.

Beyond that, the newly inaugurated Kennedy administration in
Washington was threatening right-wing dictatorships with the loss of
American aid unless they reformed. To prevent that, Stroessner had
to make some nod in the direction of democracy. Finally, compromise
might work to his advantage by dividing the opposition. Radicals and
moderates might split their parties over whether to accept the proffered olive branch. Moreover, Stroessner let it be known that as part
of the compromise the opposition parties would have to dissolve all
political fronts, such as the Unión Paraguaya, which had been established recently by the Liberals and Febreristas to coordinate their
policy against the regime.

In return for acting moderately and "responsibly" the opposition
parties would be allowed to return, to participate in the political

process, and to get their views before the public through their newspapers, political campaigns, and the minority of seats accorded them in Congress. To put it another way, by accepting this bargain the Liberals, Radical Liberals, and Febreristas agreed to become what Juan Linz calls an "a-legal" opposition. Instead of challenging the regime's legitimacy they would offer "constructive" criticism. In return, they would be tolerated.[18]

As Linz points out, however, an a-legal opposition runs the risk of getting a reputation as a pseudoopposition. The relatively easy life of a tolerated party contrasts badly with the martyrdom suffered by the regime's intransigent enemies, who continue to be jailed, exiled, or shot. In time, the party's younger generation may come to view their moderate elders as having sold out. Then they may either desert them or try to replace them. As the next chapter will show, that is just what happened in Paraguay.

Moderates can do little to defend themselves against their radical critics except to insist that their strategy will pay off in the long run. That defense always appears weak, however, because of the many restrictions on what they can do to be effective at the moment. They may protest the regime's measures, but only mildly, and their protests often do not get much publicity in the daily press. Since they are only a minority in Congress, they cannot hope to stop any government bill or even impose any amendments. Thus, the a-legal opposition cannot hope to make any real impact. If, in frustration, it tries to appeal to the public directly—to organize, say, a mass demonstration—it risks a confrontation with the police and the loss of its legality.

Having gotten a toehold in the system, the moderate opposition leaders are loath to surrender what they consider as hard-won gains. Besides, they know that most of the rank and file do not want to return to exile—and indeed, would probably not follow them there. What is more, even verbal radicalism may backfire by frightening off some of the groups—the military, the economic elites, and influential foreign embassies—which the opposition hopes to entice away from the dictator's coalition. Still, a revolt by the younger party members is a traumatic experience. It is disturbing to think that the organization is losing its appeal to the coming generations. So the moderates have a dilemma. Linz summarizes it well: "The main victims in this process are the men who could be the leaders of a democratic center-right. . . . They are carried by their younger collaborators—students and intellectuals—into positions that do not fit either their own social backgrounds or the constituencies they might successfully appeal to."[19]

Nevertheless, those dilemmas were not so obvious in 1963, when

Carlos and Fernando Levi Ruffinelli, two rising young Liberals, formed the Renovationist faction of the Liberal party and sought legal recognition from the regime. That action brought their expulsion from the party, but it also met with a favorable response from Stroessner, who invited the Renovationists to participate in the general elections of that year. Although they lost, as predicted, they received seats in the Chamber of Representatives. Moreover, their presidential candidate, Ernesto Gavilán, was appointed ambassador to England. Soon afterwards the Renovationists were granted official recognition as the Liberal party.

The next group to seek recognition was the Febrerista party. Once the great party of students, labor, and the reformist military, the Febreristas had withered in exile. Nearly a generation had passed since the civil war, and they had grown out of touch with Paraguayan youth. Moreover, they had succumbed to factionalism. While the more moderate Febreristas had remained loyal to Colonel Franco, the radicals had become increasingly critical of his leadership. When he denounced the guerrilla invasions and expressed concern about the Cuban Revolution's gravitation toward communism, the radicals determined to oust him as party president. In 1962 at the party's convention the Febreristas had split, and Colonel Franco and his moderates had expelled the radicals as "Communists" and "fellow travellers." That made them acceptable to Stroessner, who granted them legality in August 1964. The Febreristas returned to Paraguay much weakened, but hopeful of rebuilding their following among the workers, students, and cadets.[20]

That left only the old Liberals and the MOPOCOs to carry on the fight. There was little hope of those two groups getting together, however. Some left-wing Liberals like Carlos Pastore were friendly with the *epifanistas*, but most Liberals could not bridge the old party hatreds. After all, those same MOPOCOs, when in power, had been happy to persecute them. By 1967 the old Liberals became convinced of the futility of carrying on the struggle from exile and agreed to petition for legal recognition too. Stroessner demanded two minor concessions: the Liberals could not call themselves the Liberal party, because that label was already officially granted to the Renovationists, and the amnesty would not extend to Pastore, or anyone else with MOPOCO connections. The Liberals accepted the terms; they renamed themselves the Radical Liberal party, left Pastore and his clique behind, and returned to Paraguay just in time to participate in the February 1967 elections for a constitutional convention.

The opposition parties quickly learned that their freedom to participate was to be strictly limited. In many cases their followers found it difficult to get registered to vote. Also, there was blatant fraud and intimidation at several of the polling places, especially in the small towns of the interior. The press gave scant coverage to their meetings, and their access to the radio was limited to brief broadcasts carried at very early or very late hours. Their candidates were heckled and harried, and their propaganda was often seized by rowdies. By contrast, the Colorados ran a slick, well-heeled campaign with plenty of publicity. As a result, they easily outdistanced their floundering rivals with 68.7 percent of the vote—to only 20.9 percent for the Radical Liberals, 6.1 percent for the Liberal party, and only 2.7 percent for the Febreristas.

The results were similar in the general elections held the following year. Stroessner won the presidency by a predictable landslide, and the Colorados—entitled to two-thirds of all congressional seats as the majority party—elected twenty senators and forty deputies. The Radical Liberals got nine senators and sixteen deputies, the Liberals got one senator and three deputies, and the Febreristas elected one deputy.

So began the new era of liberalization. The opposition parties tried to play the parliamentary game, but had not the slightest hope of coming to power. Rather than lead gradually toward real democracy or even allow the opposition parties a breathing spell in which to rebuild their bases inside the country, liberalization seemed to be simply providing Stroessner with a facade for his dictatorship—a ploy to bargain away the opposition's integrity for a few meaningless parliamentary seats. That conclusion eventually divided the Radical Liberals and Febreristas, as many of their supporters became convinced that liberalization was a dead end. The frustration they felt was aptly summarized by *Diálogo*: "The dilemma of the political parties of the opposition is that they know perfectly well they will not win the general elections, whether they run together or separately. Nor have they any hope of coming to power by force. Their chances are even slimmer there. . . . Thus, Paraguay's political life revolves around a single person. He is one of the most capable politicians of recent times. And he is perhaps the last national caudillo."[21]

The Clergy's Challenge

Stroessner's problems were still not over, however, for by 1969 a new and formidable opposition had risen against him. This time it came from an unexpected quarter: the Roman Catholic church. That posed a ticklish problem, for social life in Paraguay is closely tied to religion. Birth, marriage, and death take place in the context of Catholic ritual. Practically every home has its crucifix or pictures of saints. Outside the home scarcely a public ceremony does not include the parish priest. Religious feasts are public holidays, and even the constitution requires that the president be a Catholic.

The clergy's attack on the regime came as a surprise and aroused a particularly fierce sense of indignation. The church in Paraguay had always been politically neutral. The model of a Paraguayan churchman was the much-revered Monseñor Juan Sinforiano Bogarín, who for nineteen years—until his death in 1949—was archbishop of Asunción. His career spanned the period from the Chaco War to the civil war. During the many upheavals in between he remained on good terms with all the parties and tried to use his prestige to moderate political conflict whenever possible, without taking sides. In the second place, the state traditionally assumed the burden of paying for the maintenance of church buildings and the support of the clergy. In return for this, the president had the right to participate in the nomination of priests and bishops. This was the legacy of the old *patronato real* exercised by the Spanish crown, by which church and state were to be mutually supportive.

After Monseñor Bogarín's death his place was taken by Archbishop Anibal Mena Porta. Following his predecessor's example, Mena Porta concentrated on such matters as reinvigorating the faith among parishioners and improving ecclesiastical administration. The problems of the declining numbers of young men entering the priesthood and of the constant need to find money to support the church's charity work occupied his attention. What little politics he engaged in was limited to sitting on the Council of State, where he seldom spoke, or to lobbying Stroessner for more aid. Since the archbishop accepted ecclesiastical patronage as the government's duty, he saw nothing wrong in its allowing the church to import, duty-free, such things as cars, typewriters, or electrical appliances. Nor did he feel guilty when Stroessner provided him with a limousine and a chauffeur, or when he presented him with a medal for his "patriotic services."[22]

The first sign of any trouble came on 22 February 1958 when Father Ramón Talavera, a parish priest in a poor *barrio* of Asunción, grew so indignant over the regime's brutality that he openly criticized it before his congregation. He excoriated the fraudulent elections and the unfair treatment of the opposition parties, and he spared no one in his attack, even accusing the army of being more interested in graft than in upholding the constitution. Finally the sermon ended with a call for "active resistance to the tyranny."

News of this event traveled fast, and by the end of the day Father Talavera was under arrest. The police held him only a few hours, however, and released him with a warning. Not only did they hesitate to beat up a priest, but Talavera's family were wealthy and prominent Colorados. Father Talavera did not heed his first warning, however. On 10 March he spoke in public again, this time to a crowd of over two thousand. Again he called on the Paraguayans to rise up and demand their rights. This time his words set off a chain of demonstrations in churches all over the country, with priests and parishioners protesting the continued state of siege. There were even a few brief demonstrations in Asunción's downtown streets, and in movie theatres. The Colorado faithful responded to these in time-honored fashion. That night young hoodlums cruised the city in jeeps, hurling stones through church windows and shouting progovernment slogans.

Nevertheless, an ugly mood was building up which worried Stroessner. He called Monseñor Bartolomé Adorno, Talavera's immediate superior, to the Presidential Palace to ask him to silence the young priest. The vicar-general not only refused, but he would not even let a progovernment priest use Talavera's pulpit to refute him. Having failed there, Stroessner then appealed to Archbishop Mena Porta, but that didn't work either. Mena Porta was reluctant to discipline a priest who was so popular with his parishioners and the other priests. In fact, support for Talavera was so strong among the clergy that Mena Porta was pressured by them to circulate a pastoral letter, dated 23 March, which criticized government waste and extravagance and called for a freer political climate.

With that a chill began to settle over church-state relations. Now the archbishop began to worry. Finally he called in Talavera and ordered him not to make any more public statements without his permission. That upset the young priest's plans, for he had scheduled a large public demonstration in August to protest Stroessner's inauguration. However, he soon hit on a solution. Complying with the letter, but not the spirit, of the archbishop's order, he went on a fast. Word spread quickly of what he was doing, and for the next two weeks his nonviolent protest was more talked about than the presidential ceremonies.

Talavera's crusade was drawing to a climax. The next stage in the battle was initiated by Stroessner. In November, Father Talavera's parish, El Carmen, was selected as the site for a new army officers' quarters and parade ground and the occupants of the *barrio* were ordered to evacuate. Talavera was irate. As the wrecking crews moved in, he tried to organize his parishioners to block the bull-dozers. The government replied by sending soldiers in. When a few shots were fired over the heads of the demonstrators, all resistance collapsed, and the work of demolition went on. Talavera then called for a mass protest rally to be held in downtown Asunción the very next day. When the time came for him to address the crowd, however, he could not be found. He had last been seen in his office, working on his speech, but now he had disappeared. The mystery of his absence was solved the following day. Talavera was discovered on a lonely country road about fifteen miles from town, stumbling along, barefoot and dazed, his clothes torn. Though he was unable to speak coherently, it was apparent that he had been kidnapped and beaten. The government's story, however, was that he had suffered a complete nervous breakdown.

Whether Mena Porta was frightened or whether he acted to save Talavera from further harm, he also announced that the priest was deranged and had him flown to a hospital in Uruguay. He then added, somewhat gratuitously, that Talavera's recent political statements were only his personal opinions and not those of the church.[23]

The denouement of the Talavera affair reflected badly on everyone. Talavera eventually recovered his health, but the government refused him permission to return to Paraguay. Mena Porta also refused him help. At that the young priest became bitter and began to vent his feelings once more from the pulpit. He called the archbishop a "collaborationist," to which Mena Porta replied that Talavera was mentally ill and "lacking a true vocation." At last Cardinal Barbieri, the Uruguayan primate, forbade Talavera to say Mass.

The Paraguayan clergy were by no means pleased with Mena Porta's handling of this matter, but Stroessner had won him over by holding out the promise of compulsory religious education in the public schools. Besides, Mena Porta could not risk alienating the government, which could cut off the church's funds. "They say it is a dictatorship here," he told an interviewer, "but you can work and study. You just can't make a revolution against the government." Accordingly, he cautioned his priests against attacking the regime.[24]

Meanwhile, all the exile groups lionized Talavera, who was traveling all over Argentina and Uruguay to harangue enthusiastic audiences. Interspersed with the speaking engagements were more fasts and more frustrated attempts to reenter Paraguay. His behavior, however, was becoming questionable. Blocked from saying Mass, he decided to leave the priesthood and set up his own church. Then he married one of his parishioners, only to divorce her later on. Such antics confused and embarrassed his followers, and they began leaving him. By the time Stroessner began the period of liberalization, Father Talavera had ceased to be an important political figure. Even so, he was not included in any amnesty.

The Radicalization of the Paraguayan Church

Father Talavera's expulsion from Paraguay did not restore calm to the Paraguayan church. An even more powerful churchman, Monseñor Anibal Maricevich, the auxiliary bishop of Asunción, took up the cause of social criticism. Although he was directly subordinate to Mena Porta, Maricevich was much the stronger character, and before long he was nudging his superior into more open opposition to the regime. He encouraged the reformist faction of the clergy to make their views known to the archbishop, while lay groups such as the Committee of Catholic Mothers sent in petitions urging him to stop his servility toward the regime and to defend the people's rights.[25] Maricevich seized on the issue of police torture to show how morally bankrupt the government was. Confronting Duarte Vera with the evidence, he embarrassed the police chief into admitting that abuses existed and extracted a promise of reform. Not content with that, he led a campaign of angry clergy and laymen to force Mena Porta to call on Edgar Ynsfran to protest police brutality after some members of Acción Católica were beaten during a demonstration.

Archbishop Mena Porta clearly did not relish the new role chosen for him. After the government's violent reprisals against the *democráticos* in June 1959 he refused to speak out any more. Thus, when Father Juan Escalante, the pastor of the suburban parish of San Roque, criticized the beating of student protesters, Mena Porta failed to back him up. Maybe he even agreed with Edgar Ynsfran, who published a pamphlet attacking Father Escalante as a liar and a subversive. In any case, his inaction so angered Acción Católica and its auxiliary, the Catholic Workers' Youth, that they went to the papal nuncio, the Vatican's representative in Paraguay, to try to persuade him to petition the Holy See for Mena Porta's removal in favor of Bishop Maricevich.

Although the papal nuncio refused to act, a change in clerical politics was in the making. In 1960 the church opened up a Catholic University in Asunción, with branches in Concepción, Encarnación, and Villarica. Since qualified professors were lacking among the Paraguayan clergy, several Jesuits from Europe—chiefly Spain—were hired for the faculty. Those soldiers of the faith brought with them a new and militantly reformist brand of Catholicism, which

soon turned the Catholic University into a center of antiregime agitation. This came at a time when the National University was exhausted and demoralized from the student riots of 1959 and the police reprisals those had provoked. The faculty had been purged, and
all student organizations were controlled by loyalist Colorados. The
new rector was Crispín Insaurralde, a tough old Guionist who ruled
the institution with an iron hand. The least hint of rebellion in the
classroom or on campus was met with expulsion. Insaurralde was so
unpopular that, a few years later, a mob of students stoned his home.
Ynsfran backed up the rector by requiring students to have a certifi-
cate of good conduct from the police before they could graduate.

By contrast, the Catholic University, being private, was free from
government interference. No one told the Jesuit professors what to
teach. Any ideas, even the politically taboo, could be discussed. But
the chief topic of discussion was the new social encyclicals of Pope
John XXIII, *Mater et Magistra* (1961) and *Pacem in Terris* (1963),
which committed the church to social reform. It was no longer
enough to pray; the world had to be changed by action. The poor nations of Latin America, Asia, and Africa were being exploited by
greedy capitalist imperialism. If the church stood by and did nothing,
atheistic Communists would take advantage of the frustration of the
poor. Rather than watch that happen, Catholics were to make a
radical revolution of their own.[26]

Putting the papal dicta into practice, the Jesuits and their enthusiastic followers in Catholic Youth soon began setting up organizations
among workers and peasants, including the Christian Workers' Center, which was started in 1962 as an alternative to the government-
controlled CPT. Soon the center counted some three thousand recruits,
chiefly from the construction and metallurgical trades, although this
was far smaller than the CPT's membership.

The Christian Agrarian Leagues, which were launched in 1962 as
well, were even more provoking to the regime. These attracted peasants through literacy programs, stepped-up Catholic welfare services,
and local entertainments at which plays and musical shows attacked
existing social conditions. Such tactics, called *conscientización*,
created social and political consciousness in the lower classes. In the
literacy courses offered by the leagues' "free schools" peasants
learned that "personal egoism" is wrong. The schools promoted a
radical philosophy in which those with land would share it with the
landless, and all tools, cattle, produce, and money would be pooled.
Officially, there were no leadership posts in the leagues. In any given
task, including teaching in the free schools and managing the cooperatives, leadership was to arise spontaneously.[27]

Eventually the leagues had a membership of about three thousand, spread over some twenty-six local centers throughout northern and central Paraguay. But *conscientización* did not stop at that. The church also set up a radio station and a weekly news magazine called *Comunidad* to broadcast the new doctrines. Every issue of *Comunidad* hammered away at social injustices, government corruption, and American imperialism. According to Bishop Maricevich, the message was simply that elections should be free and that politics ought not to be limited to "one man, one party, and one platform." "We are peaceful revolutionaries," he told a reporter. "We are inalterably opposed to violence and bloodshed, but we solidly favor moral violence."[28] Whatever "moral violence" was, it seemed to include a lot of invective. Also, many radical priests demanded a lot more than just free elections. Besides attacking all foreign capital, especially American, they demanded the socialization of practically all land and industry.

Inevitably the church's criticism focused on the Stroessner government. Under the goading of activists like bishops Maricevich, Ismael Rolón, and Ramón Bogarín, the Episcopal Conference began to make public pronouncements on political issues.[29] For example, it came out against the proposed constitution in 1967 because it permitted Stroessner a fourth term. In the following year the bishops published an open letter to Stroessner, demanding the release of over one hundred political prisoners. And in August 1969 the conference condemned the government's proposal of a new antisubversive law and demanded an immediate agrarian reform and "profound changes" in the entire social and economic order.

The liberalization implicit in the encyclicals was certainly affecting the ecclesiastical hierarchy, but it sometimes inspired unfortunate incidents for the church's public dignity. For instance, in October 1970, Monseñor Pedrozo, one of the members of the Episcopal Conference, announced that he was leaving the clergy in order to marry "a sweet brunette."[30]

Stroessner's Backlash

As the church moved more openly into opposition, it was no longer possible for the government to ignore the challenge. The long-awaited collision came after a spate of student demonstrations in April 1968, in response to the case of a medical student named Alfredo Carrillo, who had his military deferment canceled because of his participation in militant Catholic Youth activities.[31] That action touched off a strike at the National University's medical school, which was promptly seconded by the students of the Catholic University. But a joint demonstration by the two groups ended bloodily when plainclothesmen wielding billy clubs and wire whips attacked the protesters as they were leaving the grounds of the medical faculty. Several students were injured before they could get away.

Immediately the Episcopal Conference met and resoundingly condemned the government's action. Far from apologizing or admitting any blame, however, the regime accused the radical clergy of provoking the recent disturbances. Raúl Peña, the education minister, claimed that Jesuit professors at the Catholic University were spreading subversive propaganda and demanded that the church dismiss them. When the bishops indignantly rejected that demand, the government sent police onto the Catholic University's campus. Four of the Jesuits were arrested and subsequently expelled from Paraguay as troublemakers.

The response to that action was immediate and forceful. Once again the Episcopal Conference met, and it issued a blistering statement that accused the regime of "flagrant violations of human rights." In Concepción, where Bishop Maricevich headed the diocese, Catholic students painted antigovernment slogans on the walls. When some of them were caught and forced to scratch the words off with their fingernails, the bishop held a special "protest Mass." In Asunción, *Comunidad* came out with an empassioned editorial attacking the regime and published background articles on all the deported priests. The police answered by closing down *Comunidad*.

By this time relations between the church and the government had deteriorated dangerously. Stroessner and the papal nuncio were no longer on speaking terms. In fact, Stroessner informed his staff that Monseñor Innocenti was not welcome at the Presidential Palace. Archbishop Mena Porta's career was in shambles; he was so miserable that he even asked the Vatican to replace him.

Even at this juncture, however, Stroessner offered the church a truce. He permitted *Comunidad* to reappear, a month after its closure, but its editors were neither conciliated nor intimidated. They went right back to the attack with as much verve and invective as before. Stroessner took it for awhile, but when the church leaders were out of the country, attending a Latin American bishops' conference in Colombia, he sent the police in again to close down the paper. This time it stayed closed for six months.

After that it was open warfare. Once again the government focused on the Catholic University as a center of subversion. It singled out Father Luís Ramallo, the chairman of the psychology department and accused him of having helped to foment student disorders. In order to spare the priest from possible injury, Archbishop Mena Porta had him transferred to Chile. Once safely across the border, Father Ramallo let loose a tirade against Stroessner, accusing him of persecuting students, priests, and newspaper editors.

The next priest to be sanctioned was Father Francisco de Paula Oliva. A Jesuit who directed the Catholic University's School of Communications, he had made radio broadcasts encouraging student demonstrations against Stroessner. Although the Spanish-born priest had recently become a naturalized citizen, he was arrested on 22 October 1969 and deported to Spain. The angry march by students, priests, and nuns to protest the expulsion ended in another violent confrontation with the police. As the group was proceeding downtown from the campus, they were attacked by a phalanx of club-wielding policemen. One elderly priest was beaten senseless, and many other demonstrators were injured. The incident shocked Archbishop Mena Porta into a rare show of anger. On the next day he issued decrees of excommunication against Interior Minister Sabino Montanaro and Police Chief Francisco Brítez. In announcing these measures, Mena Porta declared that repression had reached "unprecedented extremes" in Paraguay. *Comunidad,* which had recently been allowed to reappear, backed him up with an editorial accusing the government of unleashing a "wave of persecution" against the church. It also published full accounts of Father de Paula's arrest and the police attack on the protest marchers.

Stroessner refused to back down. On 24 October he sent the police into the offices of *Comunidad* to close it down again, this time for good. He also issued an order for the arrest of *Comunidad*'s editor, Father Gilberto Giménez, another Jesuit. Father Giménez received warning of the impending arrest however, and managed to escape to Argentina. In a fighting mood, Stroessner vowed no toleration for "those who, hiding behind their Holy Orders, incite people to break the law."

Yet Archbishop Mena Porta still sought some way to bridge the growing differences. Sabino Montanaro's daughter was to be married in early November, and she wanted a church wedding. But her father, being under a ban of excommunication, would not be able to attend. So the minister of interior went to Mena Porta and offered his apologies. And what is more he made Police Chief Brítez apologize too. The Archbishop was sufficiently convinced of their contrition to lift the excommunication decree and Señorita Montanaro got her church wedding after all.

The truce was short-lived, however. December 8 is the feast-day of the Immaculate Conception; in Paraguay it is always celebrated with a great pilgrimage, led by high officials of both the church and the state, to the holy shrine of Caacupé. This year, however, the bishops decided to hold a silent protest march in Asunción instead. Stroessner was furious; he sent the police to disperse the marchers with billy clubs, and once again priests and nuns were beaten. In retaliation, Mena Porta declared the suspension of all masses in Paraguay for as long as the present regime remained in power. That was one of his last acts as archbishop. An embittered old man, he finally stepped down from office later that month.

The Church in Retreat

Clerical radicals favored Bishop Maricevich to take Mena Porta's place, but Stroessner, whose powers of ecclesiastical patronage gave him a veto, refused to accept him. However, he could not have a new archbishop without the Vatican's approval, so a stalemate resulted. Therefore, Deputy Foreign Minister Alberto Nogues was sent to the Holy See to ask for a successor politically acceptable to the regime. He also demanded the withdrawal of Monseñor Innocenti, the nuncio, whom Stroessner could not abide.

Nogues came back empty handed. Not only did the Vatican turn down all of Stroessner's requests but it urged him to reconsider his present course and to make reforms. Instead, Stroessner hardened his stand. He refused any of the nominations submitted by the Vatican, and the archbishopric remained unfilled. At the same time he struck a well-aimed blow at the church by outlawing the Catholic Relief Service. Henceforth all welfare activities would be a monopoly of the state. That not only drove a wedge between the priests and the poor but it also shut off a major means for disseminating *conscientización*. Moreover, priests were forbidden to meet with laymen outside of church services. Since Mass was no longer being said, that meant that any contact between the clergy and the public was against the law. Obviously such a law could not be enforced completely, but it had nuisance value.

It was clear, too, that Stroessner could not continue indefinitely with the archbishopric unfilled. Yet neither the Episcopal Conference nor the Vatican could fill it by itself. Nor was it possible for the clergy to keep their parishioners in a state of sin by refusing to hold Mass. Eventually the parties compromised and appointed Monseñor Ismael Blás Rolón as the new archbishop. Rolón, who took office on 27 January 1970, was reform minded enough to satisfy the militant clergy yet sufficiently moderate in his manner for Stroessner to find him acceptable.

Rolón had hardly settled into his new post when a new round of conflict broke out. On 27 February the police seized Father Uberfil Monzón, a Uruguayan priest who was visiting Paraguay. During his stay, Father Monzón had called in at the Catholic University and had also gone out to the countryside to look at some of the Christian Agrarian Leagues. When he was taken into custody, the police accused him of being a contact man for a leftist terrorist organization in Uruguay called the Tupamaros. Although he denied the charges, Father Monzón was held for questioning.

Archbishop Rolón tried to intercede, but could not secure Father Monzón's release. Finally, on 8 March, Bishop Andrés Rubio García flew up from Montevideo to investigate. When he got off the plane at Asunción's airport, however, a score of screaming young women attacked him, scratching and pummeling him unmercifully. Archbishop Rolón called the attack on Bishop Rubio government inspired and accused the police of having "kidnapped" Father Monzón. Then he excommunicated Montanaro and Brítez again. Bishop Rubio returned to the relatively civilized ambience of Montevideo. At the end of the month the regime finally released Father Monzón, although it added that it rejected Rolón's "unconstitutional interference" with its procedures.

Although Rolón had won a victory of sorts, he was not mollified. He sent Bishop Bogarín, the chairman of the Episcopal Conference, to Stroessner with a list of demands which included the recall of all exiled priests, amnesty for more than one hundred political prisoners, and an end to the government harassment of the Christian Agrarian Leagues. Moreover, Rolón announced that until the government mended its ways he would not take his seat in the Council of State.

Far from backing down, Stroessner stepped up the pressure. The Catholic University generated a particularly visceral hatred in him. Its corridors and patios were covered with antigovernment posters and graffiti. It had the atmosphere of a revolutionary party's convention, in permanent session. It was the intelligence center of the enemy camp, and Stroessner was determined to punish it.

A severe clash occurred on 12 September 1972, when the Catholic law school sponsored a protest meeting to demand the release of some students arrested in a demonstration earlier that month. Before the meeting began, burly, suspicious looking men joined the crowd. Fearing trouble, some students began to leave, but just then the Chamber of Deputies, which is located just across the grassy square from the

Catholic University, finished its session for the day, and some of the congressmen came over to watch the meeting. Their arrival gave courage to the student organizers, for surely the government would not risk trouble with such prominent men there. They decided to go ahead with the meeting. No sooner had the first speaker mounted the platform, however, than the government's hecklers began shouting loudly. One of the police toughs demanded the floor. The student speaker tried to ignore him and to raise his voice over the din, but a sudden shower of rocks drove him off the platform. Fistfights broke out; then the plainclothesmen brought out clubs and began bashing all around them. The meeting broke up in pandemonium as the panic-stricken spectators fled from the patio with the club-wielding bully-boys chasing them down the halls, smashing windows and furniture and tearing down banners and posters as they went. They drove the students and guests from room to room, beating them unmercifully whenever they cornered them and sparing not even the congressmen. They knocked down, kicked, and clubbed two Radical Liberal deputies, Domingo Laíno and Carlos Alberto González, and also slugged the young Colorado president of the National University law students, who was trying to protect them. Finally friends dragged the two congressmen out of the building and shoved them into waiting police cars for protection. Before they could complete their escape, however, a mob of Colorado hoodlums surrounded the cars, screaming and cursing as they beat on the fenders and windows. It was like a scene from the worst days of the Guión Rojo. When the police and the Colorado toughs finally left, the Catholic University was in a shambles.[32]

The Christian Agrarian Leagues were the other major target for Stroessner's wrath. They had gone beyond merely preaching *con-scientización* to the peasants and were becoming bolder in their attacks on the status quo. For example, on 9 November 1971 about 150 Liga peasants occupied the Church of the Immaculate Conception in the town of Caaguazú to dramatize their disapproval of the demolition of some shanties in the vicinity of the market square.[33] They also demanded that local priests pay more service calls on the poor. The incident naturally caused considerable excitement in the sleepy little town, especially when it became known that the parish priests were in strong disagreement with the bishop of the diocese, Monseñor Jerónimo Pechillo, who approved of the sit-in.

The government acted quickly. The next day soldiers surrounded the church and cordoned it off, permitting only the local priests and the department's *delegado* to enter the building. After long discussions with those mediators the peasants agreed to go, but as they walked outside, ten of their ringleaders were grabbed by the soldiers and hustled immediately into jail, where one of them died several months later after a long hunger strike.

A second sit-in (again with the approval of Bishop Pechillo) took place in April 1973, when hundreds of Liga peasants occupied the churches of Coronel Oviedo. That time the *py nandí* were sent in. After marching through the streets of the town chanting "Death to the Christian Communists," the Colorado peasants stormed the churches and ejected the demonstrators. Although the government blacked out news of the event, it was said that the *py nandí* badly mauled the Liga demonstrators, many of whom were arrested as they fled the buildings.

In the meantime more Jesuits were expelled from the country on the grounds that they were subversives. Father José Luis Caraívas, a Spaniard who had been the Christian Agrarian Leagues' archivist, and Father Vicente Barreto, a Paraguayan, were accused of distributing Communist propaganda to the peasants. In response to their deportation, Archbishop Rolón canceled any Catholic student participation in the Independence Day parade on 14 May and refused to celebrate the traditional Te Deum Mass.

By the following year, however, the church was showing signs of wanting to compromise. People had not rallied to the Cross as expected. Instead of bringing Stroessner to his knees, the bishops found themselves confronted by a regime whose discipline and ability to mobilize the masses were superior to their own. Moreover, the government had too many weapons in its arsenal: it could cancel the Catholic University's charter, it could reduce its financial support to the clergy, it could tax church property. Rolón began to moderate his public pronouncements and replaced the radical Bishop Bogarín as chairman of the Episcopal Conference with the more conservative Bishop Felipe Benítez.

Rather than accept the proffered olive branch, however, Stroessner became bolder. The Christian Agrarian Leagues were still agitating in the countryside. In Bishop Maricevich's diocese a peasant commune had been started at Colonia San Isidro, near the village of Jejuí. Shortly before dawn on 8 February 1975 a squad of soldiers led by Colonel Joaquín Grau, an old guerrilla fighter, surrounded the commune and called on the sleeping inhabitants to surrender. The fifty or so peasants awoke in panic, and some of them tried to run. When they did the soldiers opened fire, killing eight of them. Then they moved in.

A church report on the attack claimed that besides killing the eight peasants and wounding several others, the soldiers also beat the survivors, raped some of the women, smashed huts and broke tools, and seized some one million *guaranies* (about $8,000) from the cash box. Among those who were taken into custody were two American representatives of the Catholic Relief Service, a French priest, and a number of Christian Agrarian Youth leaders. All of the arrested were taken to Asunción, to be held indefinitely.[34]

In March soldiers invaded another Liga commune, the Communitarian Colony of Acaray. The colony's leader, Brother Anastasio, a young Franciscan, was arrested, along with five peasants. Although the colony was not dispersed, Brother Anastasio was expelled from Paraguay and his companions were detained in Asunción.[35]

Still other deportations were to follow. In April 1976 the police unearthed another guerrilla operation, the so-called Politico-Military Organization (OPM), which they claim was formed by radical Catholic students and linked to the Argentine Trotskyite People's Revolutionary Army (ERP). The guerrillas were well armed, for when police raided their headquarters, they fought back ferociously, killing five policemen. Thirty of their own followers fell before the gun battle was over. Following this shootout more than fifteen hundred suspects were rounded up. In their search for damning evidence the police broke into the Jesuit-run Cristo Rey College for high school students, and even into the offices of the Episcopal Conference. Sabino Montanaro accused the Jesuits of being the secret advisers of the OPM and expelled seven of them for "spreading Communist propaganda" and supporting guerrilla terrorism.[36]

Refusing all attempts at compromise, Stroessner kept the pressure on. He had already broken the power of the opposition parties. The radical Catholic church represented the last political resistance to his regime, and he was determined to crush it.

Chapter 11. The Tolerable
and the Intolerable

While the Catholic church carried the brunt of the struggle against Stroessner, Paraguay's opposition parties tried to discover some exit from the cul-de-sac in which they found themselves. Those who had achieved legal recognition had discovered that their hopes of rebuilding were cleverly blocked by the regime. Yet though the party elders were frustrated, they still clung to legality, preferring their powerless status to the uncertainties of exile. Such a policy hardly appealed to the younger party members, who demanded more forceful resistance to the regime's tactics. Over time this generational conflict would shatter the parties' unity, an event that would play into Stroessner's hands.

On the other hand, those groups still in exile were faring no better. They, too, had fallen to bickering and splintering. Moreover, their ability to act was badly hampered by the Argentine, Brazilian, and Uruguayan governments' moves to the right in the 1970s. While those countries had had democratic regimes they had enjoyed unofficial support against Stroessner, but now their left-wing character attracted the attention of the police. In addition Stroessner's own spies and undercover agents had thoroughly riddled the émigré communities. Thus, on all sides, a malaise settled over the opposition.

The Tolerated Opposition

The Febrerista Party

No group better displayed the confusion that now plagued Stroessner's opposition than the Febreristas. Of course, they had always lacked unity. From its very beginnings the Febrerista movement had attracted an indigestible mélange of liberals, nationalists, democratic socialists, and Communist sympathizers.[1] For the first ten years or so of its existence, Colonel Rafael Franco provided a respected symbol for all Febreristas to rally around, but even he was only partially successful in drawing all the factions together. At the movement's first convention, in 1945, the Marxist and non-Marxist elements were so far apart that the convention deferred a final decision on a basic charter. The result was the makeshift Revolutionary Febrerista Concentration (Concentración Revolucionaria Febrerista)—a confederation of groups, rather than a party. A centralized organization and discipline were achieved only in 1951, after the expulsion of a pro-Soviet faction called the Bloc For the Defense of the Revolution.

That was only the first of many purges to come. Febreristas continued to quarrel throughout the 1950s. Personal ambitions, arguments over how much socialism a multiclass party could espouse, and differences of opinion about the insurrectionist thesis all served to keep the party in turmoil. To its credit, however, democratic procedures were remarkably well observed. Not only were party elections held regularly, but the right and left factions alternated in power. This was probably due, in large measure, to Colonel Franco's use of his personal prestige to enforce an observance of the rules.

After losing control of the party's executive committee in 1958, however, the young radicals became impatient. They even turned on Colonel Franco, complaining that he was surrounded by a *camarilla* of elderly reactionaries. When the Febreristas met at their 1962 convention Franco found that, for the first time, he was opposed for the party presidency. The radicals put forward as their candidate a respected physician and guerrilla leader, Doctor Benigno Perrotta. Charges of fraud were hurled back and forth as the results of the party elections were challenged. In the end the radicals walked out, and the incumbent conservatives proceeded to expel them from the party. That paved the way for a deal with Stroessner to permit the Febreristas to return to Paraguay.

Even discounting Colorado fraud, the Febreristas' poor showing of only 2.7 percent of the vote in the 1967 elections was a disheartening measure of just how far the party had slipped. Its only representation in Congress was one seat in the lower house, held by Juan Speratti. It could not even keep a newspaper in business, for lack of funds. A weekly, *Febrero*, was started soon after the party returned to Paraguay, but it had to shut down after a year. Another weekly, *El Pueblo*, appeared in 1970, but it too had to give up after about twenty weeks because of financial difficulties.

Such disappointments led to renewed criticism of the party leaders.

Although Colonel Franco had come back to Paraguay under the amnesty, he had grown tired of the interminable quarrels and had stepped aside in favor of Carlos Caballero Gatti. Caballero Gatti had been Franco's second in command and was said to be a good negotiator in dealing with the government. But he was also a large landowner, rich and aloof, all of which made him unpopular with the younger Febreristas. In the 1968 presidential elections he ran last in a four-man race, and his colorless campaign did little to raise his prestige.

As the 1969 Febrerista convention approached, the party was split along lines similar to those that had plagued it before. A new left wing had emerged behind the candidacy of Ignacio Iramaín, a pediatrician who had once supported Perrotta. A small, thin man with sorrowful eyes and a wispy moustache, Iramaín was a well-known martyr for the Febrerista cause. He had twice served time in Stroessner's jails and was said to have been cruelly tortured. He was much admired by the younger generation, and he gained their enthusiastic support all the more by advocating that the party abstain from future elections until the government guaranteed fair play.

The right wing had a martyr too in Juan Speratti, the party's general secretary. But Speratti had a military man's reserved manner and, being much older than Iramaín, was more out of touch with the relatively youthful rank and file. His good friend Colonel Franco might have helped by supporting Speratti, but Franco decided to stay out of the campaign rather than risk dividing the party again.

The convention elected Iramaín president, and with that the party took a sharp swing to the left. The Febrerista Youth considered the victory as their own, and they now began to take over as the voice of the organization. Among the many pamphlets they published during this time, *¿Domesticación o revolución permanente?* furnishes a typical sample of their thinking. Its main points are: (1) capitalism is nothing but a vicious system of exploitation, (2) capitalism's hours are numbered all over the world, (3) only a violent socialist revolution can save Latin America; anything short of that is reactionary and treasonous to the working classes, (4) despite its great economic success the Soviet Union cannot be a model for the Latin American revolution because its system is not humanistic enough, and (5) the new humanism means that every vestige of authority will be abolished—no government, no army, no managers in the factory, no teachers or homework for students.[2]

That program alienated the majority of the older Febreristas, many of whom became inactive in the party, and so declined to contribute any more of their time or money to it. Despite the proselytizing zeal of the Febrerista Youth, who claimed to have brought in two thousand new recruits in 1971 alone, the morale of the party was very low. Iramaín decided to step down after his term was over in September 1971, and a fusion ticket of conservatives and moderate leftists tried to restore unity behind Manuel Benítez, an economist who taught at the National University. At fifty-eight, Benítez was a respected author of many economic studies, and it was hoped that his being a professor would gain the support of the younger generation. His politics might be described as democratic socialist. After his election he told reporters that the Febrerista party stood for "progressive nationalism" and the creation of a modern state that would "protect the exploited sectors."[3]

Under Benítez the party abstained from voting in the 1970 municipal elections and the 1973 general elections. Even so, the Febrerista Youth were not satisfied. Taking the propaganda lead once more, they published a manifesto in April 1973 lambasting the government and the "pliable" leadership of the Paraguayan Workers' Confederation, which they claimed was in the pay of the United States embassy. Only "revolutionary syndicalism" and the violent "seizure of power by the working class" could liberate Paraguay. "It is utopian," they said, "to think about the happiness of the people unless the means of production are in their hands."[4] None of this had been cleared with Benítez beforehand, yet the Febrerista Youth claimed to speak for the whole party. The issue was clear: although a majority of the party had chosen Benítez as president, the youth repudiated his authority. If the president happened to agree with them, so much the better; but if he did not, then they would go their own way. He had no means to discipline them.

By mid-1973 Benítez had taken enough. He was tired of trying to hold together an impossibly divided party, and his relations with the Febrerista Youth had become too acrimonious. He resigned in disgust and turned the leadership over to his vice-president, Francisco Sánchez Palacios. The interim president then called for a convention to be held in December.

Before the convention was held, however, *febrerismo* suffered another severe blow. Colonel Franco, who had been in poor health, died that October. Although he had recently removed himself from politics, he was the party's greatest symbol and asset. Many Paraguayans remembered him as the hero of the Chaco War and the president of the country's first truly revolutionary government. He was widely respected for having sacrificed his brilliant military career to the service of a humanitarian ideal, for which he had suffered a life of poverty and exile. He died in simple circumstances, surrounded by his followers, whom time and disillusion had thinned out.

The December convention reelected Ignacio Iramaín. This time, however, he announced a more moderate course. The party was in a shambles, he warned, and unless all Febreristas were brought back to the fold, it would not survive. The first order of business was to restore discipline. Drawing heavily on the personal admiration that many young Febreristas had for him, he purged the Febrerista Youth of its most rebellious elements. Next, he appealed to the disenchanted moderates to reincorporate themselves into the party ranks. Bit by bit the party treasury began to grow again. A permanent headquarters building was rented and plans were made to bring out the weekly, *Febrero*, once more. But it was an uphill struggle. Some Paraguayans surmised that the historical hour of *febrerismo* had come and gone and that it would never survive without Franco's charisma. Moreover in the face of Stroessner's awesome power, it could offer its members little. Iramaín's task was to rebuild the party practically from scratch. It was probably as much from fear of the results as it was from political principle that he refused to enter candidates in general elections.

The Liberal Party

Like the Febreristas, the Liberals also split into radical and conservative factions. In this case, however, the breakdown of party unity was even more significant, for the Liberals were the only group that possessed a mass base sufficient to challenge Stroessner. Unfortunately, instead of capitalizing on this potential the Liberals fell to squabbling over programs, tactics, and party offices. Consequently the Liberals, like the Febreristas, weakened as their followers became disillusioned and politically inactive. Their collapse left the field entirely to Stroessner.

The Liberal party's divisions were somewhat more complex than those of *febrerismo*. The first significant group to break off was the Renovationist wing, which after 1963 was officially recognized in Paraguay as the Liberal party. The main party branch, after it achieved legality in 1967, was called the Radical Liberal party. Up to 1977 the Liberal party, still headed by Carlos and Fernando Levi Ruffinelli, was considered by the other opposition parties as a collaborationist group. Radical Liberals and Febreristas speculated darkly about the Liberal party's source of funding and dismissed it contemptuously as a stalking horse for the regime. For example, during the congressional roll-call vote on the Itaipú treaty, the Liberals broke ranks with the opposition and supported the government, "with reservations." As *Diálogo* commented drily, that meant that the Liberals wanted to stay on Stroessner's good side, but wanted to avoid any responsibility if things went wrong with the project later on. As an organ for its views, the party had a four-page weekly, *El Enano*, which carried mainly crudely drawn cartoons attacking both the government and the other opposition parties.

Liberalism's second major split occurred at the Radicals' 1971 party convention. Three factions contended for control. The first faction, those who championed the party's traditional stand for individual liberty and limited government, was led by Justo Pastor (Chocho) Benítez, the son of a former party president of the same name. This group favored continued participation in the government. They argued that elections and congressional representation offered the party the only outlets, however limited, of reaching the Paraguayan public.

The second faction, led by Carlos Alberto (Beto) González and Domingo Laíno, wanted the party's program to go beyond merely advocating political democracy and embrace social reform as well. By that they meant that the state should promote agrarian reform, nationalize large foreign companies, and institute social welfare schemes to raise the living standards of the poor. In their view, the party had to abandon its laissez-faire traditions, which were sorely out of date. Moreover, they wanted to boycott Congress and all elections until Stroessner saw to it that the campaigns were conducted fairly and the votes were counted honestly. As is common in Latin America, differences in principle became personal rivalries—in this case Benítez and his *benetistas* versus González and his *betistas*.

The third faction at the convention gathered around the flamboyant personality of Senator Enzo Doldán. Doldán, a candidate for the party presidency, was a stout, colorful *cacique* with slicked-down hair and a bristling black moustache. A master of the flowery compliment and the bombastic speech, he was also a skillful practicioner of political infighting. Doldán was an opportunist and a brawler who commanded a small but loyal band of followers. His strategy was to let Benítez and González fight to a standstill and then offer himself as the compromise candidate.

Doldán's plan might have worked except that the two opponents found an even better compromise in Efraím Cardozo, one of Liberalism's most respected figures. Cardozo was perhaps Paraguay's greatest living historian, and though an elder statesman from the old guard, he was willing to support abstaining from future elections unless Stroessner agreed to reform the process. With the combined support of the two major factions, Cardozo easily won the party presidency.

Doldán was an ambitious man, however, and would not give up easily. He was now determined to disrupt the party, if need be, in order to grab power in the confusion. He started by seizing on the issue of reunifying Liberalism by bringing the Levi Ruffinelli brothers back to the fold. There was little chance that Benítez would support that, of course, because his father had been one of those who drummed the Renovationists out of the party. González and his supporters viewed the "Levi-Liberals" as even more reactionary than the *benetistas*. Nonetheless, among many rank-and-file Liberals a nostalgic sentiment favored reintegrating all *co-religionarios*, so lip service had to be paid to the idea. The Levi Ruffinelli brothers themselves had nothing to lose by endorsing the action.

Accordingly, Doldán and his clique met with Carlos Levi Ruffinelli and the executive committee of the Liberal party that October in the town of Carepeguá. The result was a manifesto which called for an end to all divisions in Liberalism. Perhaps Levi Ruffinelli's intentions were better revealed in a subsequent interview with the press, however. He predicted that reintegration would strengthen Liberalism by eliminating from its ranks "the many people of non-Liberal—and indeed, anti-Liberal—ideas, who have infiltrated the Radical Liberal party." More pointedly, he added that such elements were presently the "dominant force" in the Radical Liberal directorate.[5]

That sort of talk stung Efraím Cardozo to reply that the Levi-Liberals were the most reactionary, "obsolete," "manchesterian," and "laissez-fairist" group in all Paraguay. They had, he said, split the party back in 1963, usurped its name, and now were doing Stroessner's dirty work in trying to wreck it again. Even so, Cardozo could not ignore the desire of many Radical Liberals at least to explore the possibility of reconciliation. Against his better instincts, he called for an extraordinary convention, to be held in the second week of January 1972.

Meanwhile, not pinning all his hopes on the one issue of reintegration Doldán launched a full-scale assault on the Radical Liberal left, possibly in hopes of getting Chocho Benítez to join him. He charged that subversives had infiltrated the party and insisted that they be rooted out—although he mentioned no names in particular. Also, he demanded that the Radical Liberal party announce its intention to participate in the 1973 general elections.

All of those issues were on the agenda of the extraordinary convention when it opened on January 15. Three hundred delegates were

present, a large majority of whom cheered wildly when Doctor Cardozo entered the room to open the proceedings. Doldán's group was
quiet, however. Realizing that he faced heavy odds, the maverick
senator decided to carry the fight to his opponents. He began his attack by reiterating his charge that elements hostile to Liberalism had
infiltrated the party and were trying to take control. He said that these
elements opposed reincorporating the Levi Ruffinellis because they
preferred to keep Liberalism divided and weak. Their ideas were
socialistic and their tactics were aimed at provoking the government
so as to destroy all the gains the party had achieved since its legalization. Some of these un-Liberal schemers were actually Communists,
he said, and here Doldán pointed an accusing finger at Domingo
Laíno, the party's general secretary.

The basis of Doldán's charge was that Laíno had once visited
Czechoslovakia. Although flimsy, the accusation stung, for this was
not the first time that Laíno had been called a Communist. He was a
flashy young man who wore longish hair and stylish clothes and was
something of a hero to the Radical Liberal youth. He was also known
as an outspoken, combative deputy in the Chamber, tirelessly crusad-
ing against corruption, contraband, and the American-owned oil
refinery. During a session of Congress a Colorado deputy named
Adolfo Zayas had stood up in the Chamber with a sheaf of papers
which, he said, "proved" that Laíno was in the pay of the Soviet
Union. More specifically, he had claimed that the Russian embassy in
Paris had deposited a sum of $25,000 to Laíno's account in a Swiss
bank. When the Radical deputies had demanded to examine that
proof, however, Zayas had declined to show it. It would be turned
over to a court, he had said. At that, Laíno and his colleagues had
walked out of the Chamber in disgust. No investigation had ever been
made of the charges and the "proof" had never been made public, although the Colorados had continued to hint at it from time to time.[6]

Thus, Doldán was poking at an old sore in his attempt to arouse the
conservative delegates at the convention. He insisted that he meant
nothing personal by his accusation, and he even held out his hand to
Laíno, whom he called regretfully "my personal friend." Laíno was
too shocked and confused to refuse the handshake, but he quickly
recovered and fought back angrily. He first attacked the accusation
as old, Colorado-inspired mudslinging, then went on to accuse Doldán
of being in league with Stroessner and Levi Ruffinelli to split the
party in order to render it impotent. While Laíno was haranguing the
delegates, however, Cardozo, Doldán, and Benítez slipped out of the
room and met in a nearby office.

What the three men talked about can only be conjectured, but when they returned to the convention floor, Cardozo mounted the platform and announced that party unity was restored. Further debate or a vote was unnecessary because Senator Doldán had agreed to withdraw his motion for reincorporating the Levi-Liberals. Then, as if to heal the breach symbolically, Cardozo and Doldán clasped each other in a fraternal *abrazo*.

But Laíno was not feeling fraternal. His blood was up. When his turn came to embrace Doldán, he turned away and walked off the platform. Immediately afterward he resigned his post as secretary-general. He could not understand Cardozo's actions, he told reporters, and he was disgusted at his *abrazo* with Doldán.

Doldán explained his switch by saying that, like any true democrat, he had bowed to the majority will and dropped his demand for the Liberal party's reintegration. Now that the heat of battle had died down, he hoped that Laíno would show the same generous attitude.

Concerning the other questions on the convention's agenda, the weary delegates felt such an emotional relief after the Cardozo-Doldán *abrazo* that they were in no mood to debate. Drained and exhausted, they began leaving the convention hall, and soon the convention had no quorum on the floor. The other matters were tabled.[7]

Although it ended in compromise, the extraordinary convention had only deepened the cleavages within the party. The left wing was angry, and although Cardozo sought to mollify it by appointing Beto González as the new editor of *El Radical*, they continued to nurse a grievance. Trouble was to flare up again when the Radicals held their next convention, in November 1972.

Radical Liberal statutes require elections every two years, in which all the local committees vote for delegates to a national convention. The convention, in turn, elects the party's thirty-man executive committee and chooses its slate of congressional candidates. Each local committee is apportioned a number of delegates according to the size of its membership. The elections of 1972 were contested with particular bitterness in the local committees. Cardozo was in poor health (he died the following year), and it was clear that the convention would have to pick his successor. A real showdown between Benítez's "classical" Liberals and González's "modern" Liberals was in the making.

The local committees were presented with three slates, or "lists," to choose from. González and his followers campaigned under the slogan "Change for Liberation." They promised to step up their campaign in Congress against official corruption and to abstain from elections until the government abolished fraud. Not to be outdone in the slogan contest, Benítez and his group ran as "Radicals in Thought and Radicals in Action." They defended electoral participation as the only way to get representation in Congress, and participation in Congress, they argued, was the only viable alternative to the discredited tactics of violence and subversion. Finally, Enzo Doldán's group took the slogan "Revolutionary and Progressive Liberalism." Doldán was still attacking the party leadership as "unrepresentative," although he had to admit that his following was only a minority too. Nonetheless, he saw himself as the holder of the balance of power. "My group hasn't fixed its position yet," he told reporters. "We are a minority, but a decisive minority nevertheless. We are going to decide the issue. We'll take our position on the day of the convention, after we listen to both platforms and look over the candidates."[8]

For a party that attacked the government for electoral fraud and political chicanery, the Radical Liberals had much to be ashamed of in this convention. Questionable balloting procedures had been used in many of the local committees. Both the Benítez and González factions claimed victory in Coronel Oviedo and Yaguarón and charged their opponents with dirty practices. As a result, rival delegations from those two towns appeared at the convention, each claiming the right of admission to the floor. Also, the González faction raised a formal complaint about the fact that the local committee from Horqueta—which had gone for Benítez—had had its representation raised from eleven to sixteen delegates. Such disputes were nothing new in the party's history, and there was a method for dealing with them. A Commission of Powers was to pass on the legality of all the delegates' credentials. However, the Benítez and González factions were so evenly represented on the commission that, after eight hours of fruitless wrangling, it decided to pass those issues on to the convention floor for a final decision. Those delegates with uncontested credentials would vote on those whose legality was impugned.

However, Benítez and Doldán had already struck a bargain. Eight days before the convention they had met secretly at a private home to explore the idea of supporting each other's list. Benítez needed Doldán. Without the votes from Coronel Oviedo, Yaguarón, and Horqueta he lacked a majority. In fact, since the race was so close, he calculated that those same votes, given to González, would finish him. But if Doldán's delegates supported him, he could win. As Doldán had boasted, he was indeed the holder of the balance.

So they had made a deal. Benítez would include some of Doldán's men on his list of candidates for the party directorate and Congress, in return for which Doldán would back him for party president. But González was not to know about the deal, or he might raise an embarrassing scandal. To prevent that, Benítez and Doldán agreed to keep the contents of their final lists secret until the last moment. By that time it would be too late for González to do anything.

Emotions were high among the delegates when the convention opened its sessions 12 November. The first order of business was the question of the impugned delegates' credentials. González began the debate by moving that the Horqueta delegation be reduced from sixteen to eleven. After a brief but hot exchange the motion came to a vote. Backed by Doldán's bloc, Benítez's faction won the test by 243 votes to 164. The motion had failed and the left wing, which had thought itself the largest faction, was thrown into consternation. Some of Gonzalez's supporters began to waver. The delegation from Villarica, sensing a winner in Benítez, deserted.

The next test came over which of the rival delegations from Coronel Oviedo would be seated. This time Benítez won by an even bigger margin—303 to 135. After that the left was crushed and demoralized. The Yaguarón vote turned out to be a complete rout.

Benítez was in complete control now. When the convention took up the question of the party's platform, he had no need to placate the left. González and Laíno had tried to get the party to boycott the 1973 elections in protest over Stroessner's refusal to let Carlos Pastore return to Paraguay and run for Congress. They even persuaded the party's youth group, the Club Liberal Alón, to make an idealistic appeal to the delegates. Although the young *alonistas* were only there as observers without a vote, they were allowed to make their impassioned speeches and to pass out leaflets calling for the boycott. They told the delegates that the party was only helping to legitimize the dictatorship by participating. The conservatives listened politely, applauded the young people's speeches, and pocketed their leaflets. But their minds were already made up. In the vote they supported participation by an overwhelming margin.

The next order of business was to choose the party's president, executive committee, and congressional slate. A certain amount of uneasiness had been growing among Doldán's group because of rumors that none of the *doldanistas* were really on Benítez's list. Benítez's men tried to reassure the *doldanistas*, but they could not be sure because Benítez was guarding all their ballots himself. Doldán began to worry. Either the rumors were being spread by the left wing in order to split the coalition or his partner was pulling a double cross.

That evening, as the hour for voting drew near, Doldán cornered Benítez and confronted him with the rumors. But Benítez assured him that everything was going to work out splendidly. A few minutes after that the votes were called for. The leader of each faction produced copies of his list and passed them out to the delegates, who then had to choose the one they wanted and drop it in the ballot box. Doldán and his friends eagerly grabbed the sheets passed out by Benítez and looked for their names, but they were not on them! Benítez had used them to win the earlier test votes, which had seated his disputed delegations and caused a stampede from González's side to his. Now that he had a comfortable majority of his own, he did not need the *doldanistas*.

The subsequent balloting gave Benítez and his followers most of the seats on the party directorate, which meant that he would be the next party president. His faction also got most of the candidates for Congress. Finally, Gustavo Riart, a former army officer and an old guard backer of Benítez, was chosen for the hopeless but honorific task of running against Stroessner for president. The *betista* leftists received minority representation on the party directorate and the congressional ticket, but they were bitter. A discouraged González told reporters, "We fought at a disadvantage against a powerful traditional machine that is run from certain key places on the directorate, which we were never able to control."

As the delegates left the convention hall, a furious Doldán stopped Benítez and poured abuse on him. "You are a traitor and a cur!" he shouted. "And a cur should never be president of our party!" He might have said more, except that Benítez (who, though bespectacled, is tall and hefty) stopped him with a punch in the face. A scuffle followed which was finally broken up by the onlookers.

The next night some *doldanistas* turned up at the swearing-in ceremony at the Casa Azul—Liberal party headquarters—to heckle Benítez's men. One of the new officers was a veterinarian. "Quite right to elect a veterinarian as treasurer," they hooted. "After all, Chocho is an ass!"

Doldán, meanwhile, was at the National Senate, where a late-night meeting had been called. Rather than go inside, he was pacing up and down outside the building—like a caged lion, one eyewitness recalled later. With him were his son and another man, hurrying alongside him and talking in low voices as if to calm him. A few of his fellow senators hailed him to come inside, but he ignored them. Presently a reporter from *La Tribuna* came up, and Doldán stopped to say something to him when he suddenly spied Benítez across the street, heading for the Senate door. Benítez had just come from the swearing in of the new directorate at the Casa Azul, and the jaunty way he swung his briefcase showed that he was in the best of moods.

At the sight of his enemy Doldán lost control of himself. Waving his arms wildly, he yelled, "Come here, you bum [miserable]! You are a traitor—don't be a coward too!" While people standing by the

Senate door looked on in surprise, a quick-witted reporter, sensing a story, began to take pictures.

Benítez stopped in the middle of the street, puzzled. Three of his friends hurried over to him, and then the four men proceeded in a knot toward the Senate. "So! You've got your henchmen, you bum!" Doldán bellowed. "Well, I'm going to fix you anyway!" With that he pulled a revolver from his coat.

Several people swarmed on him to stop him. The Senate's chief of security got there first and grabbed for the pistol, which went off, wounding him in the hand. A melee followed in which the younger Doldán kicked one of Benítez's friends in the stomach, and Doldán himself took his second punch in the face in two days. Meanwhile, the senators were hurrying out of the building to watch the fight.

The Colorados were amused, of course, and none more so than Ezequiel González Alsina, their majority leader. "Leave them alone!" he shouted. "Let them fight like men!" He even tried to prevent the police from interfering. "Don't touch them!" he told the cops who came hurrying up. "Respect their parliamentary privileges! They've got immunity!"

Fortunately, the police ignored González Alsina and proceeded to separate the combatants. Friends surrounded the dazed Benítez, who was finally helped into a car by none other than his arch rival, Domingo Laíno. For perhaps the only time in his life Laíno appeared solicitous of Benítez's health. "I have been the victim of a cowardly attack!" Benítez huffed, as he was being driven off.

Doldán was also hustled away, but not before he demanded the return of his gun. The police refused his request politely. Meanwhile, González Alsina had turned indignant. "Just imagine!" he exclaimed to the Colorados. "They come to Congress armed—to take over! That sort of thing can't be allowed!"

That night Doldán issued Benítez a challenge to a duel and demanded the right to choose the weapons. He even appointed his own seconds. But nothing came of it. The Radical Liberals met soon after and expelled him from the party, whereupon he formed his own Partido Liberal Democrático. However, the new party never got enough signatures to obtain legal recognition from the Electoral Commission, and was unable to run in the 1973 elections. Failing in that, Doldán next tried to warm up his relations with the Levi Ruffinellis, suggesting that his party unite with the Liberal party, but they put him off. Privately, Carlos Levi Ruffinelli was said to have told friends that Doldán was now simply "dead weight." Doldán passed from the political scene, but not before he had nearly wrecked the Radical Liberal party. Benítez presided over an organization that was nearly in shambles. The next few months would see the situation deteriorate even more.

To begin with, the party's left wing could not forgive him for his underhanded tactics. González, Laíno, and Carmen Lara de Castro, the left's representatives on the directorate, refused to attend executive meetings. The left also had the support of the party youth. Indeed, the Club Liberal Alón was becoming rebellious. The *alonistas* ignored orders from the directorate, held common meetings with Febrerista and Christian Democratic youth without consulting the party leaders, and carried on an independent program of propaganda.

Moreover, it soon became evident that Benítez could not control even those who were supposed to be in his faction. The most prominent among his backers were the party's elder generation, the old guard, who had accepted him because they knew that he, like his father, was conservative to the core. Roundish, dull, and agreeable, he was not the sort who would be disrespectful to the "grand old men." Another group within his faction was the *geniolitos* (a pun once coined by Doldán, which played on the word *genio* (genius) and the brand name of a local patent medicine for head colds). Led by Mario Esteche, who had once been a member of the 14th of May Movement, the *geniolitos* controlled many of the local committees in the capital and formed the Radical Liberal minority on the Asunción municipal council. They were the party's ambitious city faction, and they would back Benítez only so long as he was useful. Finally, Benítez had supporters who followed him personally. Some of those had become disgruntled, however, because they felt that he had not adequately rewarded them for their loyalty.

Benítez's position began to erode soon after the 1972 convention. His backers had drawn together chiefly out of the fear of a left-wing takeover. But once that crisis was passed, Benítez offered little to hold them together. His platform contained only one positive plank: electoral participation. Thus, the Radical Liberals entered the February 1973 general elections, with the aged Gustavo Riart as their standard-bearer. Predictably, the Colorados chalked up their usual landslide, but this time the margin of victory was embarrassing. The official tally gave Stroessner and the Colorado ticket 84 percent of the vote, to only 12 percent for the Radical Liberals.[9] Considering that the Radical Liberals had gotten 20.9 percent of the vote in 1967, that represented a decline of almost two-fifths of their support. Either the Colorados had become more brazen about stuffing the ballot boxes, or the Radical Liberals were in serious decline. Either explanation was plausible, but since the *betistas* had failed to back the ticket, the latter was more probable. In any case, the strategy of electoral participation had lost some appeal.

As a result, Benítez's grip on the directorate began to be shaky, and his leadership came under increasing criticism. The *geniolitos* were the first to disassociate themselves from him. After the elections they informed him that representatives on the Asunción municipal council would no longer contribute their salaries to the party's national treasury; that was no small loss for a party plagued by a constant lack of funds. Henceforth the *geniolitos* put their financial support behind the Coordinating Committee for the Capital, which represented the twenty-four *barrio* committees of Asunción—and which they controlled.

Next, Benítez found himself deserted by the old guard. Justo Prieto, a former party president, and probably the most prestigious spokesman for the older generation, suddenly attacked the party president in an interview with *Diálogo*, claiming that he was too accommodating toward the government. Prieto had been responsible for expelling the Renovationists from the party in 1962, and now he was complaining again about the strategy of electoral participation. In his opinion, the Radical Liberals were simply playing Stroessner's game, lending him a façade of democracy behind which to hide his dictatorship. For all practical purposes, the Radical Liberals had become a tool of the regime.[10]

Prieto's blast cut away most of the rest of Benítez's support. If the old guard was preparing to abandon him, the *geniolitos* were determined to beat them to it. The latter now declared themselves "independent" from the leadership, and to underscore this they renounced all their positions on the party's committees, including the directorate. Then they called on Benítez to resign.

Petitions began to pour in from local committees all over the country, demanding the convocation of another extraordinary convention. Benítez realized, however, that such a convention would certainly remove him from the presidency. So, even though thirty such petitions was a sufficient number to require him to act, Benítez refused. That led to angry denunciations of his "dictatorship," and even his old friend Gustavo Riart withdrew his support.

Benítez was practically isolated, but the very sort of dogged qualities that had recommended him to the old guard originally now allowed him to ignore the protest swirling around him. He plodded along through the rest of 1974, getting weaker but refusing to give up. In the process, however, Paraguay's main opposition party was becoming paralyzed.

The agony could not last beyond January 1975, however, for the party's regular convention was scheduled for then. In the meantime, the left wing had revived. The conservatives' disarray had given them new hope. Moreover, a tired González had stepped aside in favor of the more dramatic Laíno, much to the enthusiasm of the younger Radical Liberals. For them, Laíno possessed charisma, and his whirl-wind style of attack, which borrowed the language of the revolutionary left, charged his followers with confidence.

By contrast, the old guard was fading. Having tried to perpetuate their influence by supporting Benítez, the party elders went down with him, despite their last-minute attempts to disassociate themselves from him. As for the *geniolitos*, they lacked a broad base in the party, a leader of national stature, or a well-defined program beyond their own self-interest. In the end, they supported Laíno because they saw he was in the ascendancy. Thus, the outcome of the 1975 convention was never in doubt: the left wing captured the party directorate, and Laíno took over as president.[11]

Laíno's platform sounded revolutionary. Not only did he demand an immediate end to the state of siege, the release of all political prisoners, and a general amnesty for those in exile, but he also en-thused his audiences by excoriating American imperialism. He praised Salvador Allende, the recently fallen Chilean president, as a martyr to *yanqui* power. Chile, he said, had been the most glorious social experiment in Latin America since Castro's Cuba. Behind his words, however, Laíno showed himself to be a pragmatist. Knowing well that the Radical Liberal Party could not stand alone against Stroessner, he called for a new National Front for Liberation and Development, which would include all the Liberal factions, the Febreristas, and the Christian Democrats.

Meanwhile, the government was putting pressure on the Radical Liberals. In May 1975, Laíno found himself the object of an attack from an unexpected quarter—the students. As a professor at the Catholic University's Villarica campus he was sure that his freedom to express his views would be protected by the reformist clergy. To his surprise, when he told his students that the opposition parties ought to boycott Congress to protest the regime's violations of human rights, he found himself the target of a student demonstration. The students in little backwater Villarica might be Catholics, but they were also peasants, and most of them were good Colorados as well. They demanded Laíno's resignation for being a Marxist and "insulting the Fatherland."

A complicated struggle now began inside the Catholic University, during which—curiously enough—liberal elements aided Stroessner and opposed Laíno. To begin with, the Villarica university authorities, with the acquiesence of their conservative bishop, gave in to the students and fired Laíno. That brought in the more radical Superior Council of the Catholic University, seated in Asunción, to review the issue. The council overruled the Villarica officials and reinstated Laíno. Instead of settling matters, however, that sparked another protest, this time by the students at the Asunción campus. As only the bizarre nature of Paraguayan politics would have it, the Asunción students saw the council's action as a violation of the Villarica campus's autonomy. So, even though they sympathized with Laíno, they went on strike to uphold his ouster. Caught by surprise, the church authorities backed down and allowed Laíno to be dismissed.[12]

Other setbacks for the Radical Liberals were soon to follow. The first involved the editor of *El Radical*, Miguel Angel Martínez. He was arrested for "slandering a military officer." Specifically, *El Radical* had charged General Otelo Carpinelli of abusing his powers as commander of the Fifth Military Region. The newspaper remained closed from July through October. The second blow came when the Radical Liberals entered the race for municipal offices in October 1975. In allowing this Laíno violated his earlier promise to abstain from participation. Perhaps he hoped that with a younger and more active leadership his party would poll a heavier vote in Asunción. Or maybe he was afraid that if the party abstained some Radicals would support the Liberals. Recently the Levi Ruffinellis and Doldán had been talking again of merging. Now it seemed that they would run a single ticket in the forthcoming elections. Whatever Laíno's reasoning, the decision to participate was a mistake. The Colorados rolled up their biggest victory yet, with 87 percent of the 665,000 votes cast. The Radical Liberals got just slightly over 10 percent, and the Liberals got 2.5 percent. The Febreristas, who presented candidates in only three districts, polled only 136 votes.[13]

The opposition's weakness seemed to make Stroessner bolder. In addition, the discovery of the November 1974 assassination plot had led to a wave of arrests and beatings on a scale unseen since the early years of the regime. Hundreds of students, radical priests, and party officials had been rounded up and interrogated, and some of them had been tortured.[14] Not even the normally acquiescent Liberal party had been spared. Carlos Levi Ruffinelli, who had recently complained about electoral fraud, charged that he had been beaten up at police headquarters.

Suddenly the opposition parties were forced to draw together for survival. When Stroessner's dutiful Congress voted on 16 July 1976 to hold elections to a constitutional convention—preparatory to changing the constitution so that Stroessner could run for a sixth term—the Radical Liberals, Febreristas, and Liberals all announced their intention of abstaining. This conversion of the Levi-Liberals into open opponents of the regime was significant, for it removed one of the main obstacles to their rejoining the parent party. So long as they had been treated favorably by Stroessner, they had been content to go along with him; but now that they too were facing extermination there was more safety in joining forces with others. Consequently, the Levi Ruffinellis sounded out Laíno about the prospects of reunification.

Laíno, in the meantime, had changed his mind about the Levi-Liberals. He had opposed them bitterly in the past, and their conservative outlook was far removed from his own. On the other hand, though, Stroessner was the main enemy, and he was waging an all-out war. Anyone opposed to him must be treated as an ally. Therefore the negotiations prospered. With Laíno's blessing, the issue of reunification was placed on the agenda when the Radical Liberals held their next convention, in January 1977.

That convention was a stormy one, for Benítez and the old guard attacked Laíno's record, asking what had actually been accomplished by the left. They contended that Stroessner was not one bit weaker today than he had been in 1975. Indeed, they said, the intemperate rhetoric of the left had actually goaded the regime into its new show of its strength, and this new crackdown showed the futility of adopting a belligerent position. Moreover, they charged that Laíno's leadership was not as strong and uncompromising as his language: after condemning electoral participation by the Benítez faction, he had changed his position and entered the municipal elections—and with even more disastrous results. Now, they pointed out, he was again abandoning his former principles by proposing that the Radical Liberals invite the Levi-Liberals back to their ranks. The one principle on which party radicals and conservatives had been able to agree was that the Levi Ruffinellis could not be trusted, but now Laíno was proposing to bring this Trojan horse inside the party's gates.

Despite this attack, Laíno still had the support of a majority of the party. His slate of candidates won control of the party directorate, and he was returned as president. Moreover, the convention approved the proposed merger with the Liberal party. Henceforth, the reunited Liberals would be known as the Partido Liberal Unido. Finally, it was agreed that they would abstain from all future elections until there were guarantees of honesty.[15]

The battle was not over, however. Stroessner had scheduled general elections for February 1978, and he meant to have an opposition slate in the race. Moreover, he was determined not to be embarrassed by the opposition's surrendering its seats in Congress—which it would have to do if it failed to enter candidates in the elections. To Laíno's surprise, the party found itself the defendant in a lawsuit, brought by Benítez, which questioned its legality. The suit contended that the new United Liberal party had no official status. According to Paraguayan law, no party could enjoy a legal public character until it had been recognized by the Supreme Electoral Commission. Such recognition had been granted previously to the Liberal party and to the Radical Liberal party, but so far the commission had not taken cognizance of the "so-called" United Liberal Party. Until it did so, the reunited party could not legally function—it had no "judicial personality."

The Electoral Commission heard arguments from June through August, 1977, as both sides presented briefs. Laíno argued, of course, that since the Radical Liberal and the Liberal parties were both legal parties they had a right to enter a contract to merger. Therefore, the United Liberal party was, by implication, legal. But trouble had started already for the party. Since its status was in question, the commission ordered its bank accounts frozen, suspended the publication of *El Radical*, and closed the party's headquarters. When the final decision was handed down in September, it came as no surprise that Benítez was upheld. His faction, which had set itself up as the Radical Liberal party again, was accorded official recognition, meaning that it would now have the use of the Casa Azul, the party newspaper, and all the party's assets. Furthermore, Fulvión Celauro, an exdeputy who headed a dissident faction of the Levi-Liberals, was granted recognition as the new president of the Liberal party, thus isolating Laíno and the Levi Ruffinellis.[16]

The United Liberal party was thrown into a panic, of course. It offered to drop its abstentionist platform if the government would grant it recognition, but the government ignored the offer. Meanwhile, the loss of legality posed serious problems for certain party leaders. As members of a nonexistent party Laíno, Gonzalez, and Lara de Castro stood to lose their congressional seats—and their parliamentary immunity. The Levi Ruffinelli brothers were treated somewhat more leniently. They were told that they could stay in Congress, with the implication being that they were on probation.

The stranded United Liberals soon felt the consequences of losing legality. In addition to losing their congressional seats their leader, Laíno, was arrested in July 1978. He had just returned from a visit to

Washington, where he had denounced the Stroessner regime before the Inter-American Commission on Human Rights. Although Laíno was released a month later, after the American embassy pressured the Paraguayan government on his behalf, the dilemma faced by his faction was painful indeed: either open rebellion and worse persecution or a sort of political limbo—an impotent intransigence overshadowed by constant fear of police harassment. To understand something of what that means it is useful to consider, by way of analogy, Paraguay's third tolerated party, the Christian Democrats.

The Christian Democratic Party

The Christian Democratic party is not legally recognized, but it is permitted to function. That is to say, Christian Democrats are restricted to private meetings; they may not run in elections, hold office, or have public rallies. They claim that Stroessner fears them and wants to discourage them, but the government says that the Christian Democrats have failed to get enough petitioners to meet the law's minimum requirements for recognition. The latter is probably closer to the truth, but in any case the party continues to exist. It does so, however, in an ambience in which the slightest misstep might end the unofficial toleration and bring down the whole force of the government's police power.

The Christian Democrats launched their first organization in May 1960, when a group of Catholic laymen, concerned about what they felt was a deep moral and political crisis in Paraguay, started the Movimiento Social Demócrata Cristiano. Reflecting the ideological changes then taking place in the Catholic church, they proposed a program of "spiritual socialism," which would radically transform social institutions while offering an alternative to the materialistic and atheistic doctrine of Marxism.[17]

Headed by Jorge Escobar and Luís Resck, the *movimiento* attracted the government's suspicion from the very beginning. Although the Christian Democrats claimed to be independent of the church, it was believed that they were simply the radical clergy's attempt to form a political party. In 1962, Escobar was taken into custody during Adlai Stevenson's visit to Paraguay in order to keep him from contacting the American visitor. The following year, Resck was jailed for making an antigovernment speech over the radio.

Despite such harassment the organization continued to grow, and by 1965 it felt strong enough to hold a convention at which it drew up a formal constitution and changed its name to the Christian

Democratic party. The party's first president was Jerónimo Irala Burgos, one of the original founders of the movement. His openly revolutionary line brought a sharp escalation in government persecution. Many Christian Democrats were sent to prison and tortured. Irala Burgos himself was hounded into exile in 1970, and the party offices were raided by the police, who carried off all their records and membership lists.[18]

The next president was Alfredo Ayala Haedo, who took over in 1969. Though more conservative than Irala Burgos, he paid more attention to such details as membership recruitment. He also felt that the party was not yet strong enough to fight the regime, and so he set out to achieve its legalization. That split the Christian Democrats, however, for the party youth and the workers' Central Laboral were opposed to anything that looked like appeasement. Worse yet, the government turned down Ayala Haedo's petition for legal recognition. In order to protect the party's members and sympathizers, he had refused to comply with the Electoral Commission's requirement of a petition signed by ten thousand persons.

Unable to come up with a satisfactory solution to the party's problems, Ayala Haedo was assailed by a new left-wing faction calling itself the Vanguard. This struggle was to tear the party apart. A convention was scheduled in January 1971 to settle the leadership issue, but it was broken up by the police. A second convention, held in March, resulted in such a vicious battle between Ayala Haedo's backers and the Vanguard that all the delegates walked out after the first day. A third convention, in May, succeeded in passing a resolution repudiating Ayala Haedo's leadership, but then order broke down completely before a new National Council could be elected. Finally, in July, the Christian Democrats chose Hermógenes Rojas Silva, the chief of the Vanguard, as their next president.

The Ayala Haedo faction withdrew from any further participation. Membership declined and there was a sad lack of funds. On top of that, Rojas Silva showed little interest in leadership once he was elected president. The organization drifted aimlessly. In October 1973, Rojas Silva was replaced by Luís Resck, one of the original founders of the movement.

The party was still not finished with its agonies. Within a few months, Resck found himself challenged by his vice-president, Nicasio Martínez Díaz. To his surprise and indignation he learned that Martínez Díaz and his clique were already acting as though they ran the party and had passed around the rumor that Resck had resigned—a rumor which Resck was quick to deny. The result was two parallel party organizations, each claiming to be the real one. An extraordinary convention settled the question in June 1975 in favor of Resck. By that time, though, the Christian Democratic party was thoroughly demoralized and almost moribund. As one amused Colorado observed, "They're so tiny, and yet they still squabble!"

The Untolerated Opposition

Cut off from the country they wish to govern, the exiled parties, principally the Communist party and the Popular Colorado Movement (mopoco), struggle to keep their followers' faith alive and to maintain contact with the homeland.

Yet exile may have its advantages. Stroessner's police are not able to intervene directly and forbid people to meet or criticize the regime in public. Nevertheless, exiles are always aware that, as guests of a foreign government, they can operate only within prescribed limits. If the host government is friendly toward them—as the Perón regime from 1973 to 1975 was toward the mopocos—then exile may be preferable to harassment back home. But if the host country changes its government or its foreign policy, the exiles' activities may become a diplomatic embarrassment. When that happens they are doubly penalized: cut off from their native land, and persecuted as undesirable aliens.

The Communist Party

The Paraguayan Communist party is neither legal nor tolerated in Paraguay. Of its total membership, estimated at between three and five thousand, all but a handful are in exile.[19] Nonetheless, the Stroessner government has made much of the alleged Communist menace to justify the continual state of siege. Even in exile, however, the Communist party has had only limited success in linking itself to other opposition groups. Some of the radical Febreristas expelled in 1951 and later were obviously sympathetic to communism, and a few even joined the Communist party after being purged. Also, the Communists tried to infiltrate the Liberal and Febrerista guerrilla movements in the 1950s. However, their success was only limited and temporary, for the Liberal and Febrerista leadership never endorsed such organizations as FULNA and even ordered their members to withdraw from it.

Besides being politically isolated, the party shows a certain ossification. Since its founding in 1928 it has been dominated by the same two men, Oscar Creydt and Obdulio Barthe, both of whom are university graduates and sons of wealthy Paraguayan families. With their command of Marxist ideology and their superior contacts with the Third International—having traveled abroad to Europe—these two were the natural leaders of the unsophisticated railroad and dock workers, whose unions were started in the late 1920s. For a brief period the party controlled Paraguayan labor, but with the 1936 revolution they were displaced by a stronger rival—the new Febrerista movement. The Communist party got the upper hand again, however, after Morínigo came to power, for he was determined to crush the Febreristas' rapidly growing influence. A curious arrangement grew up by which his profascist government outlawed *febrerismo* and turned the labor unions over to the Communists' workers' councils. Nevertheless, when the civil war broke out the Communists, certain that Morínigo would fall, made the mistake of joining the rebels, thus forfeiting their privileged position and ending up in exile, where they have been ever since.[20]

Like other exile parties, the Communist party fell prey to factionalism. The old leaders were accused of poor strategy and of failing to consult the rank and file. Creydt, the president, had called only two party conferences since the founding of the party—one in 1941 and another in 1949. A third was scheduled for 1955, but never took place. Moreover, by the middle 1960s a new generation of Communists had grown up which was no longer content to follow Creydt simply because he had Moscow's blessing. Oddly enough, though, when the revolt finally happened in 1968 it was led by the party's other "grand old man," Obdulio Barthe. Calling itself the Paraguayan Leninist Communist Party, this splinter group accepted the sponsorship of Peking and attacked Creydt for creating a "cult of personality."

Although the splinter group was read out of the party, Creydt later tried to heal the breach by inviting the rebels back. That required some tricky ideological juggling in order to satisfy their Maoist demands. In the end he only split his own pro-Moscow wing and got himself supplanted by Miguel Angel Soler, Jr., a former left-wing Febrerista who had switched parties. Under Soler the party never wavered from its strict conformity to the Moscow line, but it also showed more initiative by setting up underground cells inside Paraguay. It received a severe setback in February 1977, however, when Soler and several of his aides were captured in a police raid in Asunción. With its leadership thus smashed the party was left demoralized, although its Russian backers would probably not allow it to go out of existence altogether.

The Popular Colorado Movement

The MOPOCOS claim to be the *real* Colorado party. They refer to the men around Stroessner contemptuously as *oficialistas*. They are certain that the vast majority of Colorados in Paraguay are really MOPOCOS at heart and would show it if a free convention were held. Even most of the *oficialistas*, they say, would revolt against Stroessner, if they felt that they had a chance. On one point, at least, they agree with the *oficialistas*: the Colorado party is the great party of the Paraguayan masses and that all other parties represent only minority opinions. Precisely for that reason, say the MOPOCOS—because the Colorados are a majority of the people, and the MOPOCOS are a majority of the Colorados—Stroessner is afraid to extend them a political amnesty.

The movement was formed in 1959 by exiled *epifanistas* and *democráticos* who laid aside their former bitter rivalry in order to fight Stroessner. Many prominent Colorados have served on the MOPOCO executive committee: Epifanio Méndez Fleitas, José Zacarias Arza, Osvaldo Cháves, Mario Mallorquín, General Carlos Montanaro, Colonel Enrique Giménez, Virgílio Cataldi, Evaristo Méndez Paiva, and Heriberto Braganza, a former leader of the Paraguayan Workers' Confederation. Of all these men, however, Méndez Fleitas and Osvaldo Cháves are the real brains and spirit of the movement. No one else devotes more time than they to the tasks of organization and propaganda.

The MOPOCOS have adopted an extreme nationalist and statist position. In contrast to Stroessner's friendliness to private enterprise and foreign capital, they favor the nationalization of all banking and insurance, as well as most private industry. They also want an agrarian reform that would abolish both the *latifundio* and the *minifundio* and replace them with state-regulated peasant cooperatives. All aspects of the economy would be run according to a government plan. However, labor would be free to organize and strike, and provision would be made for a measure of municipal financial autonomy—although just how that would be worked out is unclear. In any case, the general idea is that the present system of "capitalist exploitation" is to be ended.[21]

The MOPOCOS claim that they will bring about this transformation of the economy and society through democratic means. Although the first step, of course, is to get rid of Stroessner, the MOPOCOS say that they reject the insurrectionist thesis and place their confidence in the Paraguayan people to end the tyranny someday. Their apparent involvement in the November 1974 plot to assassinate Stroessner suggests that they may be trying to hurry that day along, however. Once Stroessner falls there must be an end to the state of siege, a general amnesty, a constitutional convention with the participation of all parties, and free elections.

In their international policy, the MOPOCOS are strong against imperialism—and by imperialism they mean the United States. For them, the American government bears the chief blame for keeping Stroessner in power. It is simply assumed that all the regime's supporters have been bought by American money. Indeed, sometimes the MOPOCOS approach the point of paranoia, seeing agents of the Pentagon and the CIA everywhere, plotting incessantly to keep Latin America under the thumb of American capitalism. For example, Osvaldo Cháves once concluded that Robert McNamara, the World Bank president, was fostering an imperialist plot when he urged the Third World to make greater efforts at birth control. According to Cháves, McNamara was using sinister electronic computers to generate phony statistics in order to decrease the Third World's population, and so "kill off the guerrilla fighters of tomorrow."[22]

Next to the United States, the favorite target of the MOPOCOS is Brazil, which they view as little more than an American puppet. They condemn Brazil's military government as "fascist" and interpret any evidence of Stroessner's friendliness to it as an example of his treasonous appeasement of imperialism. The Itaipú treaty was, for them, the epitome of such sellout diplomacy. By contrast, the MOPOCOS tend to be pro-Argentina. In part, that may be because they hope to capitalize on the traditional Argentine-Brazilian rivalry in order to get backing for a revolution. It would not be the first time that that has happened in Paraguayan history. Also, it may reflect the close connections that Méndez Fleitas has always had with the Argentine Peronist movement. In fact, when Perón returned to power in 1973, Méndez Fleitas, who was then the MOPOCO president, moved his headquarters from Montevideo to Buenos Aires. However, after Perón's death in 1974 and his wife's fall from power two years later the political climate in Argentina changed for MOPOCOS. The new military government of General Jorge Videla became suspicious that Méndez Fleitas and other left-leaning MOPOCOS were in touch with underground Peronist guerrilla organizations, such as the Montoneros. Méndez Fleitas was arrested and held without charge, and the MOPOCOS were in worse straits than ever before.

It is difficult to assess their real strength in exile, and it is impossible to verify how many ostensibly *oficialista* Colorados in Paraguay may really harbor MOPOCO sentiments. At one time the *epifanistas* and *democráticos* could claim between them a majority of the party, but that was a generation ago. In politics, exile is a slow, wasting disease. If treated in time, it can be cured; but if allowed to go on too long it is inevitably fatal.

Summing Up

In the preface it was noted that General Alfredo Stroessner's regime was one of the world's oldest dictatorships, and the reader was promised that a study of it would be useful for understanding politics. Politics, after all, is the pursuit and exercise of power—and this Stroessner has done with exceptional success. What is the secret of that success?

Part 1 described the physical, cultural, and historical environment that made Stroessner's kind of regime possible. First, Paraguay's political traditions, formed by geography and past experience, are very congenial to dictatorship. Stroessner would probably never have risen to power—or if he had done so, would not have survived—in a country with stronger civic traditions. But where the masses are poor and ignorant, where social values see politics as an all-or-nothing struggle for scarce resources, and where the military is customarily a governing force because it alone can impose order, Stroessner's sort of rule is not out of place.

Moreover, Stroessner's success cannot be understood without reference to the violent upheavals of the post–Chaco War period. After emerging from the second great, bloody war in its history, the nation entered a period of harsh social revolution, then an equally bitter period of reaction, next a civil war, and finally a series of brief, cynical, and violent governments led by Colorado politicians. The only situation that is analogous to this picture of utter social disruption and how it can legitimate dictatorship is modern Spain. There the terrible ordeal of the civil war produced such a social trauma, including the mass expulsion of one political camp, that Generalissimo Francisco Franco was able to rule without significant opposition for thirty-seven years. Like Spain after its civil war, Paraguay in 1954 was exhausted. Any strong man who could impose peace and order—

even if it were the peace of the club and the gun—would claim the gratitude of a large number of people, for whom democracy was an alien idea anyway. This Stroessner proceeded to do.

Yet historical opportunity is not enough. Political success requires both the favorable objective conditions and a powerful personality to take advantage of that situation. Stroessner was such a man of action. Furthermore, he had much better organizational talents than most Paraguayan *caudillos*. True, he is very much in the Latin American military strongman tradition, with his moustache and medals, his rough-and-ready manner of dealing with both friends and enemies, and his ability to build up a personal following through his reputation for resourcefulness and his distribution of patronage. But he is more than a typical *caudillo*. For instance, Stroessner devotes himself to the job of being president with exceptional energy. In a country where nature easily provides and where *mañana* is good enough, his drive makes him stand out and gives him an advantage. Also, he is a good administrator. He pays attention to details and provides himself with firsthand knowledge about the running of his political machine. When it is necessary to delegate authority, he displays a shrewd instinct in his choice of subordinates.

Above all, Stroessner is a skillful strategist. In his dealings with rival Colorado factions, with other military men, or with the opposition parties and the clergy he exhibits the qualities of a good general. A master at grasping the political situation, he knows when to hold back, or even retreat in the face of superior force, as when the military forced him to raise the state of siege in 1959, and he can strike hard and ruthlessly when he senses that the enemy is weak. Preferring to fight only when the odds are heavily on his side, he likes to divide his opponents by compromising with some but not others, and then setting them to quarrel with each other. When he first came to power his position was insecure, so he pretended to be modest and deferential as he sought to disarm everyone. First he backed the *democráticos* against the *epifanistas*; then the Guionists against the *democráticos*; and finally he suppressed the Guionists. After the fall of each rival faction he controlled a larger share of the party. Also, every upheaval was attended by the fall of key military officers as well, and their places were filled by Stroessner's appointees. In this way he captured, in piecemeal fashion, the two main pillars on which he was to base his regime—the Colorado party and the armed forces.

In his use of the Colorado party Stroessner has introduced a modern element into his dictatorship, which sets him apart from the typical Paraguayan *caudillo*. As he purged, disciplined, and centralized the party, he also created a clear chain of command that enhanced his regime's ability to mobilize a large mass of supporters. Systematizing the party's symbols and traditional hatreds into a kind of ideology, he extended its ancillary organizations into practically every major social group. Neighborhood vigilantes were exhorted to keep watch on political suspects. The party and state bureaucracies were interpenetrated. In sum, the Colorado party came as close to being a modern totalitarian movement as Paraguay's rudimentary technology would permit, and those technological shortcomings were less hampering because Paraguay is a relatively small and simple country, and therefore easier to control.

The value of such an organization has proved itself many times. The Colorados' mass base in the peasantry kept the opposition parties in exile from repeating the example of the Cuban Revolution, for the government's intelligence in the countryside was decisive in putting a quick end to every guerrilla incursion. That, plus the loyalty of the army, forced the opposition to come to terms.

The monolithic party has also been a counterweight to the military. Of course the armed forces are still the most powerful group in the state. Stroessner must cultivate them carefully by giving them lucrative jobs, prestigious posts, and access to graft. But at the same time he is by no means as dependent on them as former *caudillos* were. It is too simple to say that Paraguay is only a military regime, for it would be no easy matter for the armed forces to carry out a revolt against Stroessner. To begin with, Stroessner pays close attention to military promotions and assignments. He acts as his own commander in chief, and he takes care to cultivate the junior officers. He also has his own, handpicked Presidential Escort Battalion. But beyond all that the Colorado party represents the potential power of the masses, whose loyalty is presumably to Stroessner. A successful military revolt would probably have to involve many different units and many different levels of command. The chances of such a conspiracy escaping the attention of police spies and Colorado party *pyragüés* are practically nil. And if an attack were attempted, the officers would hardly be able to count on the loyalty of their men, many of whom are Colorado peasants.

Controlling the levers of power is still not enough, for in the modern world even dictatorships have to be concerned with public relations— hence the great effort that goes into propaganda. Moreover, policies must be pursued that make the regime popular and give it a reputation as dynamic and progressive. That may not be the image that Stroessner has in the foreign press, but a visitor to Paraguay cannot avoid the conclusion that he is held in some esteem there. Because of steadily growing prosperity, which trickles down even to the humble,

Stroessner has come to be regarded as the country's indispensable man, and economic development has become an important buttress for his regime. It provides him with more patronage and welds the economic elites more firmly to him. Economic development is also a source of national pride, for through it Paraguay is better linked to the outside world and is courted by its neighbors for its hydroelectric potential.

Stroessner also has the advantage of being surrounded by countries whose governments have a stake in his survival. The right-wing military regimes that rule Argentina, Brazil, and Bolivia need a strong anti-Communist dictatorship in Paraguay; an anarchic Paraguay might conceivably become a haven for guerrillas and terrorists. The same jungle frontiers that now encourage smuggling would then provide a cover for armed bands. Therefore, since the early 1960s Stroessner's neighbors have cooperated in keeping Paraguayan exiles under close observation to prevent them from using their territories as staging grounds for invasions. This sort of support for his regime makes it even less likely that Stroessner could be toppled by a revolution.

Nevertheless, if Stroessner has created an imposing dictatorship, it is still a personalistic one, and is therefore fragile. Someday he must pass from the scene. Then events will show whether the Stroessner era was simply an aberrant phase in the country's history or whether it has laid the foundations for important future changes. Some observers suggest that Stroessner has a statesmanlike conception of his historical role and that Paraguay's social and economic transformation is part of a conscious plan. One American economist observes, for instance, that "positive indications that President Stroessner is genuinely interested in the economic and social development of the nation are evident in many of his actions, including the caliber of men selected for development positions." This same writer also concluded that "when measured against the historical background, the present administration has made great progress." [1] Another American, this one a political scientist, predicted in 1968 that Stroessner was gradually preparing the nation for democracy, for "if Stroessner's only goal had been to remain king in his small fiefdom, he would have never permitted the opposition to regain legal status nor allowed newspapers to criticize everything but the president himself. Neither would he have undertaken development schemes that show signs of upsetting the traditional status quo. The opposition is fond of claiming that international pressures forced the recent political liberalization, but Stroessner had no reason to subject himself to any outside pressures unless he chose to do so voluntarily.

Stroessner may, therefore, have some greater plan for the country's economic and political development and a vision that transcends merely being president."[2]

The return to repression after 1969 shattered such optimistic hopes. Richard Bourne, who wrote just at the time when that shift was taking place, took a far more negative view of the regime. For him, Stroessner was an anachronism. Paraguay, he asserted, "is psychologically adjusted to being ruled by a *caudillo* in 1969, long after such figures are little more than a barbaric memory elsewhere." Nor did he credit Stroessner with any farsighted plans for the country. Rather, the regime was a crude, naked tyranny. Unlike some other contemporary dictators, who justified their regimes on the basis of material progress, Stroessner was "not interested in the military as an engine for social change or bourgeois modernization."[3]

What the present study shows is that neither the enthusiastic nor the censorious view does complete justice to Stroessner. From the perspective of the past few years, there is little evidence that the regime is moving toward democracy. Quite the opposite seems to be the case; in all probability the opposition's liberties in Paraguay are even more restricted now than they were a decade ago. On the other hand, it is simply not true to say that Stroessner is little more than a political Neanderthal. That would overlook completely the material changes that have taken place in Paraguay. Stroessner may have political motives for promoting economic development, and his policies may benefit the upper classes—nevertheless, Paraguay is being modernized. Moreover, the long-term effects of that are impossible to predict and may have revolutionary consequences.

For one thing, modernization may make regimes like Stroessner's obsolete in Paraguay. That is not to say that it will necessarily lead to democracy, either. Given Paraguay's political traditions, a more sophisticated type of dictatorship with greater technical control and elaborate organization may result. As the urban population continues to grow and the traditional apathy of the countryside breaks down, the likelihood of an old-fashioned military dictatorship succeeding Stroessner becomes remote. No doubt the military will continue to play a large role in Paraguay's politics for the foreseeable future, but unless economic growth is to be sacrificed, it will have to co-opt the talents of civilian technicians to help it govern. Moreover, it is unlikely that the country—elites and masses alike—would tolerate a government that mismanaged the economy. Therefore, the old cynical *caudillo* politics of the past, which produced Stroessner, may have been rendered obsolete by his administration. If so, then his long rule constitutes an important watershed in Paraguay's political evolution.

Alternatively, Stroessner might be succeeded by a party dictatorship. The Colorado party has a mass base, incorporates most of the country's important social groups, and has a well-trained organization. Under Stroessner's tutelage it has become an efficient political machine, capable of undertaking the coordination of a large number of tasks and of mobilizing popular support. It is questionable, however, whether party discipline will survive Stroessner. Without a strongman at the top the Colorados may break apart again into petty warring factions. Stroessner has seen to it that no politician acquires enough stature to rival him; consequently, no one on the scene now looks strong enough to take over the organization and guide it through the crisis that is certain to erupt after Stroessner goes.

The possibility that any one of the opposition parties, or any coalition of them, would be capable of governing seems more remote still. So far the Liberals, Febreristas, and Christian Democrats have not shown the slightest aptitude for rule. Parties that cannot govern themselves, that cannot preserve their own unity under pressure, have no claim to the public's confidence. In any case, the more radical among them would probably not be accepted by the military, which would certainly fear revenge by the opposition for its support of Stroessner.

Paraguay will most likely continue, therefore, to be true to its long tradition of dictatorial government. The present combination of military and party rule, but with a greater emphasis on recruiting technocrats, is probably the safest prediction for the future. As urban and industrial ways spread, bringing with them the usual problems of restless masses and rising expectations, the government will be faced with more difficult challenges to its preserving order. While such ferment might conceivably result in democracy, it is more likely to bring only anarchy. Until the Paraguayans discover the art of give and take—which seems to be a long way off—their choice after Stroessner will be between a strong dictator or a weak one, and since a society lacking in social discipline is inimical to economic progress, the chances are that only a truly powerful regime will be respected. For although Paraguayans like to talk of democratic ideals, they have always, as a nation, displayed their greatest reverence for their most ironfisted tyrants. So it can be predicted that Stroessner, however brutal and corrupt his regime may seem, will someday find his place in the Pantheon of Heroes.

Notes

Chapter 1

1. Paraguayan and Argentine troops clashed along the border as late as 1978. At a meeting of the Latin American Free Trade Association (LAFTA) in July 1965 the Argentine foreign minister walked out during an argument with the Paraguayan foreign minister over the right of free navigation on the Paraná River.

2. Philip Raine, *Paraguay*, p. 340.

3. República del Paraguay, Ministerio de Hacienda, Dirección General de Estadística y Censo, *Anuario Estadístico de la República del Paraguay, 1948–1953.*

4. Raine, *Paraguay*, pp. 369–80, *Anuario Estadístico*, pp. 74–76.

5. *Anuario Estadístico*, p. 23. Raine, *Paraguay*, pp. 309–13, disagrees with the official figures. His own estimates are almost double those of the official census.

Chapter 2

1. The most thorough biography of Francia is by Julio César Cháves, *El supremo dictador*. Also useful for Francia's economic policies is Atilio García Mellid, *Proceso a los falsificadores de la historia del Paraguay*, vol. 1.

2. Luís Vittone, *Las FF.AA. paraguayas en sus distintas épocas*, pp. 92–95.

3. See especially García Mellid, *Proceso*, vol. 1, chaps. 16, 17, 21, and 22.

4. Standard anti-López works are R. B. Cunninghame Graham, *Portrait of a Dictator*; Charles Ames Washburn, *The History of Paraguay, with Notes and Personal Observations.* The standard pro-López work is Juan O'Leary, *El Mariscal Solano López.* For a serious but sympathetic treatment of López in English, see Charles J. Kolinski, *Independence or Death!*

5. Henry D. Ceuppens, *Paraguay, año 2000*, pp. 227–28; and Gerardo Fogel, et al., *Paraguay, realidad y futuro*, pp. 25–26.

6. Teodosio González, *Infortunios del Paraguay*, pp. 108–21.

7. On the rise of the *latifundios* in Paraguay and their social consequences, see Carlos Pastore, *La lucha por la tierra en el Paraguay*, pp. 253–57. Also, Teodosio González, *Infortunios*, chaps. 7, 8, and 25; García Mellid, *Proceso*, vol. 2, chap. 11; Carlos A. Caroni, *Síntesis histórico del problema agrario en el Paraguay*, p. 19.

8. Policarpo Artaza, *Que hizo el Partido Liberal en la oposición y en el gobierno*, pp. 21–32. Also, Alonso Ibarra, *Cien años de la vida política paraguaya*, pp. 24–37.

9. On the Liberal factions of this period, see Artaza, *Que hizo*, pp. 28–38; Efraím Cardozo, *23 de octubre*, pp. 19–25.

10. Concerning Paraguay's war preparations, Policarpo Artaza defends the Liberals in his *Ayala, Estigarribia, y el Partido Liberal*. But the opposition's case is better documented in Antonio E. González, *Preparación del Paraguay para la Guerra del Chaco*. Even the Liberals' commander in chief, Marshal Estigarribia, is critical in his memoirs. See José Felix Estigarribia, *The Epic of the Chaco*, p. 7. On the *23 de octubre* incident, see Artaza, *Ayala, Estigarribia*, pp. 53–63, for a defense of the Liberal government. Other pro-Liberal works are Cardozo, *23 de octubre* (see esp. pp. 229–349); Justo Prieto, *Llenese los claros*. The anti-Liberal side is presented in Juan Stefanich, *El 23 de octubre de 1931*; Enrique Volta Gaona, *23 de octubre: caireles de sangre en el alma de la patria paraguaya*; and Antonio E. González, *Preparación*, vol. 1, pp. 151–64.

11. For a history of the revolution by an insider, see Juan Stefanich's four volumes: *El Paraguay en el febrero de 1936; Renovación y liberación; La restauración histórica del Paraguay; La diplomacía de la revolución*. All of the revolutionary government's decrees and proclamations were published in a single volume. See República del Paraguay, *La revolución paraguaya*. Artaza's *Ayala, Estigarribia* is the best single work for criticizing the revolution. Harris Gaylord Warren, "Political Aspects of the Paraguayan Revolution, 1936–1940," pp. 2–25, provides an excellent overview of this period.

12. See Warren, "Political Aspects," pp. 21–23.

13. Amos J. Peaslee, *Constitutions of Nations*, vol. 2. See especially Estigarribia's essay at the end of the section, justifying and explaining the principles behind the new constitution.

14. The best general description of Morínigo's dictatorship is in Harris Gaylord Warren, *Paraguay*, pp. 333–53.

15. Events surrounding this revolt are described in *La Prensa* (Buenos Aires), 10–12 June 1946; *New York Times*, 10–13 June 1946; Warren, *Paraguay*, pp. 348–49.

16. *New York Times*, 5 August 1946, p. 14; Warren, *Paraguay*, p. 350.

17. The coalition cabinet consisted of Febreristas—Arnaldo Valdovinos (agriculture, industry and commerce), José Soljancic (public health), Miguel Angel Soler, Sr. (foreign relations); Colorados—Federico Cháves (public works), Juan Natalicio González (finance), Guillermo Enciso Velloso (education); Military—General Juan Rovira (interior), General Amancio Pampliega (defense). When General Rovira later resigned, General Pampliega shifted to the Ministry of Interior and General Vicente Machuca became minister of defense.

18. Much of the biographical data on Natalicio González is from Gilberto González y Contreros, *J. Natalacio González, descubridor del Paraguay*. The book is highly prejudiced in his favor, but remains the only full-length account of his career.

19. Other important works for understanding González's ideas are *Como se construye una nación; El estado servidor del hombre libre*; and "Teoría y fundamentos de la libertad," pp. 5–34.

20. *La Prensa*, 26 July 1946, p. 6.

21. *La Prensa*, 15 August 1946, p. 5; and 17 August 1946, p. 6.

22. *La Prensa*, 8–16 September 1946; 19 September 1946; 13 December 1946.

23. *New York Times*, 12 August 1946, p. 5; 13 October 1946, p. 3. Some

estimates of the Communist party's membership ran as high as eight thousand; see *New York Times*, 30 December 1946, p. 5.

24. The new cabinet consisted of Colorados—Juan Natalicio González (finance), Federico Cháves (foreign relations), Victor Morínigo (interior), Guillermo Enciso Velloso (agriculture, industry, and commerce), Victor Boettner (education); Military—Naval Captain Ramón Martino (defense), Colonel Mushuito Villasboa (public works), Colonel César Gagliardone (public health). Victor Morínigo was no relation to President Morínigo, but he was a close friend of Natalicio González and one of the cofounders of the Guión Rojo.

25. On the 1947 civil war, see O. Barcena Echeveste, *Concepción, 1947*; Antonio E. González, *La rebelión de Concepción*; Warren, *Paraguay*; Oscar Peyrón, *Morínigo*; *La Prensa*, March–August 1947; and *New York Times*, March–August 1947.

26. Barcena Echeveste denies this charge, but Febreristas and Liberals insist that aid was sent. See Artaza, *Que hizo*, pp. 68–69; Manuel J. Cibils, *Anarquía y revolución en el Paraguay*, p. 58. Warren, *Paraguay*, p. 353, quotes General J. A. Flores of the Brazilian General Staff to the effect that shipments of aid were sent by Perón to Morínigo. Barcena Echeveste himself quotes Colonel Federico Weddell Smith's letter to a Buenos Aires journalist, in which he condemns Argentine intervention in the civil war. See *Concepción, 1947*, pp. 208, 255–56. Also, on 29 March 1959, *La Prensa*, p. 8, quotes a passage from the daily record of the Argentine Chamber of Deputies for the session cf 22 August 1947. In it, a Radical party deputy, objecting to a government request for additional defense appropriations, accused the Perón regime of having sent Morínigo "arms, projectiles, fuel, and all manner of war materiel," to the amount of five million *pesos*.

27. The only book-length account of the naval revolt is Edgar Ynsfran, *La irrupción muscovita en la marina paraguaya*, which is very pro-Colorado. Nevertheless, it contains important descriptive material.

Chapter 3

1. Juan F. Pérez Acosta, *Migraciones históricas del Paraguay a la Argentina*, p. 17; Domingo M. Rivarola, "Aspectos de la migracíon paraguaya," pp. 56–58.

2. Manuel J. Cibils, *Anarquía y revolución en el Paraguay*, pp. 59, 68.

3. Philip Raine, *Paraguay*, p. 265; *La Prensa*, 17–21 November 1947; *New York Times*, 20 November 1947, p. 19.

4. Cibils, *Anarquía y revolución*, p. 59.

5. Besides Estigarribia and Zacarias Arza, other prominent *democráticos* to be expelled were Juan R. Cháves, Fabio da Silva, J. Bernardino Gorostiaga, Epifanio Méndez Fleitas, Evaristo Méndez Paiva, Rigoberto Caballero, and Roberto L. Petit. All of them were to become leading government figures after Cháves came to power in 1949, and the first three were to hold high positions in the Stroessner regime.

6. *New York Times*, 15 February 1948, p. 3. Those elected to Congress represented an "honor roll" of Guión Rojo activists: Manuel Talavera, Abel dos Santos, Mario Mallorquín, Felipe Molas López, Leandro Prieto, Mario Ferrario (who was also police chief), Sabino Montanaro, J. Augusto Saldivar, Edgar Ynsfran, and Enrique Volta Gaona. The last four men were to become prominent figures in the Stroessner regime.

7. Sindulfo Martínez, *Hombres y pasiones*, pp. 115–16.

8. Details of the plot are from Gilberto González y Contreras, *J. Natalicio*

González, descubridor del Paraguay, pp. 341–42; *La Prensa*, 4 June 1948, p. 7.

9. Molas López became minister of education; Mario Mallorquín was minister of public works; Domingo Montanaro (brother of Colonel Carlos Montanaro) became interior minister. Colonel Montanaro was made army commander in chief, and Liberato Rodríguez stayed on as head of the police. Other posts went to Crispín Insaurralde (public health), a Guionist writer and intellectual; Leandro Prieto (economy), a close friend of Natalicio González; and Colonel Raimundo Rolón (defense).

10. The composition of González's cabinet was Molas López (education), Mallorquín (economics), Insaurralde (public health), Prieto (finance), Domingo Montanaro (foreign affairs), Victor Morínigo (public works), Colonel Rolón (defense), and J. Augusto Saldivar (interior and justice). The last-named was the only new face, and he was pro–Molas López. The fact that Victor Morínigo had been "demoted" from the key post of interior minister under Morínigo to minister of foreign relations under Frutos and to minister of public works in the new cabinet was another gauge of Natalicio González's gradual decline in power.

11. *La Prensa*, 26–28 October 1948; *New York Times*, 26–29 October 1948; 2–3 December 1948.

12. *La Prensa*, 1 February 1949, p. 6.

13. *La Prensa*, 31 January 1949, p. 4.

14. J. Natalicio González, *Como se construye una nación*, p. 29; González y Contreras, *J. Natalicio González*, p. 376.

15. *New York Times*, 1 February 1949, p. 16.

16. *New York Times*, 20 February 1949, p. 22; 24 February 1949, p. 13.

17. William S. Stokes, "Violence as a Power Factor in Latin American Politics," *Western Political Quarterly* 5 (September 1959): 458–59.

18. The full cabinet consisted of Liberato Rodríguez (interior), Mario Mallorquín (justice), and J. Augusto Saldivar (economics), from the *molaslopista* faction; José Zacarias Arza (defense), Rigoberto Caballero (public works), Ramón Méndez Paiva (finance), J. Eulogio Estigarribia (education), and Hugo Peña (public health) from the *democráticos*. Federico Cháves served as minister of foreign affairs until April and then resigned to run for Congress.

19. Asociación Nacional Republicana (Partido Colorado), *Manifiesto de la Junta de Gobierno*, pp. 5–11; *La Prensa*, 11 September 1949, p. 1.

20. *Ibid.*; Asociación Nacional Republicana (Partido Colorado), *El caso Estigarribia*, pp. 6, 22–23. Information in these pamphlets was supplemented by an interview with Mario Mallorquín in Buenos Aires, 17 July 1973.

21. *Hispanic American Report*, September 1949, pp. 24–25.

22. *Hispanic American Report*, December 1949, p. 30; *New York Times*, 22 November 1952, p. 5.

23. Raine, *Paraguay*, p. 269.

24. *Hispanic American Report*, July 1952, p. 36.

25. G. A. Costanzo, *Programas de estabilización económica en America Latina*, p. 93; Epifanio Méndez Fleitas, *Diagnosis paraguaya*, p. 305.

26. *New York Times*, 22 November 1952, p. 5.

27. For background information on Colorado leaders in this period, see Ricardo Almeida Rojas, *Guía de la Asociación Nacional Republicana (Partido Colorado)*.

28. República de Argentina, Ministerio de Relaciones Exteriores y Culto, *Unión económica argentino-paraguaya*.

29. Méndez Fleitas, *Diagnosis paraguaya*, pp. 305–14.

30. A recent sample of anti-Méndez literature in which those same

themes are repeated is "Veritas," *Epifanio.* In defense of Méndez, see Guillermo Enciso Velloso, *El valor moral del coloradismo;* Asociación Nacional Republicana (Partido Colorado), Comisión de Desagravio a Epifanio Méndez, *Manifiesto de desagravio al líder colorado Epifanio Méndez.* The committee was headed by José Zacarias Arza.

31. Méndez Fleitas, *Diagnosis paraguaya,* pp. 319–21.
32. Petit's background is also from Almeida Rojas, *Guía de la Asociación.*
33. Raymond Estep, *The Latin American Nations Today,* p. 217.
34. *La Nación,* 8–9 May 1954; *New York Times,* 6–11 May 1954.
35. Biographical data on Romero Pereira are from *New York Times,*
9 May 1954, p. 34; *La Nación,* 9 May 1954, p. 1.

Chapter 4

1. Richard Bourne, *Political Leaders of Latin America,* pp. 98–130.
2. Ibid., p. 98.
3. Asociación Nacional Republicana (Partido Colorado), Seccional Colorada de Paraguarí, *Biografía del Gral. de Div. don Alfredo Stroessner,* p. 11; Comando en Jefe de las FF.AA. de la Nación, Dirección General del Personal, *Biografía del excelentisimo Señor Presidente de la República y comandante en jefe de las FF.AA. de la nación, General de Ejército don Alfredo Stroessner,* p. 16. The data on Stroessner's early career are mainly from these two sources.
4. Asociación Nacional Republicana, *Biografía,* pp. 12–13; Comando en Jefe de las FF.AA., *Biografía,* pp. 18–19.
5. Edgar Ynsfran, *La irrupción muscovita en la marina paraguaya,* pp. 63–66.
6. Accounts of the subsequent military actions are from *La Prensa,* 19 July 1947, p. 6; 21 July 1947, p. 7; 23 July 1947, p. 8. For more about the mutiny aboard the two gunboats, see *La Prensa,* 22 June 1947, p. 7; *New York Times,* 8 May 1947, p. 12; 19 May 1947, p. 12.
7. The Argentine medal was awarded on 21 December 1953 and the Brazilian medal on 22 December.

Chapter 5

1. Interview with Osvaldo Cháves, Buenos Aires, 4 July 1973; interview with Mario Mallorquín, Buenos Aires, 17 July 1973.
2. Dr. Florentín Peña was gotten out of the way by appointing him ambassador to Chile.
3. On Estigarribia's plot, see *La Nación,* 26–29 January 1955.
4. George Pendle, *Paraguay,* p. 44.
5. London *Times,* 7 October 1955, p. 8; 10 October 1955, p. 8.
6. Ibid.
7. For one version of the party proceedings that led up to this decision, see Epifanio Méndez Fleitas, *El reencuentro partidario.*
8. Edgar Ynsfran, "La barbarie colorado," *Guaranía,* pp. 141–50.
9. Epifanio Méndez Fleitas, *Diagnosis paraguaya,* p. 332. The events of the coup are also covered in *La Nación,* 23–29 December 1955; *New York Times,* 23–27 December 1955.
10. Stroessner's gradual consolidation of military support is covered in *La Nación,* 9 January–17 May 1956; *New York Times,* 6 January–15 May 1956.
11. Martínez Miltos was later named to the Supreme Court.

Chapter 6

1. Edgar Ynsfran, *Tres discursos*, p. 12.
2. *La Nación*, 21 February 1956, p. 1, gives a rundown on the political factions at this time.
3. Alfredo Stroessner, *Mensaje presidencial a la honorable Cámara de Representantes*, p. 8.
4. Richard Bourne, *Political Leaders of Latin America*, p. 117.
5. For a discussion of the military pressure on Stroessner, see *La Prensa*, 25–28 February 1959; *New York Times*, 18–28 February 1959.
6. Osvaldo Cháves, *Contribución a la doctrina de la revolución paraguaya*, pp. 183–92. The manifesto was signed by seventeen leading Colorados, including José and Enrique Zacarias Arza, Osvaldo Cháves, Mario Mallorquín, and Evaristo Méndez Paiva. The latter was a follower of Eulógio Estigarribia—whose own name, however, was missing.
7. *La Tribuna*, 2 April 1959, p. 3.
8. *Hispanic American Report*, June 1959, pp. 289–91.
9. For the antigovernment version of this, see Osvaldo Cháves, *Contribución*, pp. 196–98. For the progovernment version, see the statement by Eulógio Estigarribia in *La Tribuna*, 7 June 1959, p. 3. According to Estigarribia, the *democrático* majority was "circumstantial" because not all of the deputies were in attendance. And in any case, he claimed, Lovera's resolution passed by a bare three-vote majority. Osvaldo Cháves says, however, that the vote was 36 to 21. Since there were sixty members of Congress that would mean that the only missing deputies were the three arrested *democráticos*, Carlos Zayas Valle, Abel dos Santos, and José D. Miranda.
10. *La Prensa*, 6 June 1959, p. 1.
11. See Ynsfran, *Tres discursos*, pp. 31–39; Edgar Ynsfran, *Tapejuasá*, pp. 12, 23–28, for the flavor of his anticommunism. *Tapejuasá* means crossroads in Guaraní, and of course the title of his book on the 1947 naval revolt, *La irrupción muscovita*, sums up his argument on that subject.
12. On the subject of the Communists' relations with the Febrerista party, both during the civil war and after, see Paul H. Lewis, *The Politics of Exile*, pp. 78, 80–85, 91, 95, 116, 129–32.
13. In June 1960, Adlai Stevenson visited Asunción as President Kennedy's representative on a fact-finding tour of Latin America. Shortly before his arrival, Colonel Franco of the Febrerista party and Carlos Pastore, a prominent Liberal exile, tried to enter the country to talk with him. Although they were stopped by the police, the incident was reported to Stevenson, who then issued a sharp statement expressing the repugnance of the United States for dictatorships. Considering that about $30 million of aid had been granted to Paraguay since 1954, and that more might be forthcoming through the Alliance for Progress, Stroessner had good reason to appease his foreign critics.
14. The only other contested election was in 1928. Also, the 1963 elections were remarkable for one other thing: women voted in Paraguay for the first time.
15. Now renamed the Radical Liberal party, since the Renovationists had been accorded official recognition previously as the Liberal party.
16. César R. Gagliardone, *Plan de organización política del Partido Colorado*, pp. 11, 59.
17. Ibid., pp. 71, 75, 89–90, 92, 103–4.
18. *Le Monde*, 8 February 1975, p. 4, has the most details about this affair. But see also *Latin America*, 25 January 1975, p. 28; *Diálogo*, November 1974, p. 28; *La Prensa*, 7 December 1974, p. 1; 12 December 1974, p. 6; 16 December 1974, p. 1.

19. Roberto Thompson, editor of Asunción's daily *ABC Color* was arrested and held for three months for violating the news blackout and reporting Ynsfran's arrest.
20. *Latin America*, 7 March 1975.

Chapter 7

1. *New York Times*, 18 August 1958, p. 8.
2. A record of Stroessner's public activities, day by day, for one year, is to be found in República del Paraguay, Presidencia de la República, Sub-Secretaria de Informaciones y Cultura, *Relación sintética de los principales acontecimientos nacionales, agosto de 1962 a julio de 1963*.
3. Jacques Lambert, *Latin America*, chaps. 16–18.
4. See articles 79 and 181 of the constitution. A useful discussion of presidential powers may be found in Leo B. Lott, *Venezuela and Paraguay: Political Modernity and Tradition in Conflict*, pp. 300–303.
5. See Ibid., pp. 203–6, on local government. Also, George Pendle, *Paraguay*, pp. 52–53.
6. Paul H. Lewis, "The Spanish Ministerial Elite, 1938–1969," *Comparative Politics* 5 (October 1972): 83–106; Lewis, "Salazar's Ministerial Elite, 1932–1968," *Journal of Politics* 40 (August, 1978): 622–47.
7. Lott, *Venezuela and Paraguay*, p. 125, also emphasizes the upper-class character of Stroessner's ministers by noting that about one-third of them have university doctorates.
8. Juan Linz, "An Authoritarian Regime," pp. 327–28.

Chapter 8

1. T. N. Dupuy and Wendell Blanchard, *The Almanac of World Military Power*, pp. 58–59; Thomas Weil, et al., *Area Handbook for Paraguay*, pp. 273–74.
2. The estimates are my own, based on Dupuy and Blanchard, *The Almanac of World Military Power*; Weil, et al., *Area Handbook for Paraguay*; *Time*, 13 April 1959, p. 46.
3. *New York Times*, 19 February 1959, p. 8.
4. Institute for Strategic Studies, *The Military Balance, 1977–1978*; Charles Lewis Taylor and Michael C. Hudson, *World Handbook of Political and Social Indicators*, pp. 38–40.
5. Taylor and Hudson, *World Handbook*, pp. 34–36.
6. Henry D. Ceuppens, *Paraguay, año 2000*, p. 21.
7. Weil, et al., *Area Handbook for Paraguay*, p. 279.
8. Taylor and Hudson, *World Handbook*, pp. 34–36.
9. Dupuy and Blanchard, *Almanac*, pp. 58–59; Robert C. Sellers, ed., *Armed Forces of the World*, pp. 187–88.
10. Edwin Lieuwin, *Arms and Politics in Latin America*, p. 157; Willard Barber and C. Neale Ronning, *Internal Security and Military Power*, p. 226; *New York Times*, 19 February 1959, p. 8.
11. On the contrary, the combined Defense and Interior allocations declined under Stroessner from slightly over 45 percent of the budget in 1955–56 to less than 40 percent by 1957. Since 1968 they have been less than 30 percent, as a rule. By contrast, during the last three years of the Cháves administration they received 47.2, 50.2, and 47.8 percent. See Servício Técnico Interamericano de Cooperación Agrícola, *Manual estadístico del Paraguay, 1941–1961*, pp. 87–88; Banco Central de Paraguay, Departa-

mento de Estudios Económicos, *Boletín estadístico mensual*, May 1973, p. 85.

12. Dupuy and Blanchard, *Almanac*, pp. 58–59.

13. Taylor and Hudson, *World Handbook*, pp. 30–32.

14. Leo B. Lott, *Venezuela and Paraguay*, p. 257. Also, Thomas Weil, et al., *The Area Handbook for Paraguay*, pp. 264, 276–78; *New York Times*, 19 February 1959, p. 8.

15. *Revista de la Policía del Paraguay*, July–August 1970, pp. 11–15.

16. *New York Times*, 29 May 1966, p. 2. Also, Richard Bourne, *Political Leaders of Latin America*, p. 127.

17. *Latin America*, 30 November 1973, p. 378.

18. *Latin America*, 5 March 1976, p. 76.

19. Ibid., p. 76; Lester A. Sobel, ed., *Latin America, 1976*, p. 152.

20. Nathan Adams, "Tráfico de heroína en Iberoamerica," pp. 151–92.

21. Ibid., p. 166. Also, *Latin America*, 9 June 1972, p. 188; 25 August 1972, p. 269.

22. He was unsuccessful. Rodríguez was dangerous also because it was thought that he might be purchasing additional weapons through unofficial channels out of the proceeds of his smuggling operations. See *Latin America*, 2 January 1970, p. 6; 20 July 1973, p. 229.

23. *Latin America*, 20 May 1970, p. 176; 25 August 1972, p. 269.

24. Delegates are not permitted to represent more than one local committee. Members of the Junta de Gobierno attend the convention sessions, but do not vote.

25. Article 12, sections 21 and 22 of the party statutes. See Asociación Nacional Republicana (Partido Colorado), *Acta de fundación del Partido Colorado y estatutos*.

26. Except that no extraordinary convention was called, this was how the *Re-encuentro* of October 1955 came about. See Epifanio Méndez Fleitas, *El reencuentro partidario*.

27. Articles 15 through 17 of the party statutes.

28. *Diálogo*, April 1973, pp. 6–7.

29. Frederick Hicks, "Interpersonal Relationships and Caudillismo in Paraguay," p. 105.

30. Ibid.

31. Byron A. Nichols, "Las espectativas de los partidos políticos en el Paraguay."

32. Hicks, "Interpersonal Relationships," pp. 89–111.

33. Nichols, "Las espectativas." On reasons for joining a party, other possible choices were: (a) because of my family; (b) because of my friends; (c) because it represents best my personal interests; and (d) because it offers me the best opportunity for a job. On how a party should increase its membership, other possible choices were: (a) by representing certain classes or groups; (b) by representing as many different classes and groups as possible; (c) by showing how the country's traditions are important to the party; and (d) by having dances and fiestas.

34. Letter to the author from Epifanio Méndez Fleitas, 3 April 1975.

35. Justo Prieto, *Manual del ciudadano liberal paraguayo*, pp. 12–14.

36. For example, see Ezequiel González Alsina, "La línea nacional," pp. 11–37; Carlos Yaryes, "Francia y Stroessner," pp. 31–40.

37. Alfredo Stroessner, *Programa de gobierno del Gral. de Ejército Alfredo Stroessner, candidato del Partido Colorado a la Presidencía de la República*.

38. Prieto, *Manual del ciudadano liberal*, pp. 18, 123, 127.

39. Bacon Duarte Prado, *Bosquejo de la doctrina del Partido Colorado*.

40. *Diálogo*, July–August 1973, p. 20.

Chapter 9

1. For example, see Hipólito Sánchez Quell, *Alfredo Stroessner, el programa colorado, y el desarrollo paraguayo,* pp. 22–23.
2. G. A. Costanzo, *Programas de estabilización económica en America Latina,* pp. 93–94.
3. For a comprehensive discussion of the plan, see Costanzo, *Programas de estabilización,* and República del Paraguay, Banco Central, *La reforma cambiaria de la República del Paraguay.*
4. The National Development Bank's charter also stipulates that its loans are to go primarily for starting new businesses, in accordance with government guidelines for encouraging production, as opposed to merely speculative investments. It also disburses any foreign loans received by Paraguay. The board of directors includes the ministers of agriculture, industry and commerce, and treasury, as well as representatives from private industry and agriculture. See, Escuela Paraguaya de Administración Pública, Facultad de Ciencias Económicas, Universidad Nacional de Asunción, *Manual del gobierno paraguayo.*
5. Among the more important are the National Development Bank (1961), the National Council on Foreign Trade (1962), the Technical Secretariat of Planning for Economic and Social Development (1962), the Council on Educational Planning (1962), the Institute of Rural Welfare (1963), the National Council on Agriculture (1964), the National Electricity Administration (ANDE, 1963), the Paraguayan Institute on Housing and Urbanization (1964), the Corporation for Sanitary Works (CORPOSANA, 1966), and the National Council on Industrial Development (1967). To these should be added the three national airline companies, the Valle Mí Cement Corporation, the expanded and modernized merchant fleet, and the Puerto Presidente Stroessner Port Authority. See, Gerardo Fogel, et al., *Paraguay, realidad y futuro,* pp. 79–81.
6. Henry D. Ceuppens, *Paraguay, año 2000,* pp. 167, 193, puts the foreign companies' participation in the export sector at 80 percent. On the structure of local private capital and its attitudes, see Enzo Faletto, "El empresario industrial en el Paraguay," pp. 32–40; Domingo M. Rivarola, "Los empresarios en el Paraguay," pp. 123–28.
7. Among FEPRINCO's affiliates are the National Society of Agriculture, the Paraguayan Rural Association, the Chamber of Commerce, the Chamber of Exporters, the Chamber of Importers, the Association of Insurance Companies, and the Association of Real Estate Proprietors, to name only the most prominent. It has a twelve-man directing council, composed of four members each from industry, commerce, and agriculture. One representative from each sector takes his turn chairing the council for one-third of the year. See, Fogel, *Paraguay, realidad y futuro,* pp. 87–90.
8. Founded in 1936, the UIP's affiliates include almost all manufacturing firms, most food processors, the construction industry, as well as such nonindustrial groups as the Hotel Association and the Association of Tourist and Travel Agents.
9. Faletto, "El empresario industrial," pp. 33–34; Rivarola, "Los empresarios," p. 126; *Diálogo,* September 1972, pp. 5–12, and July 1974, pp. 6–12.
10. *Diálogo,* September 1972, pp. 5–12.
11. The Paraguayan Rural Association's membership is limited to ranchers with more than one hundred head of cattle. The National Society of Agriculture represents large producers of export corps such as cotton, tobacco, soybean, wheat, sugar, coffee, citrus, and yerba mate. On rural colonization, see Adlai F. Arnold, *Foundations of an Agricultural Policy in Paraguay,* pp. 102–3.

12. *Statistical Abstract of Latin America,* 1977, p. 306; *BOLSA Review,* November 1978, pp. 637–38; *Business Latin America,* 21 January 1976, p. 20.

13. Alfredo Stroessner, *Mensajes y discursos,* p. 3.

14. On the 1955 law, see República del Paraguay, Banco Central, *Ley no. 246, de fecha 25 de febrero de 1955.* For a description of the more recent law, see *BOLSA Review,* January 1971, pp. 47–48, and April 1971, p. 233.

15. *Statistical Abstract for Latin America,* 1977, p. 306; *Business Latin America,* 22 January 1975, p. 28; 20 January 1976, p. 20; 13 October 1976, pp. 326–27; *BOLSA Review,* January 1977, p. 38, March 1977, p. 162; Inter-American Development Bank, *Economic and Social Progress in Latin America, 1976 Report,* p. 336.

16. Alfredo Stroessner, *Mensaje presidencial a la honorable Cámara de Representantes* (April 1957).

17. The cost of Itaipú has been estimated at about $6.5 billion, of which three-fourths is to come from Brazilian sources and the remainder from international lending agencies. Paraguay's share was loaned it by Brazil, and to pay it back the country has agreed to sell Brazil most of its share of the energy—at a fixed price over fifty years. That latter condition has generated much criticism of the government in Paraguay, for inflation would result in Brazil getting increasingly cheap energy. Also, Brazil is to name the president of the joint commission administering Itaipú.

18. *Latin America,* 4 May 1973, p. 141.

19. *Latin America, Political Report,* 6 May 1977, pp. 133–34; 10 June 1977, pp. 174–75; 30 September 1977, pp. 297–98; 18 November 1977, p. 360; 25 November 1977, p. 360; 25 November 1977, pp. 365–66; 23 December 1977, p. 394.

20. Ceuppens, *Paraguay, año 2000,* pp. 238, 246; Fogel, *Paraguay, realidad y futuro,* p. 67.

21. Unless otherwise indicated, the statistics in this section are from the following sources: República del Paraguay, Ministerio de Hacienda, Dirección General de Estadística y Censos, *Anuario estadístico,* 1950–75; República del Paraguay, Banco Central, *Boletín estadístico mensual,* 1953–78; *Statistical Abstract for Latin America;* Inter-American Development Bank, *Economic and Social Progress in Latin America,* 1976 and 1977 reports; Organization of American States, Institución Interamericano de Estadística, *America en cifras, 1977,* vol. 2; United Nations, Economic Commission for Latin America, *Economic Survey of Latin America, 1976.*

22. *Statistical Abstract for Latin America,* 1977, pp. 33, 208.

23. Organization of American States, *America en cifras,* pp. 126, 137.

24. Inter-American Development Bank, *Economic and Social Progress in Latin America, 1977 Report,* pp. 344–45.

Chapter 10

1. Robert Dix, "Latin America: Oppositions and Development," p. 294.

2. W. Howard Wriggins, *The Ruler's Imperative,* p. 161.

3. Amnesty International, *Report on Torture,* pp. 214, 216.

4. T. N. Dupuy and Wendell Blanchard, *The Almanac of World Military Power,* p. 59.

5. The phasing out of many aid programs to Paraguay is described in U.S., Congress, House, Committee on International Relations, *Hearings before the Subcommittee on International Organizations: Human Rights in Uruguay and Paraguay,* appendix 4, pp. 150–52.

6. *Latin America,* 25 August 1972, p. 269.

7. See U.S., Department of State, *Human Rights Practices in Countries Receiving U.S. Security Assistance: Report Submitted to the Committee on International Relations, U.S. House of Representatives*, p. 131.
8. *Latin America*, 22 September 1978, p. 294; *Diálogo*, June–July 1973, p. 19; April 1974, pp. 21–22; Amnesty International, *Report on Torture*, p. 215.
9. *La Prensa*, 30 March 1959, p. 8.
10. *The Hispanic American Report*, August 1959, p. 403, for the Miranda case; Thomas Weil, et al., *Area Handbook for Paraguay*, p. 142, for the Farias case.
11. E. Rene Speratti, *Campos de concentración en el Paraguay*, pp. 8–9.
12. Amnesty International, *Report on Torture*, p. 216.
13. Juan Linz, "Opposition To and Under an Authoritarian Regime," p. 229.
14. *Latin America, Political Report*, 24 January 1975, p. 28.
15. On *Comunidad*, see Kenneth Westhues, "Curses Versus Blows," pp. 8, 11; on the seizure of *El Radical*, see *Latin America, Political Report*, 8 July 1977, p. 207.
16. On the guerrilla organizations and invasions, see Paul H. Lewis, *The Politics of Exile*, pp. 133–39; *The Hispanic American Report*, 1958–1961.
17. F. G. Bailey, *Stratagems and Spoils*, p. 115.
18. Linz, "Opposition," pp. 191, 219.
19. Ibid., p. 223.
20. Lewis, *Politics of Exile*, pp. 144–66.
21. *Diálogo*, 24 January–7 February 1972, p. 8.
22. Frederick C. Turner, *Catholicism and Political Development in Latin America*, p. 120. Turner, who interviewed Mena Porta in 1968, felt that the archbishop was sincere in believing that he was really politically neutral.
23. Ibid., pp. 117–19; *The Hispanic American Report*, March–December 1968.
24. Turner, *Catholicism*, p. 120; *The Hispanic American Report*, April 1974, p. 174.
25. Comité de Madres Católicas, *Mensaje al Arzobispo del Paraguay, Monseñor Anibal Mena Porta*.
26. On the radical impact of the encyclicals and Vatican II on Catholic political movements in Latin America, see Richard Shaull, "The Church and Revolutionary Change: Contrasting Perspectives," in Henry A. Landsberger, ed., *The Church and Social Change in Latin America*, pp. 135–53.
27. The revolutionary potential of the leagues as training grounds for a new political order is noted in Westhues, "Curses Versus Blows," p. 13.
28. *New York Times*, 9 May 1969, p. 10.
29. Marícevich was shifted from auxiliary bishop of Asunción to bishop of Concepción. Rolón was bishop of Villarica, and Bogarín was bishop of San Juan Bautista de Misiones.
30. London *Times*, 23 October 1970, p. 1.
31. Carrillo was exempted from the draft originally on the grounds that he was the only son of a disabled Chaco War veteran. Later, the government revised his father's disability rating from 50 to 30 percent, thus making Carrillo eligible for service.
32. *Diálogo*, 26 September–13 October 1972, pp. 4–12.
33. *Diálogo*, 24 November 1971, p. 18.
34. *Sendero* (the official organ of the Paraguayan Episcopal Conference), 4–18 April 1975, pp. 3, 8, and 12.
35. Ibid., pp. 6–7.
36. *Facts on File* 36 (1976): 403; *Keesing's Contemporary Archives* 22 (1976): 27976.

Chapter 11

1. For a more complete history of the Febrerista party, see Paul H. Lewis, *The Politics of Exile.*

2. Juventud Febrerista, *¿Domesticación o revolución permanente?.*

3. *Diálogo,* 8–12 December 1971, pp. 18–19. The Febreristas joined the Democratic Socialist International in 1966, and so are linked fraternally to the German and Scandinavian social democrats.

4. *Diálogo,* April 1973, p. 9.

5. *Diálogo,* October 1971, p. 8.

6. This kind of smear tactic is nothing new to the Colorados. They made a similar charge in Congress against Carmen Lara de Castro, another Radical Liberal deputy. She was accused of pocketing $10,000 she allegedly received from a French organization to further the work of the Human Rights Commission. As in Laíno's case, the Radical Liberals were never able to force a public airing of the charge.

7. The events of the extraordinary convention are related in *Diálogo,* 10–24 January 1972, pp. 20–21; 24 January–7 February 1972, pp. 5–11.

8. The 1972 convention and the events immediately preceding it are described in *Diálogo,* 12 November 1972, pp. 4–15.

9. The Levi-Liberals got 3 percent of the vote, one percent of the ballots were blank or spoiled, and the Febreristas did not run.

10. *Diálogo,* January 1974, p. 13.

11. For coverage of the 1975 convention, see *Diálogo,* January–February 1975, pp. 11–13; *Latin America,* 7 March 1975, p. 74.

12. *Latin America,* 30 May 1975, p. 167.

13. *New York Times,* 28 October 1975, p. 14.

14. *New York Times,* 21 January 1975, p. 2.

15. *Latin America,* 11 February 1977, p. 45.

16. *Latin America,* 8 July 1977, p. 207; 23 September 1977, pp. 293–94.

17. Edward J. Williams, *Latin American Christian Democratic Parties,* pp. 38, 100, 164.

18. Thomas Weil, et al., *Area Handbook for Paraguay,* p. 149.

19. Ibid., p. 150; Rollie E. Poppino, "Paraguay," p. 355; *New York Times,* 6 January 1956, p. 5.

20. For a complete history of Paraguayan communism, see Poppino, "Paraguay"; Robert J. Alexander, *Communism in Latin America.*

21. Osvaldo Cháves, *Contribución a la doctrina de la revolución paraguaya,* pp. 122, 150, 213–17.

22. Ibid., pp. 172–73.

Summing Up

1. Adlai F. Arnold, *Foundations of an Agricultural Policy in Paraguay,* pp. 162–63.

2. Byron A. Nichols, "Paraguay—A Future Democracy?" pp. 32–33.

3. Richard Bourne, *Political Leaders of Latin America,* pp. 129–30.

Bibliography

Newspapers and Periodicals

ABC Color. Asunción.
Acción (Catholic). Asunción.
Apepú (Colorado). Asunción.
El Ateneo (Febrerista). Buenos Aires. October 1961.
BOLSA Review (Bank of London and South America). 1954–79.
Business Latin America, 1975–78.
Cartillas Políticas (Partido Colorado.) Asunción.
El Colorado. Fourth week of June 1974.
Comunidad (Catholic). 1965–69.
Cuadernos Republicanos (Colorado). Asunción. 1971.
El Dia. Montevideo.
Diálogo. Asunción.
The Economist. London.
The Europa Yearbook.
Facts on File.
Febrero (Febrerista). Buenos Aires.
Guaranía. Asunción and Buenos Aires.
Heraldo (Liberal). Buenos Aires.
Hispanic American Report.
Keesing's Contemporary Archives.
Latin America. London.
Latin American Digest.
The *Times* (London).
La Nación. Buenos Aires.
New York Times.
La Opinión Republicana con Stroessner (Colorado).
Patria (Colorado).
Political Handbook of the World.
La Prensa. Buenos Aires.
El Pueblo (Febrerista).
El Radical (Radical Liberal).
Reflexiones Republicanas (Colorado).
Revista Paraguaya de Sociología.
Revista de la Policía del Paraguay.
Revolución (Liberal). Buenos Aires.
Sendero (Catholic). Asunción.

La Tribuna. Asunción.
Visión Paraguaya (Colorado). Published in Asunción for distribution abroad.

Documents, Speeches, and Manifestos

Almeida Rojas, Ricardo. *Guía de la Asociación Nacional Republicana.* Asunción: El Arte, 1951.
Asociación Nacional Republicana (Partido Colorado). *Acta de fundación del Partido Colorado y estatutos.* Asunción, 1969.
————. *El caso Estigarribia.* Asunción: El País, 1952.
————. *Epifanio Méndez Fleitas y sus secuases unidos al legionarismo.* Asunción, [1956?].
————. *Estatutos del Centro Colorado "Blas Garay."* Asunción, 1947.
————. *Manifiesto de la Junta del Gobierno.* Asunción, September 1949.
————. *Al pueblo de la República.* Asunción, June 1948.
————. *El reeligido: adhesión del pueblo a la reelección del Pte. Cháves.* Asunción, 1952.
————. *Comisión de Desagravio a Epifanio Méndez. Manifiesto de desagravio al líder colorado Epifanio Méndez.* Asunción, [1951?].
Aswell, Washington; Valiente Marcial E.; Florentín Hernen; Duarte Ruben; and Servín Aristíbulo. *El Centro de Estudiantes de Ciencias Económicas y el "pronunciamiento" de la Federación Universitaria del Paraguay sobre la nueva ley universitaria,* Asunción, June 1956.
Comité de Madres Católicas. *Mensaje al Arzobispo del Paraguay, Moñsenor Anibal Mena Porta.* Asunción, March 1959.
Concentración Revolucionaria Febrerista, Comité de Resistencia. *Construyendo el febrerismo.* Buenos Aires, 1951.
Constitución de la República del Paraguay. Asunción, 1960.
Constitución de la República del Paraguay. Asunción, 1971.
Foro de la Libre Empresa. Asunción: Emasa, 1967.
Juventud Revolucionaria Febrerista. *V. Convención Ordinaria, 31 de marzo–7 de abril, 1974.* Asunción, 1974.
————. *¿Domesticación o revolución permanente?* Asunción: El Gráfico, 1971.
Méndez Fleitas, Epifanio. Letter to the author. Buenos Aires, 3 April 1975.
Partido Revolucionaria Febrerista. *Carta organica.* 1969.
————. *Ideario.* 1969.
————. *VII Convención Ordinaria. Pronunciamientos.* Asunción, 1973.
Prieto, Justo. *Manual del ciudadano liberal paraguayo.* Buenos Aires: Lucanía, 1953.
República de Argentina, Ministerio de Relaciones Exteriores y Culto. *Unión económica argentino-paraguaya: Afirmación de un destino común.* Buenos Aires, 1953.
República del Paraguay. *Ley 248 de impuesta a la renta.* Asunción, 1971.
————. *La revolución paraguaya.* Asunción, 1937.
————, Banco Central. *Ley no. 246, de fecha 25 de febrero de 1955: Que establece el regimen para la incorporación de capitales privados procedentes del extranjero.* Asunción, 1955.
————, Banco Central. *La reforma cambiaria de la República del Paraguay.* Asunción, 1957.
————, Banco Central, Departamento de Estudios Economicos. *Boletín estadístico mensual.* Asunción, 1954–78.
————, Cámara de Diputados. *Diario de sesiones.* Asunción, 1968.
————, Cámara de Senadores. *Diario de sesiones.* Asunción, 1968.

————, Ministerio de Agricultura y Ganadería. *Censo agropecuario, 1956.* Asunción, 1961.
————, Ministerio de Hacienda, Dirección General de Estadística y Censos. *Anuario estadístico del Paraguay.* Asunción, 1948–75.
————, Ministerio de Hacienda, Dirección General de Estadística y Censos. *Boletín estadístico del Paraguay,* Asunción, 1971 and 1973.
————, Ministerio de Hacienda, Dirección General de Estadística y Censos. *Demografía: hechos vitales.* Asunción, 1973.
————, Ministerio de Industria y Comercio. *Paraguay: primero censo industrial.* Asunción, 1958.
————, Presidencía de la República, Sub-Secretaria de Informaciones y Cultura. *Relación sintética de los principales acontecimientos nacionales, agosto de 1962 a julio de 1963.* Asunción, 1963.
Servício Técnico Interamericano de Cooperación Agrícola, *Manual estadística del Paraguay, 1941–1961.* Asunción: Ministerio de Agricultura y Ganadería, 1963.
Stroessner, Alfredo. *Mensaje a la honorable Cámara de Representantes.* Asunción, April 1965.
————. *Mensaje al honorable Congreso Nacional.* Asunción, April 1973.
————. *Mensaje presidencial a la honorable Cámara de Representantes.* Asunción, April 1957.
————. *Mensajes y discursos.* Asunción: Presidencía de la República, 1960.
————. *Programa de gobierno del Gral. de Ejército Alfredo Stroessner, candidato del Partido Colorado a la Presidencía de la República.* Asunción, 1962.
U.S., Department of State. *Human Rights Practices in Countries Receiving U.S. Security Assistance: Report Submitted to the Committee on International Relations, U.S. House of Representatives.* Washington: U.S. Government Printing Office, 1977.
U.S., House Committee on International Relations. *Hearings before the Subcommittee on International Organizations: Human Rights in Uruguay and Paraguay.* Washington: U.S. Government Printing Office, 1975.

Paraguayan Authors

Artaza, Policarpo. *Ayala, Estigarribia, y el Partido Liberal.* Buenos Aires: Ayacucho, 1946.
————. *Que hizo el Partido Liberal en la oposición y en el gobierno.* Buenos Aires: Lucanía, 1961.
Asociación Nacional Republicana (Partido Colorado), Seccional Colorada de Paraguarí. *Biografía del Gral. de Div. don Alfredo Stroessner: Hijo honorario de Paraguarí.* Paraguarí, 1954.
Barcena Echeveste, O. *Concepción, 1947.* Buenos Aires: Juan Pellegrini, 1948.
Bejarno, Ramón C. *Contribución de la FF.AA al bienestar y progreso del país.* Asunción: Toledo, 1959.
Bibolini Quaranta, Juan Carlos. "El Coloradismo: Su nacionalismo, su representatividad y autenticidad," *Reflexiones Republicanas,* no. 3, 1969, pp. 73–76.
Cardozo, Efraím. *22 de octubre: Una pagina de historia contemporánea.* Buenos Aires: Guayrá, 1956.
Caroni, Carlos A. *Síntesis histórica del problema agrario en el Paraguay.* Buenos Aires: Tupá, 1948.

Ceuppens, Henry D. *Paraguay, año 2000.* Asunción: Zamphirópolos, 1971.

Cháves, Julio César. *El supremo dictador.* Buenos Aires: Nizza, 1958.

Cháves, Oscaldo. *Contribución a la doctrina de la revolución paraguaya.* Buenos Aires: Canendiyú, 1971.

Cibils, Manuel J. *Anarquía ye revolución en el Paraguay: vórtice y asíntota.* Buenos Aires: Editorial Americalee, 1957.

Comando en Jefe de las FF.AA. de la Nación, Dirección General del Personal. *Biografía del excelentisimo Señor Presidente de la República y comandante en jefe de las FF.AA. de la nación, General de Ejército don Alfredo Stroessner.* Asunción, [1965?].

Confederación Paraguaya de Trabajadores en el Exilio. *Los trabajadores paraguayos frente a la tiranía de Stroessner.* Buenos Aires, 1975.

Corvalán, Grazziella. "Ideologias y origen social de los grupos políticos en el Paraguay." *Revista Paraguaya de Sociología* 9 (January–April 1972): 106–18.

Duarte Prado, Bacón. *Bosquejo de la doctrina del Partido Colorado.* Asunción: Partido Colorado, 1959.

Enciso Velloso, Guillermo. *El valor moral del coloradismo.* Asunción, November 1952.

Escuela Paraguaya de Administración Pública, Facultad de Ciencias Económicas, Universidad Nacional de Asunción. *Manual del gobierno paraguayo.* Asunción, 1965.

Estigarribia, José Felix. *The Epic of the Chaco: Marshal Estigarribia's Memoirs of the Chaco War.* Translated and edited by Pablo Max Insfran. Austin: University of Texas Press, 1950.

Faletto, Enzo. "El empresario industrial en el Paraguay." *Revista Paraguaya de Sociología* 2 (December 1965): 32–40.

Fogel, Gerardo. "El desarrollo regional y el cambio rural en el Paraguay." *Revista Paraguaya de Sociología* 5 (April 1968): 96–122.

———. Santacruz Galeano, Oscar; Fogel, Ramón; and de Vela, Ruth. *Paraguay, realidad y futuro.* Asunción: Instituto de Desarrollo Integral y Armónico, n.d.

Fogel, Ramón B. "Determinantes negativos de la movilización social en sistemas sociales rurales del Paraguay." *Revista Paraguaya de Sociología* 9 (May–August 1972): 149–62.

Gagliardone, César R. *Plan de organización política del Partido Colorado.* Buenos Aires: López, 1968.

García Mellid, Atilio. *Proceso a los falsificadores de la historia del Paraguay.* Vols. 1 and 2. Buenos Aires: Theoría, 1964.

Gómez Fleytas, José Gaspar. "Ubicación histórica de los partidos políticos en el Paraguay." *Revista Paraguaya de Sociología* 7 (September–December 1970): 144–66.

González, Antonio E. *Preparación del Paraguay para la Guerra del Chaco.* Vols. 1 and 2. Asunción: El Gráfico, 1957.

———. *La rebelión de Concepción.* Buenos Aires: Guaranía, 1947.

González, Juan Natalicio. *Como se construye una nación.* Buenos Aires: Guaranía, 1949.

———. *El estado servidor del hombre libre.* Mexico City: Guaranía, 1940.

———. "Teoría y fundamentos de la libertad." *Guaranía,* November–December 1947, pp. 5–34.

González, Teodosio. *Infortunios del Paraguay.* Buenos Aires: L. J. Rosso, 1931.

González Alsina, Ezequiel. "La linea nacional." *Cuadernos Republicanos,* no. 6, November 1971, pp. 11–37.

González y Contreras, Gilberto. *J. Natalicio González, descubridor del Paraguay.* Asunción: Guaranía, 1951.

Ibarra, Alonso. *Cien años de vida política paraguaya, posterior a la epopeya de 1865 al 70.* Asunción: Comuñeros, 1973.
Juventud Democrata Cristiana. *Geografía electoral.* Asunción: Revolución, n.d.
Levi Ruffinelli, Fernando. *Meditaciones.* Asunción, 1974.
López, Berta H. de. "Estudio de la migración interna paraguaya: Utilización de una muestra censal, 1962." *Revista Paraguaya de Sociología* 9 (May–August 1972): 73–127.
Martínez, Sindulfo. *Hombres y pasiones.* Asunción: El Gráfico, 1966.
Méndez Fleitas, Epifanio. *Diagnosis paraguaya.* Montevideo: Prometeo, 1965.
————. *Ideologias de dependencia y segunda emancipación.* Buenos Aires: Emancipación, 1975.
————. *Psicología del colonialismo: Imperialismo yanqui-brasilero en Paraguay.* Buenos Aires: Instituto Paraguayo de Cultura "Pané-Garay," 1971.
————. *El reencuentro partidario.* Montevideo: "Firmeza," 1958.
Moreno, Augusto. *La época de Alfredo Stroessner.* Asunción, 1967.
Nuñez, Monseñor Secundino. "Nueva imagen del sacerdote rural." *Revista Paraguaya de Sociología* 5 (April 1968): 93–95.
O'Leary, Juan. *El Mariscal Solano López.* Madrid: Felix Moliner, 1925.
Paciello, Oscar. "Revolución colorada." *Cuadernos Republicanos*, No. 6, November 1971, pp. 41–69.
Pastore, Carlos. *La lucha por la tierra en el Paraguay.* Montevideo: Antequera, 1972.
Pérez Acosta, Juan F. *Carlos Antonio López: Obrero máximo.* Asunción: Guaranía, 1948.
————. *Migraciones históricas del Paraguay a la Argentina.* Buenos Aires: Optimus, 1952.
Peyrón, Oscar. *Morínigo: Guerra, dictadura, y terror en Paraguay.* Buenos Aires: Centro Editor de America Latina, 1972.
Prieto, Justo. *Llenese los claros.* Buenos Aires: Lucanía, 1957.
————. *Manual del ciudadano liberal paraguayo.* Buenos Aires: Lucanía, 1953.
Ramírez, Miguel Angel. "Ideario social del coloradismo." *Reflexiones Republicanas*, no. 1, 1968, pp. 21–30.
Rivarola, Domingo M. "Aspectos de la migración paraguaya." *Aportes* 1 (January 1967): 25–72.
————. "Los empresarios en el Paraguay." *Revista Paraguaya de Sociología* 5 (April 1968): 123–28.
Sánchez Quell, Hipólito. *Alfredo Stroessner, el programa colorado, y el desarrollo paraguayo.* Asunción: Partido Colorado, 1972.
Speratti, E. René. *Campos de concentración en el Paraguay.* N.p.: Partido Febrerista, 1957.
Speratti, Juan. *Los partidos políticos.* Asunción: Emasa, 1967.
Stefanich, Juan. *El 23 de octubre de 1931.* Buenos Aires: Editorial "Febrero," 1951.
————. *La diplomacía de la revolución.* Buenos Aires: El Mundo Nuevo, 1945.
————. *El Paraguay en el febrero de 1936.* Buenos Aires: El Mundo Nuevo, 1946.
————. *Renovación y liberación: la obra del gobierno de febrero.* Buenos Aires: El Mundo Nuevo, 1946.
————. *La restauración histórica del Paraguay.* Buenos Aires: El Mundo Nuevo, 1945.

Velázquez, Americo. "Los derechos humanos y políticos en el programa del Partido Colorado." *Reflexiones Republicanas*, no. 1, 1968, pp. 57–62.
"Veritas." *Epifanio: El mago de las finanzas*. Asunción: 1970.
Vittone, Luís. *Las FF.AA. paraguayas en sus distintas épocas*. Asunción: El Gráfico, 1968.
Volta Gaona, Enrique. *23 de octubre: caireles de sangre en el alma de la patria paraguaya*. Asunción: El Arte, 1957.
Yaryes, Carlos. "Francia y Stroessner." *Reflexiones Republicanas*, no. 1, 1968, pp. 31–40.
Ynsfran, Edgar. "La barbarie colorada." *Guaranía*, November–December 1947, pp. 143–52.
————. *La irrupción muscovita en la marina paraguaya*. Asunción: 1947.
————. *Tapejuasá*. Asunción: 1961.
————. *Trés discursos*. Asunción: America-Suacaí, 1956.

Foreign Sources on Paraguay

Adams, Nathan. "Tráfico de heroína en Iberoamerica," *Selecciones del Reader's Digest*, June 1973, pp. 151–92.
ALAC-BID-INTAL. *Transporte y comercio exterior del Paraguay*. Buenos Aires: Instituto para la Integración de America Latina, 1967.
Alba, Victor. "Latin American Militarism." In *The Role of the Military in Under-Developed Countries*, edited by John J. Johnson. Princeton: Princeton University Press, 1962.
————. *Politics and the Labor Movement in Latin America*. Stanford: Stanford University Press, 1968.
Alexander, Robert J. *Communism in Latin America*. New Brunswick: Rutgers University Press, 1957.
————. *Organized Labor in Latin America*. Glencoe: Free Press, 1965.
Amnesty International. *Report on Torture: World Survey on Torture*. London: Duckworth, 1975.
Arnold, Adlai F. *Foundations of an Agricultural Policy in Paraguay*. New York: Praeger, 1971.
Barber, Willard, and Ronning, C. Neale. *Internal Security and Military Power: Counterinsurgency and Civic Action in Latin America*. Columbus: Ohio State University Press, 1966.
Bourne, Richard. *Political Leaders of Latin America*. Baltimore: Penguin, 1969.
"The Case of Father Talavera," *The Economist*, 17 October 1959, p. 254.
Costanzo, G. A. *Programas de estabilización económica en America Latina*. Mexico City: Centro de Estudios Monetarios Latinoamericanos, 1961.
Cunninghame Graham, R. B. *Portrait of a Dictator: Francisco Solano Lopez*. London: William Heinemann, 1933.
Dahl, Robert. *Regimes and Oppositions*. New Haven: Yale University Press, 1973.
Dix, Robert. "Latin America: Oppositions and Development." In *Regimes and Oppositions*, edited by Robert Dahl. New Haven: Yale University Press, 1973.
Dupuy, T. N., and Blanchard, Wendell. *The Almanac of World Military Power*. New York: Bowker, 1972.
Estep, Raymond. *The Latin American Nations Today*. Maxwell Air Force Base: Aerospace Institute, 1964.
Hicks, Frederick. "Interpersonal Relationships and Caudillismo in Paraguay." *Journal of Interamerican Studies and World Affairs* 13 (January 1971): 89–111.

————. "Politics, Power, and the Role of the Village Priest." *Journal of Inter-American Studies* 9 (April 1967): 273–82.

Institute for Strategic Studies. *The Military Balance, 1977–1978.* Boulder, Colorado: Westview Press, 1978.

Inter-American Development Bank. *Economic and Social Progress in Latin America.* Washington, 1976, 1977.

Johnson, John J. *The Role of the Military in Under-Developed Countries.* Princeton: Princeton University Press, 1962.

Kolinski, Charles J. *Independence or Death! The Story of the Paraguayan War.* Gainesville: University of Florida Press, 1965.

Lewis, Paul H. "Leadership and Conflict Within the Febrerista Party of Paraguay," *Journal of Inter-American Studies* 9 (April 1967): 283–95.

————. *The Politics of Exile: Paraguay's Febrerista Party.* Chapel Hill: University of North Carolina Press, 1968.

Lieuwin, Edwin. *Arms and Politics in Latin America.* New York: Praeger, 1961.

Lott, Leo B. *Venezuela and Paraguay: Political Modernity and Tradition in Conflict.* New York: Holt, Rinehart, and Winston, 1972.

Martin, Percy Alvin. *Who's Who in Latin America.* Stanford: Stanford University Press, 1940.

Mitchell, Glenn H. "Notas sobre hábitos de compra y consumo de comestibles en familias de la clase trabajadora de Asunción." *Revista Paraguaya de Sociología* 8 (September–December 1971): 132–62.

Nichols, Byron A. "La cultura política del Paraguay." *Revista Paraguaya de Sociología* 8 (January–April 1971): 133–60.

————. "Las espectativas de los partidos políticos en el Paraguay." *Revista Paraguaya de Sociología* 5 (December 1968): 22–61.

————. "Paraguay—A Future Democracy?" *SAIS Review* 12 (Summer, 1968).

Organization of American States, Institución Interamericano de Estadística. *America en cifras, 1977.* Vol. 2, 1978.

Peaslee, Amos J. *Constitutions of Nations.* Vol. 2. The Hague: Martinius Nijhof, 1956.

Pendle, George. *Paraguay: A Riverside Nation.* London: Royal Institute of International Affairs, 1956.

Pincus, Joseph. *The Economy of Paraguay.* New York: Praeger, 1968.

Poppino, Rollie E. "Paraguay." In *World Communism: A Handbook, 1918–1965,* edited by Witold S. Sworakowski. Stanford: Hoover Institution, 1973.

Raine, Philip. *Paraguay.* New Brunswick, N.J.: Scarecrow Press, 1956.

Rengger, J. R. *The Reign of Doctor Joseph Gaspard Roderick de Francia in Paraguay.* London: T. Hurst, E. Chance, and Co., 1827.

Sellers, Robert C., ed. *Armed Forces of the World: A Reference Handbook.* New York: Praeger, 1971.

Sobel, Lester A., ed. *Latin America, 1976.* New York: Facts on File, 1977.

Statistical Abstract of Latin America. Vol. 18 (UCLA Latin American Center, 1977).

Sworakowski, Witold S. *World Communism: A Handbook, 1918–1965.* Stanford: Hoover Institution, 1973.

Taylor, Charles Lewis, and Hudson, Michael C. *World Handbook of Political and Social Indicators.* New Haven: Yale University Press, 1972.

Turner, Frederick C. *Catholicism and Political Development in Latin America.* Chapel Hill: University of North Carolina Press, 1971.

United Nations, Economic Commission for Latin America. *Economic Survey of Latin America, 1976.* Santiago de Chile, 1977.

Warren, Harris Gaylord. *Paraguay: An Informal History.* Norman: University of Oklahoma Press, 1949.

————. "Political Aspects of the Paraguayan Revolution, 1936–1940." *Hispanic American Historical Review* 30 (February 1950): 2–25.

Washburn, Charles Ames. *The History of Paraguay, with Notes and Personal Observations.* Boston: Lee and Shepard, 1871.

Weil, Thomas; Black, Jan K.; Blustein, Howard I.; McMorris, David S.; Munson, Frederick P.; and Townsend, Charles. *Area Handbook for Paraguay.* Washington: American University Press, 1972.

Westhues, Kenneth. "Curses Versus Blows: Tactics in Church-State Conflict." *Sociological Analysis* 36 (Spring 1975): 1–16.

Williams, Edward J. *Latin American Christian Democratic Parties.* Knoxville: University of Tennessee Press, 1967.

General Works

Allardt, E., and Littunen, Y. *Cleavages, Ideologies, and Party Systems.* Helsinki: Westermarck Society, 1964.

Bailey, F. G. *Stratagems and Spoils.* New York: Schocken Books, 1969.

Huntington, Samuel P. *Political Order in Changing Societies.* New Haven: Yale University Press, 1968.

Jennings, Eugene E. *Anatomy of Leadership: Princes, Heroes, and Supermen.* New York: Harper, 1960.

Lambert, Jacques. *Latin America: Social Structures and Political Institutions.* Berkeley: University of California Press, 1967.

Landsberger, Henry A., ed. *The Church and Social Change in Latin America.* Notre Dame: University of Notre Dame Press, 1970.

Linz, Juan. "An Authoritarian Regime: Spain." In *Cleavages, Ideologies, and Party Systems,* edited by E. Allardt and Y. Littunen. Helsinki: Westermarck Society, 1964.

————. "Opposition To and Under an Authoritarian Regime: The Case of Spain." In *Regimes and Oppositions,* edited by Robert Dahl. New Haven: Yale University Press, 1973.

Wolf, Eric R., and Hansen, Edward C. "Caudillo Politics: A Structural Analysis." *Comparative Studies in Society and History* 9 (January 1967): 168–79.

Wriggins, W. Howard. *The Ruler's Imperative.* New York: Columbia University Press, 1969.

Index

DATE DUE
